THE
GUNFIGHTERS

THE
GUNFIGHTERS

Edited by Bill Pronzini
and
Martin H. Greenberg

G.K.HALL & CO.
Boston, Massachusetts
1991

Published in Large Print by arrangement with
Ballantine Books, a division of Random House, Inc.

G.K. Hall Large Print Book Series.

Set in 18 pt. Plantin.

Library of Congress Cataloging-in-Publication Data

The Gunfighters / edited by Bill Pronzini and Martin H.
   Greenberg.
      p.   cm. — (G.K. Hall large print book series)
      ISBN 0-8161-5273-X
      1. Western stories.   2. Large type books.   I. Pronzini, Bill.
   II. Greenberg, Martin Harry.
   [PS648.W4G8   1991]
   813′.0874—dc20   91-23885

ACKNOWLEDGMENTS

"First Kill," by Will C. Brown. Copyright © 1959 by The Western Writers of America, Inc. First published in *Frontiers West*. Reprinted by permission of Scott Meredith Literary Agency, Inc., 845 Third Avenue, New York, N.Y. 10022.

"The Makings," by Norman A. Fox. Copyright © 1948 by The Crowell-Collier Publishing Co. First published in *Collier's*. Reprinted by permission of Richard C. Fox, executor for the estate of Rosalea S. Fox (Mrs. Norman A. Fox).

"The Streets of Laredo," by Clay Fisher. From *Nine Lives West*. Copyright © 1978 by Clay Fisher. Reprinted by permission of Henry W. Allen.

"Too Good With a Gun," by Lewis B. Patten. Copyright © 1950 by The Hawley Publications, Inc. First published in *Zane Grey's*

v

CONTENTS

Introduction

The Gunfighters is the ninth in our series of Best of the West anthologies. In the previous volumes, we offered some of the most entertaining Western fiction written over the past half century—stories about the men who wore badges of courage and brought order to a lawless land (*The Lawmen*); the desperate and ruthless with whom those law officers did battle (*The Outlaws*); cowpunchers and trailhands (*The Cowboys*); the brave and fearless among the Indian tribes (*The Warriors*); those who built and operated the iron horse (*The Railroaders*) and the riverboats grand and small (*The Steamboaters*); the ranchers who settled, shaped, and sometimes bloodied the Old West landscape (*The Cattlemen*); and the officers and troops who manned the forts and fought Indians both valiantly and shamefully (*The Horse Soldiers*). Now in these pages, we bring you fifteen exciting tales of the gun throwers good and bad, real and fictional, who tamed and terrorized the

Western frontier, tales penned by such craftsmen as Norman A. Fox, Clay Fisher, Lewis B. Patten, L. L. Foreman, Wayne D. Overholser, Thomas Thompson, Elmore Leonard, T.V. Olsen, and William R. Cox.

We're confident that you'll find these stories as authentic, action-packed, and absorbing as those in the first eight Best of the West volumes—even more so, perhaps, for no other figure in Western myth stirs the blood and the imagination quite so much as the gunfighter.

—Bill Pronzini and
Martin H. Greenberg

THE GUNFIGHTERS

This grim and stirring verse about a gunman in old Mexico is one of many fine Western rhymes by poet, novelist, and short-story writer Henry Herbert Knibbs. Others can be found in two previous Best of the West *volumes,* The Warriors *and* The Steamboaters, *and in three collections published between 1914 and 1920:* Songs of the Outlands, Riders of the Stars, *and* Songs of the Trail.

The Killer

Henry Herbert Knibbs

Got to kill to live . . . that's right . . .
   Trail is mighty hot and dusty;
Sleepin' in the brush at night,
   Both my guns a-gettin' rusty;
Sun a-burnin' high and bright,
   On the trail to Malachite.

Yonder through the blindin' glare,
   Dreamin' down the lazy hours
Stands the 'dobe; and the air

Just plumb rich with scent of flowers!
Roses bloomin' everywhere . . .
   Wonder if she's livin' there

Now? I'll light right down and see.
   Buenos Dios! Yes, I'm back;
Knew that you'd remember me . . .
   Concho outfit 's on my track?
Señorita, thanks! I'm goin'
   Down to pay the debt that's owin'.

No, I'm goin'. Won't you shake—
   Say Adios? For I'll miss you.
Life is short. I always take
   What I want, and so, I'll kiss you.
Sho! There's no one 'round to see us;
   Just one more and then, Adios!

Better ride the other way?
   Thanks again. That smile is winnin'.
Sheriff now is your José!
   Gosh! That makes a tough beginnin',
But that kiss is worth a fight
   Any time, in Malachite.
   · · · · · · · · · · · · · · ·

Bronc, you take your drink and I'll
   Sift in here and see what's doin'.
Same old sign—"The Forty-Mile"—
   Old saloon is most a ruin;

How, Amigo! Some hot day!
　　Howdy, Pedro! How, José!

Don't get nervous. Have a drink.
　　Yes, I'm on the job to buy it.
Sho! Why, I can hear you think;
　　Keep your hands still—don't you try it!
I come friendly . . . Call me, eh?
　　Take it then, you fool, José.

Had to kill to live . . . The fool
　　Might 'a' downed his glass of liquor,
But a Chola can't keep cool,
　　And he knew my hand was quicker,
But he had to call my hand . . .
　　Wonder if she'll understand?

The most notorious of all Old West gunfighters was, of course, Henry McCarty, alias William H. Bonney and better known as Billy the Kid. The Kid's infamous exploits have been told and retold in fact, fiction, and on film; but the one person who perhaps knew him best, and was, therefore, best qualified to tell his story, was the man who shot him dead—Sheriff Pat Garrett. Garrett's account of the life and death of Billy the Kid may be fact (with a few relatively minor historical inaccuracies), but as you'll discover it has all the drama and excitement of the best Western fiction.

Billy the Kid

Pat F. Garrett

In the month of October 1880, the author of this history first became in an official capacity actively engaged in the task of pursuing and assisting in bringing to justice the Kid and others of his ilk. As it would be awkward to speak of myself in the third person

4

throughout the rest of this narrative, I shall run the risk of being deemed egotistical and use the first person in the future pages of this book.

In October, Azariah F. Wild, a detective in the employ of the Treasury Department, hailing from New Orleans, La., visited New Mexico to glean information in regard to the circulation of counterfeit money, some of which had certainly been passed in Lincoln County. Mr. Wild sent for me to come to Lincoln to confer with him and assist in working up these cases. I met him there, and in the course of our interview, I suggested that it would be policy to employ a reliable man to join the gang and ferret out the facts. Wild at once adopted the idea, giving me authority to act in the matter according to my judgment. I returned to my home near Roswell and immediately sent to Fort Sumner for Barney Mason, whom I had tried and knew I could trust.

Mason came to me at once, but before I could present the matter to him, he told me that he had stopped at Bosque Grande, twenty-eight miles above, at the ranch of Dan Dedrick and that Dan had read him a letter from W. H. West, partner of his brother, Sam Dedrick, in the stable business at White

Oaks. The gist of the letter was that West had $30,000 in counterfeit greenbacks and that he intended to take this money to Mexico, there buy cattle with it, and then drive them back across the line. He wanted to secure the services of a reliable assistant whose business would be to accompany him to Mexico, make sham purchases of the cattle as fast as they were bought, receive bills of sale therefor so that in case of detection the stock would be found in the legal possession of an apparently innocent party. West's letter went on to suggest Barney Mason as just the man to assume the role of scapegoat in these nefarious traffickings.

Mason was considerably surprised when he knew that this was the very business about which I had sent for him. Accompanied by Mason, I returned to Lincoln; and Wild, after giving Mason full instructions and finding that he comprehended them, employed him at a stipulated per diem salary and expenses to go to White Oaks and fall in with any proposition that might be made to him by West, Dedrick, or any other parties.

Mason left Lincoln for White Oaks on November 20th. The night of his arrival he went at once to West & Dedrick's stable to look after his horse. Let it be understood that there are three Dedrick brothers—Dan, who lived at this time at Bosque Grande, but was later a partner of Sam at Socorro, being the oldest; Sam, who lived then at White Oaks and was the partner of West, being the next in age; and Mose, the youngest, who was floating promiscuously over the country, stealing horses, mules, and cattle, and who at the time of this writing [1882] is now on the wing, having jumped a bail bond. As Mason entered West & Dedrick's corral he met the Kid, Dave Rudabaugh, and Billy Wilson. Rudabaugh had killed a jailer at Las Vegas in 1879 while attempting to liberate a friend named Webb. He was on the dodge and had associated himself with the Kid. Billy Wilson had sold some White Oaks property to W. H. West and received in payment $400 in counterfeit money. This he had spent, so it was alleged, and accordingly he, too, was on the dodge. There was no graver charge at that time against Wilson than that of passing counterfeit money, but the murder of Carlyle a few days subsequently rendered him liable to indictment for complicity in that crime.

Mason was well known to the three outlaws and had always been on friendly terms with them. They addressed him in their usual good-natured manner, the Kid asking what brought him there. Mason's reply intimated that a chance to "take in" a band of horses near by was the cause of his presence. The Kid at once "smelled a rat," and, in a consultation shortly afterward with his companions and Dedrick, wanted to kill Mason then and there. Dedrick, however, vetoed the plan at once, for he knew it could be dangerous to him and his business. Mason knew J. W. Bell, afterward my deputy, and so he sought Bell and advised him of the presence of the Kid and his party at the corral. Bell promptly raised a posse of citizens, and then went alone to the stable. He interviewed West, who assured him that those he sought were not there. He then inquired about their horses, and West declared that they had no horses there. That statement, however, was false, as Dedrick and West slipped the horses out to the gang during the night.

Mason remained at White Oaks several days, but owing to the intense excitement caused by the presence of the Kid and his pursuit by the citizens, he did not deem it a fitting time to broach the subject of his visit to West. I had told him to be sure to see me before he started for Mexico and to come to Roswell in a few days at all hazards. He reached my house on the 25th. In the meantime I was daily hearing of the depredations of the Kid and his gang in the vicinity of White Oaks. I had heard that they were afoot and guessed that they would go to Dan Dedrick at Bosque Grande for horses. I sent word to my neighbors, requesting them to meet me at Roswell, five miles from my house, at dark. I imparted my plans to Mason, and he volunteered to accompany me.

We left home in the evening, and when near Roswell, we saw a man riding one horse and leading another. He was going south in the direction of Chisum's ranch. We went on to Roswell and found that this wayfarer had avoided that place, and so we concluded that he was dodging. Knowing that the Kid's party had become separated, we thought he might be a straggler from that band trying to get out of the country. Mason knew all the Kid's party; so, taking him with me, I pursued and caught up with the supposed fugitive near Chisum's ranch. Mason at once recognized him as Cook, who had fled from the fight at Coyote Springs. We disarmed him, took him back to Roswell, and put him in irons. There he remained in charge of Capt. J. C. Lea for some three or four weeks, and was then sent to the jail at Lincoln, whence he made his escape.

My neighbors had responded to my call, and about 9 o'clock that night I started up the Rio Pecos with a posse consisting of the following citizens: Messrs. Lawton, Mitchell, Mason, Cook, Whetston, Wildly, McKinney, Phillips, Hudson, Ollinger, Roberts, and Alberding. At daybreak we surrounded Dedrick's ranch at Bosque Grande. Here we found two escaped prisoners from the Las Vegas jail; one was Webb who had been sentenced to hang for the killing of a man named Kelleher at Las Vegas, and who had taken an appeal; the other was Davis who was awaiting trial for stealing mules. These two had made their escape in company with three others, two of whom had been killed while resisting rearrest, and the other had been captured and returned to the jail at Las Vegas. We found nobody else that we wanted; and so, causing Webb and Davis to fall into ranks, we proceeded up the Rio Pecos, arriving at Fort Sumner about daylight on the 27th of November.

Here I received a letter from Capt. Lea detailing further depredations of the Kid and his band about White Oaks together with the killing of Carlyle and the incidents that supervened. From a buckboard driver I gained some further information, and I thereupon determined to leave the prisoners, Webb and Davis, under guard at Sumner and pursue the outlaws. I went to A. H. Smith, a citizen of Sumner, and made inquiries. He assured me that the Kid and his two companions had not yet returned from the vicinity of White Oaks, but that O'Folliard, Bowdre, and Pickett were at Cañaditas, about twenty miles northeast from Fort Sumner, where Bowdre was in the employ of T. G. Yerby. Stopping at Fort Sumner only long enough to get breakfast, I left four of my men in charge of the prisoners, and with the balance started for Las Cañaditas. Ollinger and myself were both commissioned as deputy United States marshals and held United States warrants for the Kid and Bowdre for the killing of Roberts on an Indian Reservation.

The country between Fort Sumner and Las Cañaditas was well known to me, and in order to approach Yerby's ranch unobserved, we took across the prairie, intending to make observations from the surrounding hills through our field-glasses. When yet some eight miles distant from the ranch, we dis-

11

covered a horseman riding in that direction who was evidently coming from another ranch about twelve miles from Fort Sumner and was bound for Las Cañaditas. He was a long distance from us, but, with the assistance of excellent fieldglasses, we recognized Tom O'Folliard. There was a pass through the hills, unknown to any of my party except myself, which would surely enable us to intercept him if we could get through in time. But it was certainly a "hard road to travel"; it was so overgrown with weeds and brush and encumbered with loose rock that it was almost impassable.

With much difficulty we made our way through the pass and came out on the beaten road within three hundred yards of O'Folliard, who had not before suspected our presence. He was, however, equal to the situation. As soon as he saw us, the splendid animal he was riding sprang away under whip and spur and his Winchester pumped lead fast and furiously. We pursued hotly, but, instead of overtaking him as I had expected, he left us like the wind. He fired twenty-six shots, as he afterward declared; I fired but three times. There were only Lawton and Mitchell with me, as the others had fallen behind in the almost inaccessible ravine; but these two used their rifles industriously. No harm was done by this fusillade on either side, except that O'Folliard's horse was wounded in the thigh. O'Folliard made a splendid run and a brave horseback fight, reaching the ranch and giving the alarm in time, for when we arrived there the birds had flown to the hills.

We, however, approached the ranch with caution, for we were not sure whether O'Folliard had reached the ranch or not. We knew that if he had done so and if the Kid's party had elected to remain there, they would give us a fight. I had with me only Lawton, Mason, McKinney, and Roberts, as I had sent Mitchell back to bring up the rear. When we arrived at the ranch, I proposed to divide the force we had and charge on the house. But I was overruled, my companions advising that we await the rest of the posse. When we did walk up to the ranch unopposed, our precautions appeared rather ludicrous to us, for we found only Bowdre's wife and another Mexican woman who hailed our advent with "terror-born lamentations." Our labor was not without its reward, for we captured a pair of mules stolen from a stage company on the Rio Grande by Mose Dedrick and by

13

him turned over to the Kid. We also secured four stolen horses.

We returned to Fort Sumner, stayed one night, and relieving the guard over the two prisoners, Webb and Davis, started for the Kid's stronghold, Los Portales, where he was wont to harbor his stolen livestock. This place was sixty miles east of Fort Sumner and was the veritable castle so graphically described by newspaper correspondents, with its approaches impassable except to the initiated and inaccessible and impregnable to foes. Here was where romance surrounded the young brigand with more than oriental luxury, blessed him with the loves of female beauties whose charm would shame the fairest tenant of an eastern seraglio, and clothed him in the most gorgeous splendor. It seems cruel to rob this fairy castle of its magnificence, to steal the romance from so artfully woven a tale, but the naked facts are as follows: Los Portales is but a small cave in a quarry of rock, not more than fifteen feet high, lying out and obstructing the view across a beautiful level prairie. Bubbling up near the rocks are two springs of cool clear water capable of furnishing an ample supply for at least one thousand head of cattle. There is no building or corral; all the signs of habitation are a snubbing post, some rough working utensils, and a pile of blankets—"just that and nothing more."

The Kid was supposed to have had about sixty head of cattle in the vicinity of Los Portales, all but eight of which were stolen from John Newcomb at Agua Azul (Blue Water). On our visit we found only two cows and calves and a yearling, but we heard afterward that the Kid had moved his stock to another spring about fifteen miles east. We had brought no provisions with us and only found some musty flour and a little salt in the cave; so we killed the yearling and banquetted on beef straight while there. The next day we circled the camp but found no more stock. Then we returned to Fort Sumner, the expedition having taken four days.

On our return trip, we took dinner at Wilcox's ranch, twelve miles from the Fort. Wilcox told me that Bowdre was very anxious to have an interview with me in order to see if he would be allowed to make bond in case he came in and gave himself up. I left word with Wilcox for Bowdre to meet me at the forks of the road about two miles from Sumner at 2 o'clock of the following day. He kept the appointment, and I showed him a letter from Capt. J. C. Lea of Roswell, which contained a promise that, if he would change his lawless life and forsake his disreputable associates, every effort would be made to procure his release on bail and to give him an opportunity to redeem himself. Bowdre did not seem to place much faith in these promises, and evidently thought I was playing a game to get him into my power. He did, however, promise to cease all connection with the Kid and his gang. He said he could not help but feed them when they came to his ranch, but he promised that he would not harbor them any more than he could help. I told him that if he did not quit them or surrender, he would be pretty sure to get captured or killed, as we were after the gang and would sleep on their trail until we took them dead or alive.

On my arrival at Fort Sumner, I dismissed the posse, all except Mason, and they returned to Roswell. I hired C. B. Hoadley to convey the two prisoners to Las Vegas. On my arrival at Sumner with them from below on the Rio Pecos where I had found them, I had written to Desiderio Romero, sheriff of San Miguel County, advising him that I had them under guard at Fort Sumner and requesting him to come after them. As I had heard nothing from him, I concluded to take them to Las Vegas myself and get them off my hands. The day we were to start Juan Roibal and two other Mexicans came into Sumner from Puerto de Luna to inquire about the horses of Grzelachowski stolen by the Kid. They returned as far as Gearhart's ranch with us and assisted Mason and myself in guarding the prisoners. At Gearhart's, they took the direct route to Puerto de Luna; and after some delay, we started by the right-hand road. We were only three or four miles on our way when a messenger from Roibal overtook us with the information that a sheriff's posse from Las Vegas was at Puerto de Luna on its way to Fort Sumner after the prisoners. This changed my route, and I took the other road.

We met the Las Vegas posse about eight miles from Puerto de Luna and found it was led by two deputy sheriffs, Francisco Romero and a Dutchman, who *was* a Dutchman. They had arrived at Puerto de Luna with three men in a spring wagon and had there swelled the party of five to twenty-five, all Mexicans except the irrepressible Dutchman. The spring wagon had been discarded, and now they were all mounted. They came toward my small party like a whirlwind of lunatics, their steeds prancing

17

and curveting and the riders with loud boasts and swaggering airs. One would have thought this crowd had taken a contract to fight the battle of Valverde over again, or that an army of ten thousand rebels opposed them instead of two manacled prisoners. At Puerto de Luna, the deputies receipted to me for the prisoners; and as I was turning them over, Webb made a request of me. He said he had but $10 in the world, but he would give me that if I would accompany him to Las Vegas and protect him on the journey. He argued that it was my duty to do this inasmuch as I had arrested him and he had surrendered to me rather than to such a mob as this that had come from Las Vegas. I told him that if he looked at the matter in that light and feared for his safety, I would go on, but I, of course, refused to take his money.

While the deputies were gone with the prisoners to have them ironed, I happened to be sitting in the store of A. Grzelachowski, when Juanito Maes, a noted desperado, thief, and murderer, approached me, threw up his hands, and said that having heard I wanted him, he had come to surrender. I replied that I did not know him, had no warrant for him, and did not want him. As

Maes left me, a Mexican named Mariano Leiva, the big bully of the town, entered. With his hand on a pistol in his pocket, he walked up to me and said he would like to see any damn Gringo arrest him. I told him to go away and not annoy me. He went out on the porch, but there he continued in a tirade of abuse, all directed against me. I finally went out and told him that I had no papers for him and no business with him. I assured him, however, that, whenever I did, he would not be put to the trouble of hunting me, for I would be sure to find him. With an oath, he raised his left arm in a threatening manner, his right hand still on his pistol. I thereupon slapped him off the porch. He landed on his feet, drew his pistol, and fired without effect. My pistol went off prematurely, the ball striking at his feet; the second shot went through his shoulder. Then he turned and ran, firing back as he went, very wide of the mark.

I entered the store to get my Winchester, when in a few minutes Romero, one of the deputy sheriffs, came in and informed me that I was his prisoner. I brushed him aside and told him I did not propose to submit, at the same time asking the ground of my arrest. He replied that it was for shooting at

Leiva and extended his hand for my gun. I told him I had no intention of evading the law, but I would not allow him to disarm me. I added that I did not know what sort of a mob I had struck, for one man had deliberately shot at me; and I therefore proposed to keep my arms and protect myself. Mason, who by this time had come in, picked up his rifle and said, "Shall I cut the damn son of a b—— in two, Pat?" I told him not to shoot, adding that I did not mind the barking of those curs. My friend, Grzelachowski, now interfered in my defense, and the bold deputy retired. The next morning I went before an alcalde, had an examination, and was discharged.

Romero had written to the sheriff at Las Vegas that he had arrested the two prisoners and was on his way up with them. He had also stated in his letter that he had Barney Mason, one of the Kid's gang, in his charge. The sheriff immediately started Romero's brother with five or six men to meet us at Major Hay's ranch. They came in all the paraphernalia of war—if possible, a more ludicrously bombastic mob than the one that had appeared at Puerto de Luna. Threats and oaths and shouts made a pandemonium. The Romero who had just joined us swore that he had once arrested the Kid at Anton Chico, which was a lie out of the whole cloth, although he proved his assertion by his posse. He also bragged that he wanted no weapons to arrest the Kid—all that was needful was for him to get his eyes on the outlaw. Yet it is pretty sure that this poodle would have ridden all night to avoid sleeping within ten miles of an old camp of the Kid's. Rudabaugh once remarked that it only required lightning bugs and corncobs to stampede the officers of Las Vegas or Puerto de Luna.

Before we reached Hay's ranch, I had heard that Frank Stewart, agent for cattle owners on the Canadian River, was at or near Anton Chico with a large party, and was hotly on the trail of the Kid and his band with the determination not merely to recover the stolen stock but also to capture the thieves. On this information I had started Mason to Anton Chico with a message to Stewart. The Las Vegas officers objected strongly to his leaving the posse, as they had by some process of reasoning got it into their heads that Mason was their prisoner, although they had no warrant for him and had made no direct effort to arrest him. I paid no attention to their senseless gabble, except to tell them that Mason would be in Las

Vegas nearly as soon as we would and that, if they wanted him then, they could arrest him. A few days afterward in Las Vegas I pointed Mason out to them, but the officers had changed their minds and did not want him. A few miles from Las Vegas this delectable posse stopped at a wayside *tendejon* to take on a cargo of *aguardiente*. I seized the opportunity to escape their society and rode on alone into town. I was ashamed to be seen with that noisy, gabbling, boasting, senseless, undignified mob whose deportment would have disgusted the Kid and his band of thieves.

As Mason and myself had left the direct road from Fort Sumner to Las Vegas in order to meet the San Miguel officers at Puerto de Luna, we had by so doing missed the Kid, Rudabaugh, and Wilson, who were then on their way to Las Cañaditas. I had understood that Frank Stewart, the agent of the Panhandle stockmen, was going down the Pecos to hunt the Kid, and the message I had sent to him at Anton Chico by Mason was to the effect that I wished to see him before he started. He responded by coming with Mason and meeting me at Las Vegas. His party he had sent on to White Oaks. Stewart, I learned, was planning to search in the vicinity of White Oaks first, and then, should he miss the gang, to cut across the mountains, strike the Rio Pecos below, and follow it up. I opposed this course because I was sure it would give the outlaws time to leave the country or find a safe hiding place. Stewart was readily convinced that his plan would not work, and about 1 o'clock in the afternoon of the 14th of December, Stewart, Mason, and myself left Las Vegas to overtake Stewart's posse and turn them back.

We stopped at Hay's ranch, eighteen miles from Las Vegas, got supper, and continued our ride. About 1 o'clock at night we fell in with some Mexican freighters, camped with them by the roadside, and slept until daylight. We rode hard until about 9 o'clock on the morning of the 15th, when we hove in sight of Stewart's party.

While eating a hearty breakfast, Stewart, who wanted to sound the disposition of his men, but did not wish to confide all our plans to them, said, "Boys, there's a bunch of steers down near Fort Sumner which I am anxious to round up and take in."

Their countenances fell when they learned what he was expecting to seize in the vicinity of Fort Sumner, but some of them were even more dismayed when they learned that a conflict with the Kid and his gang might be on the program, whereas the others were more than willing to take a hand.

Finally, Stewart said, "Do as you please, boys, but there is no time to talk. Those who are going with me, get ready at once. I want nobody that hesitates."

In a moment Lon Chambers, Lee Hall, Jim East, "Poker Tom," "The Animal," and "Tenderfoot Bob" were in the saddle ready to accompany us.

We took a southwesterly direction, aiming to strike the Rio Pecos at Puerto de Luna. The first day we made about forty-five miles and pulled up at a Mexican ranch some fifteen miles north of Puerto de Luna about 9 o'clock that night, where we found entertainment neither for man nor beast. We, however, consoled ourselves with remembrances of buffalo humps we had consumed in days past and feasted on anticipation of good cheer on the morrow.

On the morning of the 16th, we took the road at daylight. It was intensely cold, and some of our party walked, leading their horses, in order to keep their feet from freezing. Between 8 and 9 o'clock we drew up in front of Grzelachowski's store and were cordially welcomed and hospitably entertained. For the sake of our horses, we determined to lay over until the next morning. We spent the day infusing warmth into our chilled bodies through the medium of mesquite root fires and internal applications of liquid fuel. We were entertained by the vaporings of one Francisco Arragon, who was a veritable Don Quixote—with his mouth. Over and over again, he captured the Kid and all his band, each time in questionable Spanish. His weapons were eloquence, fluency, and well-emphasized oaths, inspired by frequent potations of a mixed character. This redoubtable warrior did not take to me kindly, but lavished all his attention and maudlin sentiment on Stewart and Mason, and threw before them the aegis of his prowess and infallibility.

At last he invited my two companions to accompany him to his house, just across the street, where he promised they could regale themselves with rock and rye *ad infinitum*. Little persuasion was necessary to start my friends. The rock and rye was produced, and after two or three libations, Don Francisco opened his combat with the windmills. It was his philosophy that, as they were run by wind, they must be fought by wind, and he launched whole tornadoes against invisible foes. It was evidently the object of this hero to impress the wife of his bosom with his bravery, and he succeeded to such an extent that his raving elicited from her a thousand passionate entreaties that he would stay his dreadful hand and refrain from annihilating the Kid and all his cohorts, thus endangering his own precious life. This was what Arragon was playing for, and if she had failed to exhibit distress and alarm, he would doubtless have hammered her black and blue as soon as he had her alone. And yet her entreaties only redoubled his profane threatenings.

He was eager to get at the bloody desperadoes; he wanted neither me nor any of my party to accompany him; he alone would do all the fighting, would round them up, bring them in, and turn them over to me. He seemed to think Americans were scarce, and he seemingly wanted to save them. He was going to get me all the volunteers I wanted in the morning—ten, twenty, thirty. After fighting this long-range battle until nearly night, he concluded to start out immediately and bring them in right away. He expected that they would take to shelter when they saw him coming, but he would tear the walls down over their heads and drag them out by the heels. At last, the trio of listeners,

Stewart, Mason, and the Mexican's wife, elicited from him a solemn pledge that he would for the time being give the Kid and his followers a few hours' lease of life.

In the morning I thought I would waste a little time and see if I could get this doughty ally to come along with us. Stewart begged of him the privilege of being allowed to go along with him just to see how he made his capture. Arragon said he would be ready at 10 o'clock, and mounting his horse, he rode furiously up and down the streets and the plaza pretending to be enlisting recruits, but secretly dissuading citizens from going. When 10 o'clock arrived we asked him if he was ready. He was not but would be almost immediately. About 2 o'clock, the bold Arragon announced to us that he had no legal right to interfere with the outlaws and declined to accompany us. It was with difficulty I prevented Stewart from roping and dragging him along with us by the horn of his saddle.

We got away from Puerto de Luna about 3 o'clock in the afternoon with but one recruit—Juan Roibal. Of all the cowardly braggarts in the place, not one could be induced to go when the time came. They were willing to ride in any direction but that in which the Kid might be encountered. I must, however, except two young men, Americans—Charlie Rudolph and George Willson—who did not start with us, having neither horses nor arms, but, ashamed of the pusillanimity of their townsmen, they borrowed horses and arms and overtook us at John Gearhart's ranch, eighteen miles below Puerto de Luna and twenty-five above Fort Sumner. We reached Gearhart's about 9 o'clock on the night of December 17th in a terrible snowstorm from the northwest. We got a meal, rested a while, and by 12 o'clock were again in the saddle with a ride of twenty-five miles before us which we were determined to make by daylight.

The day before I had started a spy, José Roibal, brother of Juan, from Puerta de Luna to Fort Sumner. He was a trustworthy fellow, who had been recommended to me by Grzelachowski. He had ridden straight through to Fort Sumner without stopping, obtained all the information possible, and on his return reported to me at Pablo Beaubien's ranch, a mile above Gearhart's. His appearance at Fort Sumner had excited no suspicion. He kept his eyes open and his mouth closed; when it was necessary to talk, he pretended he was a sheepherder looking for strays. He learned that it was certain that the Kid, with five adherents, was at Fort Sumner and that he was decidedly on the *qui vive*. It seemed that George Farnum, a buckboard driver, had told the Kid that Mason and I were on the way down toward Fort Sumner, but both Farnum and the Kid were ignorant of the fact that we were not alone. The Kid and his crowd, it was said, kept horses saddled all the time, and were prepared either to give us a warm reception when we should appear on the scene, or to run, as occasion demanded. After gaining all the information possible without exciting suspicion, José rode leisurely from Fort Sumner, crossing the river on the west. O'Folliard and Pickett followed him across the river, and asked him who he was, what his business was, etc. He replied that he was a herder and was hunting stray sheep. This satisfied his questioners, and they allowed him to depart.

After the Kid, O'Folliard, Bowdre, Rudabaugh, Wilson, and Pickett had all met at Las Cañaditas, they had gone directly to Fort Sumner and were putting in a gay time at cards, drinking, and dancing. The Kid had heard of our capture of the mules and other stolen stock at Yerby's ranch, and was terribly angered thereat. The gang squandered many precious hours in cursing me and threatening me with bloody death. The Kid had written to Capt. Lea at Roswell that if the officers of the law would give a little time and let him alone until he could rest up his horses and get ready, he would leave the country for good. But he added threateningly that if he was pursued or harassed, he would start a bloody war and fight it out to the fatal end.

With all this information from our faithful spy, we left Gearhart's ranch about midnight and reached Fort Sumner just before daylight. I made camp a little above the plaza, then took Mason and went prospecting. We understood that the outlaws kept their horses when in Fort Sumner at A. H. Smith's corral, and we first visited him. We found that their horses were not there; then we awakened Smith and learned from him that they had left after dark the night before. We all turned in at Smith's except Mason, who went to the house of his father-in-law. He came back, however, immediately with the news that he had heard that the Kid and his gang were in an old deserted building nearby. This report served to excite us, rouse us out of bed, and disappoint us, as there was no one at the house designated. We concluded perforce that we would possess our souls in patience until daylight.

On the morning of the 18th of December, before anyone was stirring in the plaza of Fort Sumner, I left our party with the exception of Mason in concealment and started out to make observations. I met a Mexican named Iginio Garcia in my rounds, whom I knew to be a tool of the Kid's, and I spoke to him. I warned him not to betray my presence to any of the Kid's gang and not to leave the plaza. He represented that he had urgent business down the river but assured me that he would keep my presence a secret. I consented for him to go, as it didn't matter much. If the Kid and his associates found out I was there, they would labor under the impression that my only support in the engagement would be Mason, and perhaps a Mexican or two. The fact of the presence of Stewart and his party I felt sure had not been betrayed to anyone. Garcia lived twelve miles south of Fort Sumner and started in that direction.

A day or two previous to these events, A. H. Smith had sent Bob Campbell and José Valdez to Bosque Grande to drive up a bunch of milk cows he had bought from Dan Dedrick. Garcia happened to meet these two near his home. He knew that Campbell was a friend and an accomplice of the Kid and that Valdez was, at least, a friend. He told them I was in Fort Sumner, and they immediately turned the cows loose and separated. Campbell at once went to a camp close by, hired a Mexican boy, and sent him to the Kid with a note. The Kid and his gang were then at the ranch of Erastus J. Wilcox, twelve miles east of Sumner.

Valdez rode into Sumner, and there, when I met him, I inquired if he had seen Garcia. He said he had seen him at a distance, but had not spoken to him. I asked no further questions, as I was convinced I would get no word of truth from him. On receipt of Campbell's note, the Kid sent Juan, a stepson of Wilcox, to the Fort to see how the land lay and with instructions to return and report as soon as possible. Wilcox and his partner, Brazil, were law-abiding citizens, and subsequently rendered me invaluable assistance in my efforts to capture the gang. Seeing Juan in the plaza, I suspected his errand, accosted him, and found my surmise was correct. After a little conversation I concluded that I could fully trust him; and when

I made known my business to him he promised faithfully to follow my instructions. From him I gathered the following information about the Kid's movements.

The Kid and all his band were intending to come to Fort Sumner the next day in a wagon with a load of beef. That morning, however, the Kid had received by a Mexican boy a note from Bob Campbell wherein Bob told how he and Valdez met Garcia and how Garcia had notified them of my presence in Sumner. So from this I knew that Valdez had lied to me. This note had disarranged the Kid's plans. He had sent Juan in to try to learn something of my movements, the number in my posse, etc. I asked Juan if he would work with me to deceive the outlaws. He said he would do anything I told him. Thereupon I left him and went to Valdez. I made the latter write a note to the Kid saying that all my party and I had gone to Roswell and there was no danger. I then wrote to Wilcox and Brazil, stating that I was at Fort Sumner with thirteen men, that I was on the trail of the Kid and his gang, and that I would never let up until I caught them or ran them out of the country. I closed with the request that they cooperate with me. When Juan had finished his business in the plaza and came to me, I gave him the two notes, warning him not to get them mixed.

The Kid and his party were impatiently awaiting Juan's return. They read Valdez's note eagerly—then shouted their scorn at my timidity, saying that this news was too good for them; that they had intended to come in after me anyhow; that they had a great notion to follow me and my party; that if they could kill me they would not be further molested; and that if we had not run away they would have "shot us up a little" and set us on foot. Juan was discreet, and when the opportunity arose, he gave the other note to Wilcox.

I was confident that the gang would be in Fort Sumner that night and made arrangements to receive them. There was an old hospital building on the eastern boundary of the plaza—the direction from which they would come. The wife of Bowdre occupied one of the rooms of the building, and I felt sure they would pay their first visit to her. So I took my posse there, placed a guard about the house, and awaited the game. They came fully two hours before we expected them. We were passing away the time playing cards. There were several Mexicans in the plaza, some of whom I feared would convey information to the gang, as I had them with me in custody. Snow was falling on the ground, the fact that increased the light outside. About 8 o'clock the guard cautiously called from the door.

"Pat, someone is coming!"

"Get your guns, boys," said I. "No one but the men we want would be riding at this time of night."

With all his reckless bravery, the Kid had a strong infusion of caution in his composition when he was not excited. He afterward told me that as they approached the building that night he was riding in front with O'Folliard. As they rode down close to our vicinity, he said, a strong suspicion arose in his mind that they might be running into unseen danger.

"Well," said I, "what did you do?"

He replied, "I wanted a chew of tobacco bad. Wilson had some that was good and he was in the rear. I went back after tobacco, don't you see?" And his eyes twinkled mischievously.

One of the Mexicans followed me out, and we joined the guard, Lon Chambers, on one side of the building, while Mason with the rest of our party went around the building to intercept them should they try to pass on into the plaza. In a short time we saw the Kid's gang approaching, with O'Folliard and Pickett riding in front. I was under the porch and close against the wall, partly hidden by some harness hanging there. Chambers was close behind me and the Mexican behind him.

I whispered, "That's him." They rode on up until O'Folliard's horse's head was under the porch. When I called "Halt!" O'Folliard reached for his pistol, but before he could draw it, Chambers and I both fired. His horse wheeled and ran at least a hundred and fifty yards. As quick as possible I fired at Pickett, but the flash of Chambers' gun disconcerted my aim, and I missed him. But one might have thought by the way he ran and yelled that I had put a dozen bullets in him. When O'Folliard's horse ran with him, he was uttering cries of mortal agony, and we were convinced that he had received a death wound. But he wheeled his horse, and as he rode slowly back, said, "Don't shoot, Garrett. I am killed."

Mason, from the other side of the house, where he had been stationed, called out, "Take your medicine, old boy; take your medicine," and was going to O'Folliard's assistance. But fearing it might be a feint and that O'Folliard might attempt revenge on Mason, I called out a warning to the latter to be careful how he approached the wounded man. Then I called to O'Folliard to throw up his hands, adding that I would give him no chance to kill me. He replied that he was dying and couldn't throw up his hands, and begged us to take him off his horse and let him die as easy as possible. Holding our guns down to him, we went up to him, took his gun out of the holster, lifted him off his horse, carried him into the house, and laid him down. Then taking off his pistol, which was full-cocked, we examined him and found that he was shot through the left side just below the heart, his coat having been cut across the front by a bullet.

During this encounter with O'Folliard and Pickett, the rest of our party on the other side of the house had seen the Kid and the others of his gang. My men had promptly fired on them and killed Rudabaugh's horse, which, however, ran twelve miles with him to Wilcox's ranch before the animal died. As soon as our men fired, these four ran like a bunch of wild Nueces steers. They were, in truth, completely surprised and demoralized.

As soon as the outlaws had disappeared,

Mason came around the building just as O'Folliard was returning, reeling in his saddle. After we had laid him down inside, he begged me to kill him, saying that if I was a friend of his I would put him out of his misery. I told him I was no friend of his kind who tried to murder me because I tried to do my duty; and I added that I did not shoot at my *friends* as he had been shot.

Just then Mason entered the room again. O'Folliard at once changed his tone and cried, "Don't shoot any more, for God's sake. I am already killed." Mason again told him to take his medicine.

O'Folliard replied, "It's the best medicine I ever took." He also asked Mason to tell McKinney to write to his grandmother in Texas and inform her of his death. Once he exclaimed, "Oh, my God, is it possible that I must die?"

I said to him just before he died, "Tom, your time is short."

He answered, "The sooner the better; I will be out of pain then." He blamed no one and told us who had been in the Kid's party with him. He died about three-quarters of an hour after he was shot.

Pickett, who was riding by O'Folliard's side, was unhurt, but he was nearly scared to death. He went howling over the prairie yelling blue murder, and was lost until the next night. He ran his horse to exhaustion and then took out on foot, reaching Wilcox's ranch about dark. He had run his horse fully twenty-five miles in a northeasterly direction before the animal gave out, and then had to walk twelve or fifteen miles to the ranch. There he hid himself in a haystack and remained there crouching in fear and trembling until he saw his companions ride in from the hills.

The Kid, Rudabaugh, Bowdre, and Wilson first went to Wilcox's ranch where Rudabaugh got another horse. Then they lost no time in going to the hills from which they watched the ranch and the surrounding country all the next day with their fieldglasses. At dark they rode back to the house, when Pickett showed himself. It must have been amusing to witness this fellow's sudden change from abject cowardice to excessive bravado as soon as he realized he was actually alive and unharmed and had friends within reach to whom he could look for protection. He swaggered about and blew his own horn somewhat in this strain: "Boys, I got that damn long-legged fellow that hollered 'halt.' I had my gun lying on my saddle in front of me and just as he yelled I poured it into him. Oh, I got him sure."

The gang, now reduced to five, remained at Wilcox's ranch that night, depressed and disheartened. After a long consultation they concluded to send someone to Fort Sumner the next morning to spy out the lay of the land. They took turns at standing guard throughout the night to prevent surprise, and the next morning sent Wilcox's partner, Brazil, to the plaza. They had been made suspicious of treachery on the part of Wilcox and Brazil when they were so effectually surprised at the old hospital building, but had been entirely reassured by them after returning to the ranch.

Brazil came to me at Fort Sumner on the morning of the 20th of December. He described the condition of the crestfallen band of outlaws and said they had sent him in to gather news and report to them. I told him to return, and, as a ruse, to tell them that I was at Sumner with only Mason and three Mexicans and that I was considerably scared up and wanted to get back to Roswell, but feared to leave the plaza. Brazil remained in town until the next day; then, when he was ready to start, I told him that, if he found the gang still at the ranch when he arrived there, he should remain; but if they had left, or should leave after his arrival, he was to come and report to me. I had it understood further between us that if he did not come to me before 2 o'clock in the morning, I would start for the ranch, and if I did not meet him on the road, I would feel sure that the Kid's gang were still on the ranch. Brazil went home and almost immediately returned, reaching Summer about 12 o'clock in the night.

There was snow on the ground, and it was so desperately cold that Brazil's beard was full of icicles. He reported that the Kid and his four companions had taken supper at Wilcox's, then mounted their horses and departed. My party and I all started for the ranch immediately. I took the precaution to send Brazil ahead to see whether the gang had returned, while with my posse I took a circuitous route by Lake Ranch, a mile or two off the road, thinking they might be there. We reached the ranch, surrounded the house, found it vacant, and rode on toward Wilcox's. About three miles from there we met Brazil, who reported that the outlaws had not returned and showed me their trail in the snow.

After following this trail a short distance, I was convinced that they had made for Stinking Spring, where there was an old deserted house, built by Alejandro Perea. When within a half-mile of the house, we halted and held a consultation. I told my companions that I was confident we had them trapped, and cautioned them to preserve silence. We moved quietly in the direction of the house until we were only about four hundred yards distant; then we divided our party, leaving Juan Roibal in charge of the horses. Taking one-half of our force with me, I circled the house. I found a dry arroya, and by taking advantage of its bed we were able to approach pretty close. Stewart, with the rest of the posse, found concealment on the other side within two hundred yards of the building. We could see three horses tied to the porch and rafters of the house, and knowing there were five in the gang and that they were all mounted when they left Wilcox's, we concluded that they must have led two horses inside. There was no door to the house—just an opening where a door had once been. I had a messenger creep around to Stewart and propose that as the Kid's gang were surely there we stealthily enter the house, cover them with our guns, and hold them until daylight. Stewart did not view the suggestion favorably, although Lee Hall was decidedly in favor of it. So, shivering with cold, we awaited daylight or some movement on the part of the inmates of the house.

I had a perfect description of the Kid's dress, especially his hat. I had told all the posse that if the Kid made his appearance it was my intention to kill him, for then the rest would probably surrender. The Kid had sworn that he would never give himself up a prisoner, and would die fighting even though there was a revolver at each ear, and I knew he would keep his word. I was in a position to command a view of the doorway, and I instructed my men that when I brought up my gun they should all raise theirs and fire. Before it was daylight, a man appeared at the entrance with a horse's nosebag in his hand, and I took him to be the Kid. His size and dress, especially the hat, corresponded exactly with the description I had been given of the Kid. So I gave a signal by bringing my gun to my shoulder; my men did likewise and seven bullets sped on their errand of death.

Our victim was Charlie Bowdre. He turned and reeled back into the house. In a moment Wilson called to me from the house and said that Bowdre was killed and wanted to come out.

As he started, the Kid caught hold of his belt, drew his revolver around in front of him and said, "They have murdered you, Charlie, but you can get revenge. Kill some of the sons of b——s before you die."

Bowdre came out with his pistol still hanging in front of him, but with his hands up. He walked unsteadily toward our group until he recognized me; then he came straight to me, motioning toward the house, and almost strangling with blood, said, "I wish—I wish—I wish—" then in a whisper, "I am dying!" I took hold of him, laid him gently on my blankets, and he died almost immediately.

As I watched in the increasing daylight every movement about the house, I shortly saw a movement of one of the ropes by which the horses were tied, and I surmised that the outlaws were attempting to lead one of the horses inside. My first impulse was to shoot the rope in two, but it was shaking so that I was confident I would only miss. I did better than I expected, for just as the horse was fairly in the door opening, I shot him and he fell dead, partially barricading the outlet. To prevent another attempt of this kind, I shot in two the ropes that held the other horses, and they promptly walked away. But the Kid and his companions still had two horses inside the house, one of them the Kid's favorite mare, celebrated for speed, bottom, and beauty. I now opened a conversation with the besieged, the Kid acting as their spokesman. I asked him how he was fixed in there.

"Pretty well," answered the Kid, "but we have no wood to get breakfast with."

"Come out," said I, "and get some. Be a little sociable."

"Can't do it, Pat," replied the Kid. "Business is too confining. No time to run around."

"Didn't you fellows forget a part of your program yesterday?" said I. "You know you were to come in on us at Fort Sumner from some other direction, give us a square fight, set us afoot, and drive us down the Pecos."

Brazil had told me that, when he took the information to the Kid that I had only Mason and three Mexicans with me at Sumner and was afraid to leave for home, the Kid had proposed to come and "take me in." Bowdre, however, had objected to the attempt, and the idea was abandoned. My banter now caused the Kid to catch on to the fact that

45

they had been betrayed, and he became very reticent in his subsequent remarks.

Those in our party were becoming very hungry, and, getting in one group, we arranged to go to Wilcox's ranch for breakfast. I went first, accompanied by one-half of the other men. The distance was only about three miles. When we reached there, Brazil asked me what news I brought. I told him that the news was bad; that we had killed the very man we didn't want to kill. When he learned it was Bowdre, he said, "I don't see why you should be sorry for having killed him. After you had that interview with him the other day, and was doing your best to get him out of his trouble, he said to me, riding home, 'I wish you would get that son of a b—— out to meet me once more. I would just kill him and end all this trouble!' Now, how sorry are you?"

I made arrangements with Wilcox to haul out to our camp some provisions, together with wood and forage for our horses. I had no way to tell how long the outlaws might hold out, and I concluded I would make it as comfortable as possible for myself and the boys. The night previous Charlie Rudolph had frozen his feet slightly. When I and those who had gone with me returned, Stewart and the balance of the boys went to breakfast.

About 3 o'clock in the afternoon the gang turned loose the two horses from the inside. We picked them up as we had the other two. About 4 o'clock the wagon arrived from Wilcox's with the provisions and wood, and we built a rousing fire and went to cooking. The odor of roasting meat was too much for the famished lads who were without provisions. Craving stomachs overcame brave hearts. Rudabaugh stuck out from the window a handkerchief that had once been white and called to us that they wanted to surrender. I told them they could all come out with their hands up if they wanted to. Rudabaugh then came out to our camp and said they would all surrender if I would guarantee them protection from violence. This, of course, I did readily. Rudabaugh then returned to the house where he and the others held a short consultation. In a few minutes all of them—the Kid, Wilson, Pickett, and Rudabaugh—came out, were disarmed, given their supper, and started in our custody to Wilcox's. Brazil, Mason, and Rudolph I sent back from the ranch with a wagon after the body of Bowdre. They brought the corpse down to Wilcox's ranch, and, after a short stay, my party and I started for Fort Sumner, getting there before night. We turned Bowdre's body over to his wife, put irons on the prisoners, and by sundown Stewart, Mason, Jim East, "Poker Tom" and myself started for Las Vegas with our prisoners.

During the trip the Kid and Rudabaugh were cheerful and gay, Wilson somewhat dejected, and Pickett was badly frightened. The Kid said that if they had succeeded in leading the three horses, or two of them, or even one of them, into the house he and his crowd would have made a break and got away. He said also that he alone would have made a target out of himself until his mare could carry him out of the range of our guns or we had killed him—all of which might have been done had it not been for the dead horse barring his way. He said he knew his mare would not try to pass that body of a dead horse, and if she had tried to do so, she would have probably knocked the top of his head off against the lintel of the doorway. While at Fort Sumner the Kid had made Stewart a present of his mare, remarking in his usual joking way that he expected his business would be so confining for the next few months that he would hardly find time for horseback exercise.

We reached Gearhart's ranch with our prisoners about midnight, rested until eight in the morning, and reached Puerto de Luna at 2 o'clock in the afternoon on Christmas Day. My friend Grzelachowski gave us all a splendid dinner. My ubiquitous Don Quixote Arragon proffered to me again his invaluable services together with those of his original mob, which I respectfully declined. With a fresh team we got away from Puerto de Luna about 4 o'clock; but we had not traveled far before our wagon broke down and we were compelled to borrow one off Captain Clancy. We managed, however, to reach Hay's ranch in time for breakfast.

At 2 o'clock in the afternoon, December 26th, we reached Las Vegas, and through a crowd of citizens made our way to the jail. Our objective point was the Sante Fe jail, as there were United States warrants against all our prisoners except Pickett. We intended to leave him at Las Vegas, but we proposed to go on with the other three to Santa Fe the next morning, although we expected, and so did Radabaugh himself, that the authorities at Las Vegas would insist on holding him for the killing of the jailer. We had made a promise to Rudabaugh that we would take him to Santa Fe and we were determined to

49

do it at all hazards. So Stewart went before an alcalde and made oath that we were holding this prisoner on a United States warrant; this affidavit and our warrant, we believed, would enable us to hold Rudabaugh as our prisoner and take him to Santa Fe.

On the morning of December 27th, I had fresh irons placed on the Kid, Rudabaugh, and Wilson. As Michael Cosgrove, the mail contractor carrying the mail from Fort Sumner to Roswell, was well acquainted in Santa Fe, I induced him to accompany me there with the prisoners, and I therefore released two of my guards, starting with only Cosgrove, Stewart, and Mason. After breakfast we went to the jail for our prisoners. They turned over the Kid and Wilson to us, and we handcuffed them together. Then we demanded Rudabaugh, but they refused to give him up, saying that he had escaped from the jail and that he was wanted for a murder committed in Las Vegas. I argued with them that my right to the prisoner outranked theirs inasmuch as I was a deputy United States marshal and had arrested Rudabaugh for an offense against the laws of the United States and was not supposed to be cognizant of any other offense or arrest. I insisted that

I was responsible for him as my prisoner and pressed in no uncertain terms my intention to have him. Stewart drew his affidavit on them and they at last turned Rudabaugh over to us.

We had been on the train with our three prisoners but a few minutes when we noticed that a good many Mexicans scattered through the crowd were armed with rifles and revolvers and seemed considerably excited. Stewart and I concluded that their object was to take Rudabaugh off the train. I asked Stewart whether we should make a fight for it if such an attempt was made. He said we would, of course, do so; and I replied, "Let's make a good one." We felt sure that they intended to mob Rudabaugh then and there, and for that reason were unwilling to give him up. He acknowledged that he was afraid of them, and we were moreover under pledge to protect him and to take him to Santa Fe. Stewart guarded one door of the car and I the other. These armed ruffians crowded about the car, but none of them made a formal demand for Rudabaugh or stated their business. Deputy Sheriff Romero, brother of the sheriff, who had so distinguished himself when I brought Webb to him at Hay's ranch, headed a mob of five,

51

who approached the car platform where I was standing and flourished their revolvers.

One of them said, "Let's go right in and take him out of there," and with that they began to push the deputy up the car steps, while the others crowded after him. I merely requested them in my mildest tones to get down, and they slid to the ground like a covey of hard-back turtles off the banks of the Pecos. They did not seem so much frightened as modest and bashful.

Rudabaugh was, of course, excited; the Kid and Wilson seemed unconcerned. I told all three not to be uneasy, for we intended to make a fight if the mob tried to enter the car; and I added that, if the fight came off, I would arm them and let them take a hand.

The Kid's eyes glistened as he said, "All right, Pat. All I want is a six-shooter." Then, as he looked out at the crowd, he remarked, "There is no danger, though. Those fellows won't fight." He was correct in his observation, for those in the mob were evidently weakening, and all they wanted was for someone to coax them to desist so it would not look like a square backdown. Some influential Mexicans began to reason with them and they quickly subsided. We were detained by them about three-quarters of an hour. I understood afterward that they had covered the engineer with their guns and threatened him if he moved the train. One of the railroad officials had thereupon warned them of danger from the law for detaining the United States mail. Finally, Mollay, a deputy United States marshal who had had some railroad experience, mounted the cab and pulled the train out.

I had telegraphed to Charles Conklin, deputy United States marshal at Santa Fe, and when the train arrived, I found him at the depot waiting for us. I turned the prisoners over to him on the 27th of December, and he placed them in the Santa Fe jail. While they were there, they made an attempt to escape by digging a hole through the adobe walls, hiding the dirt under their bedding. This attempt was, however, frustrated through the vigilance of the officials. Rudabaugh was tried and convicted for robbing the United States mail, but no sentence was passed. Then, on demand of the territorial authorities, he was taken to San Miguel County, tried for the murder of the jailer, convicted, and sentenced to be hanged. He took an appeal and while confined in the Las Vegas jail awaiting a new trial, he made his escape.

Billy Wilson was twice arraigned for passing counterfeit money, first at Mesilla and then at Santa Fe, but he has not as yet [1882] had a trial. Should he clear himself of this charge, he still would be in jeopardy for complicity in the murder of Carlyle.

The Kid and Wilson were taken from Santa Fe to Mesilla under charge of Tony Neis, a deputy United States marshal, where the Kid was tried at the March 1881 term of the District Court, first for the murder of Roberts at the Mescalero Apache Indian Agency in March 1878. Judge Bristol, who presided at the trial, assigned Judge Ira E. Leonard, of Lincoln, to defend the Kid, and the outcome of the trial was that he was acquitted. He was again tried at the same term of court for the murder of Sheriff Brady at Lincoln on the 1st of April 1878, the outcome this time being a conviction. Judge Bristol sentenced the Kid to be hanged on the 13th of May 1881, at Lincoln. He was brought from Mesilla to Lincoln by Deputy Marshal Robert W. Ollinger and Deputy Sheriff David Woods of Dona Ana County, and turned over to me by them at Fort Stanton, nine miles west of Lincoln, April 21, 1881.

Lincoln County did not then have a jail

that would hold a cripple. The county had just purchased the large two-story building, formerly the mercantile house of Murphy & Dolan, for use as a public building, but a new and secure jail had not been constructed. Hence I was obliged to keep the Kid directly under guard all the time. For this duty I selected my deputy sheriff, J. W. Bell, and Deputy Marshal Robert W. Ollinger, and chose as a guardroom one of the rooms in the second story of the county building, separate and apart from the quarters given the other prisoners. This room was at the northeast corner of the building, and in order to reach the only door leading into it, a person had to pass from a hall and through another large room. There were two windows—one on the north, opening upon the street, and the other on the east, opening upon a large yard that ran east a hundred yards or more and projected into the street twelve or fourteen feet beyond the north, i.e., the front, walls of the building.

At the projecting corner of the yard and next to the house on the northwest was a gate that opened into a path running along the east end of the building to the south, i.e., the rear wall, where was a smaller gate opening into a corral at the rear of the house.

Inside this corral and at the southwest corner of the building was a door leading into a small hall and broad staircase, which was the only means of access to the second story. A person ascending this stairway would first face north and ascend five or six steps; he would then reach a square landing, and turning at right angles and facing the east, he would ascend twelve or fourteen steps, thus reaching the hall, which extended through the building from north to south.

If the person now turned to his right, he would find two doors, one on the east side of the hall and the other on the west. That on the east side opened into a room at the southeast corner, which was used as a place for keeping our surplus arms. If, however, at the head of the stairs, a person turned to the left, he would find two doors, one at each side of the hall, and still another door at the north end, this last door opening upon a balcony. The door on the west side of this part of the hall led into a room that I at that time used for the confinement of prisoners. The door on the east side opened into a large room, which I used as an office. In the east wall of this room was a door, which led into the northeast room I had selected as the one in which to confine the Kid under guard.

The necessity of this description will soon be understood by the reader, whether the description is lucid or not.

During the few days the Kid remained in confinement, I had several conversations with him. He appeared to have a plausible excuse for every crime charged against him, except, perhaps, the killing of Carlyle. I said to him one day, "Billy, I pass no opinion as to whether your sentence is just for the killing of Brady, but had you been acquitted on that charge, you would most surely have been hanged for the murder of Jimmie Carlyle, and I would have pronounced that sentence just. That was the most detestable crime ever charged against you."

He seemed abashed and dejected, and only remarked, "There's more about that than people know of." In our conversations, he would sometimes seem on the point of opening his heart, either in confession or justification, but it always ended in an unspoken intimation that it would all be of no avail, as no one would give him credence and he scorned to beg for sympathy. He expressed no enmity toward me for having been the instrument through which he was brought to justice, but evinced respect and confidence in me, acknowledging that I had only done my duty without malice and had treated him with marked leniency and kindness.

As to his guards, he placed great confidence in Bell, and appeared to take a great liking to him. Bell had been in no manner connected with the Lincoln County War and had no animosity or old grudge against the Kid. Although the natural detestation of an honest and law-abiding citizen like Bell for a well-known violator of the law was intensified in this instance by the murder of Carlyle, who was a friend of Bell's, yet never, by word or action, did he betray any prejudice or dislike. As to Ollinger, the case was altogether different. He and the Kid had met opposed in arms frequently during the past years of anarchy. Bob Beckwith, the bosom friend of Ollinger, had been killed by the Kid at the close of the three days' fight in Lincoln. The Kid likewise charged Ollinger with the killing of friends of his. Between these two there existed a reciprocal hatred and neither attempted to disguise or conceal his antipathy from the other.

On the evening of April 28, 1881, Ollinger took all the other prisoners across the street to supper, leaving Bell in charge of the Kid in the guardroom. We have only the Kid's story and the sparse information elicited from Mr. Geiss, a German employed about the building, to determine the facts in regard to events immediately following Ollinger's departure. From all the circumstances and indications, the information from Geiss and the Kid's own admissions, the conclusions seemed to be as follows:

At the Kid's request, Bell accompanied him downstairs and into the back corral where was the jail latrine. As they returned, Bell, who was inclined to be rather easygoing in his guarding of the Kid, allowed the latter to get considerably in advance. As the Kid turned on the landing of the stairs he was hidden from Bell, and being very light and active, he bounded up the stairs, turned to the right, pushed open with his shoulder the door of the room used as an armory, which, though locked, was easily opened by a firm push, entered the room, seized a six-shooter, and returned to the head of the stairs just as Bell faced him on the landing of the staircase and some twelve steps beneath. The Kid fired, and Bell, turning, ran out into the corral in the direction of the little gate, but he fell dead before reaching it. The Kid ran to the window at the south end of the hall, from which he saw Bell fall; then slipping his handcuffs over his hands he threw them at the body, saying, "Here, damn you, take these, too."

He then ran to my office and got a double-barrel shotgun. This gun was a very fine one, a breech-loader, and belonged to Ollinger. He had that morning loaded it in the presence of the Kid, putting eighteen buckshot in each barrel, and had remarked, "The man that gets one of these loads will feel it." The Kid then went from my office into the guard-room and stationed himself at the east window, which opened on the yard.

Ollinger heard the shot and started back across the street, accompanied by L. M. Clements. Ollinger entered the gate leading into the yard just as Geiss appeared at the little corral gate and said, "Bob, the Kid has just killed Bell."

At the same instant the Kid's voice was heard from above. "Hello, old boy," said he.

"Yes, and he has killed me, too," exclaimed Ollinger, and thereupon fell dead with eighteen buckshot in his right shoulder, breast, and side.

The Kid then left the guardroom, went through my office into the hall and passed out on to the balcony. From there he could see the body of Ollinger as it lay in the projecting corner of the yard near the gate. He took deliberate aim and fired the other barrel, the charge taking effect in nearly the same place as the first. Then breaking the gun across the railing of the balcony, he threw the pieces at Ollinger, saying, "Take it, damn you, you won't follow me any more with that gun."

He then returned to the back room and armed himself with a Winchester and two revolvers. He was still encumbered with his shackles, but hailing old man Geiss, he commanded him to bring a file. Geiss found one and threw it up to him in the window. The Kid then ordered the old man to saddle a horse belonging to Billy Burt, deputy clerk of the Probate Court, which was in the stable. While waiting for this to be done, the Kid went to a front window, which commanded a view of the street, and seating himself there, began to file the shackles from one leg. Bob Brookshire came out on the street from the hotel opposite and started down toward the plaza. The Kid saw him going in that direction, and bringing his Winchester down on him shouted, "Go back, young fellow, go back. I don't want to hurt you, but I am fighting for my life. I don't want to see anybody leave that house."

In the meantime, old man Geiss was having trouble with the horse, which broke loose and ran around the corral and yard for a while; but at last he brought him saddled to the front of the house. While this was going on, the Kid was running about all over the building, now on the porch, now watching from different windows. He danced about on the balcony, laughed and shouted as though he hadn't a care on earth. He remained at the house for nearly an hour after the two killings before he made a motion to leave. When he left the house and attempted to mount the horse, the animal again broke loose and ran down toward the Rio Bonito. The Kid thereupon called on Andrew Nimley, one of the prisoners who was standing by, to go and catch it. Nimley hesitated, but a quick and imperative gesture by the Kid started him. He brought the horse back, and the Kid remarked, "Old fellow, if you hadn't gone for this horse, I would have killed you." This time the Kid succeeded in mounting, and saying to those within hearing, "Tell Billy Burt I will send his horse back to him," and galloped away, the shackles still hanging to one leg. He took the road west leading to Fort Stanton, turned north about four miles from town, and rode in the direction of Las Tablas.

In order to understand all that happened it is necessary to go back a little in the story of this tragedy. It was found that Bell was hit under the right arm, the ball passing through the body and going out under the left arm. On examination it was evident that the Kid had made what was for him a very poor shot, and that his hitting Bell at all was a lucky accident. The ball had hit the wall on Bell's right, then caromed, and passed through his body, and buried itself in the adobe wall on his left. There were other proofs besides the marks in the wall that showed that this was the course of the bullet. The ball had surely been indented and creased before it entered Bell's body, as the grooves and crumplings on it were filled with flesh. The Kid afterward told Pete Maxwell that Bell shot at him twice and just missed him, but there is no doubt that this statement was false. One other shot was heard before Ollinger appeared on the scene, but it is believed that it was an accidental one fired by the Kid while he was fooling with the arms in the armory. Ollinger was shot in the right shoulder, breast, and side. He was literally riddled by thirty-six buckshot.

All the inhabitants of the town of Lincoln appeared to be terror-stricken. It is my firm belief that the Kid could have ridden up and down the plaza until dark without a shot being fired at him or any attempt made to arrest him. Sympathy for him might have actuated some of this, but most of the people were doubtless paralyzed with fear when it was whispered that the dreaded desperado, the Kid, had slain his guards and was at liberty again. To me the escape of the Kid was a most distressing calamity for which I do not hold myself guiltless. His escape and the murder of his two guards were the result of mismanagement and carelessness in great measure. I knew the desperate character of the man, that he was daring and unscrupulous, and that he would sacrifice the lives of a hundred men who stood between him and liberty, when the gallows stared him in the face, with as little compunction as he would kill a coyote.

And now I realized how inadequate all my precautions were. Yet, in self-defense and at the risk of being charged with shirking responsibility and laying it upon dead men's shoulders, I must say that my instructions as to caution and the routine of duty were not heeded and followed. On the bloody 28th of April, I was at White Oaks, having left Lincoln on the day before to meet an engagement to receive taxes. I was at Las Tablas on the 27th and went from there to White Oaks. On the 29th I received a letter from John C. Delaney, the post trader at Fort Stanton, which merely stated the bare fact that the Kid had escaped and had killed his guards. On the same day Billy Nickey arrived from Lincoln and gave me further particulars. I returned to Lincoln on the 30th, and went out with some voluntary scouts to try and find the Kid's trail, but we were unsuccessful. A few days later Billy Burt's horse came in dragging a rope. This seemed to indicate the Kid had either turned him loose or sent him in by some friend who had brought him in to the vicinity of the town and headed him for home.

The next thing I heard about the Kid after his escape was that he had been at Las Tablas and there had stolen a horse from Andy Richardson. This horse he rode to within a few miles of Fort Sumner, but at that point the animal managed to get away from him, and the Kid walked into town with his presence unknown to anyone there. At Sumner he stole a horse from Montgomery Bell, who lived some fifty miles above, and who happened to be in town that day on business. This horse the Kid rode out of town bareback, going in a southern direction. Bell, supposing the horse had been stolen by some Mexican, got Barney Mason and Mr. Curington to go with him to hunt it up. Bell left the others and went by himself down the Rio Pecos, while Mason and Curington took another direction, Mason carrying a rifle and six-shooter and Curington being unarmed. They came to a Mexican sheep camp, rode up close to it, and to their amazement the Kid stepped out and hailed them. Now the Kid had frequently designated Mason as an object of his direct vengeance; so on this sudden and unexpected appearance of the Kid Mason's business "laid rolling." He had "no sight on his gun," but he wore "a new pair of spurs." In short, Mason left. Curington remained, talked to the Kid, who admitted he had Bell's horse but said to tell Bell he was afoot and must have something to ride out of the country upon. He added that if he could make any arrangements he would send the horse back to Bell; if not, he would pay for it.

Subsequently to the Kid's interview with Curington he stayed for some time with one of Maxwell's sheepherders about thirty-five miles east of Sumner. He spent some time also at various cow and sheep camps; and he was often at Cañaditas, Arenoso, and Fort Sumner. He was almost constantly on the move, living in this way about two and a half months and hovering in spite of danger around the scenes of his past two years of lawless adventure. He had many friends who were faithful to him, who harbored him, who kept him supplied with Territorial newspapers and other valuable information concerning his safety. His end had not yet come, but it was fast approaching.

During the weeks following the Kid's escape, I was censured by some for my seeming unconcern and inactivity in the matter of his rearrest. I was egotistical enough to think I knew my own business best, and preferred to accomplish this duty, if at all possible, in my own way. I was constantly but quietly at work seeking trustworthy information and maturing my plan of action. I did not show my face in the Kid's old haunts, nor did I disclose my intentions and doings to anyone. Most of the time I stayed at home and busied myself about the ranch. If my seeming unconcern deceived the people as well as gave the Kid confidence in his security, my end was accomplished. I was strongly inclined to believe that the Kid was still in the country and probably in the vicinity of Fort Sumner, yet there was some doubt mingled with this belief. The Kid had never been taken for a fool; on the contrary, he was generally credited with the possession of forethought and cool judgment in a degree extraordinary for one of his age. It was therefore hard for me to believe that he would linger in the Territory in the face of all the elements in the situation—his liability to the extreme penalty of the law, the liberal reward for his detection and rearrest, and the ease with which a successful flight into safety might be made. My first task was to resolve my doubts.

Early in July I received a reply to a letter I had written to Brazil. I was in Lincoln when the letter came to me, and Brazil was dodging and hiding from the Kid. He feared the latter's vengeance on account of the part he had taken in his capture at Stinking Spring. There were many others in that section of the Territory who trembled in their boots at the news of the Kid's escape, but most of them seemed able to talk him out of his resentment or to conciliate him in some manner. Brazil's letter gave me no positive information; he merely said he had not seen the Kid since his escape but, from many indications, believed he was still in the country. He offered me any assistance in his power in the recapture of the Kid. In reply to Brazil's letter I wrote and requested him to meet me at the mouth of Taiban Arroyo an hour after dark on the night of the 13th of July.

A gentleman named John W. Poe, who had superseded Frank Stewart in the employ of the stockmen of the Canadian, was at the same time in Lincoln on business, as was also one of my deputies, Thomas K. McKinney. I first went to McKinney but did not deem it wise to disclose to him my full intentions. So I told him I wanted him to accompany me on a business trip to Arizona, but added that we would have to go down to my home first and start from there. He readily consented to this proposal. I then went to Poe, and to him I disclosed my business and all its particulars, even showing him the correspondence. He also readily agreed to my request that he accompany me on the expedition. We three then set out for Roswell and started up the Rio Pecos from there on the night of July 10th. We rode mostly in the night, followed no roads but took unfrequented routes, and arrived at the mouth of Taiban Arroyo, five miles south of Fort Sumner, about an hour after dark on the night of the 13th. Brazil was not there. We waited nearly two hours, but he did not come. We then rode off a mile or two, staked our horses, and slept until daylight. Early in the morning we rode up into the hills and prospected awhile with our fieldglasses.

Poe was a stranger in the country, and there was little danger he would meet anyone at Sumner who might know him. So, after an hour or two spent in the hills, I sent him into Fort Sumner to take observations. I advised him also to go on to Sunnyside, seven miles above Sumner, and interview M. Rudolph, in whose judgment and discretion I had great confidence. It was understood that Poe was to meet us that night at moonrise at La Punta de la Glorietta, four miles north of Fort Sumner. Poe went on up to the plaza, while McKinney and I rode down into the Pecos Valley, where we remained during the day. At night we started out circling around the town and met Poe exactly on time at the trysting place. Poe's appearance, it seemed, had excited no particular notice, and he had gleaned no news there. When he went to Sunnyside and saw Rudolph, he learned that the latter was inclined to think from all indications that the Kid was about and yet at times he doubted if this were the case. The basis of this doubtfulness was not so much an actual evidence contradicting it, as his feeling that the Kid would not be fool enough, under the circumstances, to brave such danger.

When I had heard Poe's report, I concluded to go and have a talk with Pete Maxwell, in whom I felt sure I could rely. We three rode in that direction, but when we were within a short distance of Maxwell's place, we ran upon a man who was in camp. We stopped to see who it might be, and to Poe's great surprise, he found in the camper an old friend and former partner by the name of Jacobs, with whom he had been associated in Texas. So we unsaddled here and got some coffee. Then on foot Poe, McKinney, and I entered an orchard that ran from where we were down to a row of old buildings, some of which were occupied by Mexicans, not more than sixty yards from Maxwell's house.

We approached these houses cautiously, and when within earshot heard the voices of persons conversing in Spanish. We concealed ourselves quickly and listened, but the distance was too great to hear words or even to distinguish voices. Soon a man arose from the ground, close enough to be seen but too far away to be recognized. He wore a broad-brimmed hat, dark vest and pants, and was in his shirtsleeves. With a few words that reached our ears as merely an indistinct murmur, he went to the fence, jumped it, and walked down toward Maxwell's house. Little as we then suspected it, this man was the Kid. We learned subsequently that when he left his companions that night, he went to the house of a Mexican friend, pulled off his hat and boots, threw himself on a bed, and commenced reading a newspaper. He soon, however, called to his friend, who was sleeping in the room, and told him to get up and make him some coffee, adding, "Give me a butcher knife, and I will go over to Pete's and get some beef. I'm hungry." The Mexican arose, handed him the knife, and the Kid, hatless and in his stocking feet, started to Maxwell's house, which was but a few steps distant.

When the Kid, who had been thus unrecognized by me, left the orchard, I motioned to my companions, and we cautiously retreated a short distance. In order to avoid the persons we had heard at the houses, we took another route, approaching Maxwell's house from the opposite direction. When we reached the porch in front of the building, I left Poe and McKinney at the end of the porch, and about twenty feet from the door of Pete's bedroom, while I myself entered it. It was nearly midnight and Pete was in bed. I walked to the head of the bed and sat down near the pillow and beside Maxwell's head. I asked him as to the whereabouts of the Kid. He replied that the Kid had certainly been about, but he did not know whether he had left or not. At that moment, a man sprang quickly into the door, and, looking back, called twice in Spanish, *"Quién es? Quién es?"* ("Who comes there?") No one replied, and he came on into the room. I could see he was bareheaded, and from his tread I could perceive he was either barefooted or in his stocking feet. He held a revolver in his right hand and a butcher knife in his left.

He came directly toward where I was sitting at the head of Maxwell's bed. Before he reached the bed, I whispered, "Who is it, Pete?" but received no reply for a moment. It struck me that it might be Pete's brother-in-law, Manuel Abreu, who had seen Poe and McKinney on the outside and wanted to know their business. The intruder came close to me, leaned both hands on the bed, his right hand almost touching my knee, and asked in a low tone, "Who are they, Pete?" At the same instant Maxwell whispered to me, "That's him!"

Simultaneously the Kid must have seen or felt the presence of a third person at the head of the bed. He quickly raised his pistol—a self-cocker—within a foot of my breast. Retreating rapidly across the room, he cried, *"Quién es? Quién es?"* ("Who's that? Who's that?") All this occurred more rapidly than it takes to tell it. As quick as possible I drew my revolver and fired, threw my body to one side, and fired again. The second shot was useless. The Kid fell dead at the first one. He never spoke. A struggle or two, a little strangling sound as he gasped for breath, and the Kid was with his many victims.

I went to the door, and met Poe and McKinney there. Maxwell in the excitement had leaped over the foot of the bed, dragging the bedclothes with him; and now he rushed out of the door past me and the others. Poe and McKinney threw their guns down on him, but he shouted to them, "Don't shoot, don't shoot." I told my companions I had got the Kid. They asked if I had not shot the wrong man. I told them I had made no mistake, for I knew the Kid's voice too well.

To both of them the Kid was entirely unknown. They had seen him pass by them when they were sitting on the porch, and as he stepped up on it, McKinney, who had been sitting, rose to his feet. One of his spurs caught under the boards and nearly threw him. Observing this, the Kid laughed, but the next instant he probably saw their guns, and thereupon drew his own weapon as he sprang into the doorway, calling out, *"Quién es?"* Seeing a bareheaded, barefooted man, in his shirtsleeves, with a butcher knife in his hand, and hearing his hail in excellent Spanish, they naturally supposed him to be a Mexican and an attaché of the establishment; hence their suspicion that I had shot the wrong man.

We now entered the room and examined the body. The ball had struck him just above the heart and must have cut through all the ventricles. Poe asked me how many shots I had fired; I told him two, but stated that I had no idea where the second one went. Both Poe and McKinney said the Kid must have fired also, as there were surely three reports. I told them he had fired one shot, between my two. Maxwell also said that the Kid had fired once. Yet when we came to look for bullet marks none from his pistol could be found. We searched long and faithfully—found both my bullet marks but none other. So, against the impressions and senses of four men, we concluded that the Kid did not fire at all. We examined his pistol—a self-cocker, .41 caliber. It had five cartridges and one shell in the chambers, the hammer resting on the shell. But this proved nothing, as many carry their revolvers in this way for safety. Moreover, the shell looked as though it had been shot some time before.

It will never be known whether the Kid recognized me or not. If he did, it was the first time during all his life of peril that he ever lost his presence of mind, or failed to shoot first and hesitate afterward. He knew that a meeting with me meant surrender or fight. He had told several persons about Sumner that he bore no animosity against me and had no desire to do me injury. He had also said that he knew, should we meet, he would have to choose between the several alternatives of surrendering, or killing me, or getting killed himself. So he had declared his intention in case we should meet to commence shooting on sight.

On the following morning, the alcalde, Alejandro Segura, held an inquest over the body, M. Rudolph of Sunnyside being foreman of the coroner's jury. Their verdict was that William H. Bonney came to his death from a gunshot wound, the weapon being in the hands of Pat F. Garrett; and that the fatal wound was inflicted by the said Garrett in the discharge of his official duty as sheriff and that the homicide was justifiable. The Kid's body was neatly and properly dressed and buried in the old military cemetery at Fort Sumner, July 15, 1881. His exact age on the day of his death was twenty-one years, seven months, and twenty-one days.

I have said that the body was buried in the cemetery at Fort Sumner. I wish to add that it is there today [1882] intact—skull, fingers, toes, bones, and every hair of the head that was buried with the body on that 15th of July, doctors, newspaper editors, and paragraphers to the contrary notwithstanding. Some presuming swindlers have claimed to have the Kid's skull on exhibition, or one of his fingers, or some other portion of his body, and one medical gentleman has persuaded credulous idiots that he has all the bones strung upon wires. It is possible that there is on exhibition somewhere in the States, or even possibly in this Territory, a skeleton that was procured somewhere down the Rio Pecos. We have them—lots of them—in this section. The banks of the Pecos from Fort Sumner to the Rio Grande are dotted with unmarked graves and the skeletons are of all sizes, ages, and complexions. Any showman of ghastly curiosities can resurrect one or all of them and place them on exhibition as the remains of Dick Turpin, Jack Sheppard, Cartouche, or the Kid, with no one to say him nay, so he does not ask the people of the Rio Pecos to believe it. Again I say that the Kid's body lies undisturbed in the grave, and I speak of what I know.

This robust and powerful tale marks the first Best of the West appearance of Will C. Brown, whose expert stories and novels won him a wide readership in the 1950s and 1960s. One of his novels, The Border Jumper, *was made into the successful Gary Cooper film,* Man of the West; *another,* The Nameless Breed, *received a 1960 Western Writers of America Spur Award as best novel of the previous year. Brown's fiction is distinguished by the authenticity of its characters and Texas settings, as "First Kill" amply attests.*

First Kill

Will C. Brown

Death came late to Taggert. He was thirty years old, which was ancient in the bad-man business, and ten years past the frequent predictions heard in his youth that the Taggert boy would be shot before he was twenty.

Dave Esperson, who killed him, felt no pride that it was his gun that finally did it.

He stood there smelling the powder smoke, knowing the hollowed stomach and ringing ears of one who has not killed before.

Taggert lifeless on the ground was no longer Taggert, but a dead man of no resemblance to what he had been thirty seconds ago, alive and on his legs and feared and hated. Esperson looked at the unbreathing bundle, then at the gun, and experienced a new killer's terrible awe at the enormity of killing. Once it has been done, the act is beyond retrieving, and like many a man before him he felt limp disbelief after the high surge of tension and wished that he had not done it.

Still, this thing that had taken place was nobody's fault but Taggert's. There were six staring men to say fervently that this was so. The first of them to say it, Ed Oliver, wound it up in words of foul cursing, directed to Taggert already dead.

In a twisted way Oliver meant his rough talk as a kind of friendly support for young Esperson, who, he may have noticed, was still a little white along the nose lines and lips. But to Dave Esperson's ears, still hearing the big noise of his gun, such words were uncalled for in the new presence of death, and he got no comfort from them.

Nor from what the others said. The first stunned silence that had followed Dave's play and the fall of Taggert in the dust outside the railroad loading pen now dissolved as men found their tongues. The bawling of the steers in the pen picked up again, after momentary muteness from the gun blast. The men said awkward, commending words to Esperson, and one said somebody ought to go tell Sheriff Birdwell, and another that he'd fetch a slicker off a saddle for covering Taggert.

Soon there was movement with purpose, of a sort, and Esperson, the one who had done the big thing, all at once seemed in the way and unneeded. He went over to the water can and took a drink from the tin cup.

Ed Oliver, following him over, said, "Here, this is what you need," and extended a pint bottle to Dave.

Eying the whisky, he halfway reached a hand for it, but then shook his head and said, "No thanks, Ed. Thanks just the same."

So Oliver took a slug himself, slapped the cork back in with heel of his palm, and told Dave, "You take it easy now. We'll finish loading the cattle ourselves."

When Oliver went away, Dave sat on his boot heels, his back against a mesquite trunk, and looked at his hands, rubbing the sweat off on his pants leg. He wasn't going to think of Louise, his wife. Not until he got his mind better arranged. So he steeled her picture out of his brain, or tried to. But her face, sweet and young and frightened, kept coming in, no matter how he wanted to make his thoughts go blank for a little while.

Keeping his eyes away from where the men were moving Taggert's body to the shade of another tree, he felt a craving for tobacco and ruined one try completely before he got a lumpy smoke fashioned that would hold together. The world around him was peopled as it had been. The cattle pen and the bawling steers, the loading chute and the red cars on the siding, the dust and the men and the herd-high canopy of hot sky that made a lid over Texas in August. But in a few high-fevered minutes the world about had changed, turning into unfamiliar men and sounds, that left him suspended from the rest of it, conspicuous as a giant, different from all the others, and alone.

When the sheriff had come and had spoken with the other men awhile, he moved on to Dave and squatted to his boots, pulling at grass blades and not hurrying the talk.

Dave, as tall a man as the sheriff but still

young in the face and eyes where the sheriff showed webs of calendar time, wondered what the procedure would be now, but didn't want to ask. He hoped Birdwell had got all he wanted to know from the others. He would hate to say the words again; he didn't want to have to say them, nor get his mind dirtied up again, nor talk of Louise in any way. He knew that White Flat had a proper way of law now, with a courthouse and such new things as grand juries and appearance bonds and a circuit prosecuting attorney. These loomed as strange and formidable complications but had nothing to do with the first subject that Birdwell brought up.

"I was in front of the White Flat Saloon," Birdwell said, his words slow-steady as wagon wheels, "when Johnny rode in and told me. There was a fellow inside the saloon—he didn't hear Johnny, but the word will get in there pretty soon, I expect."

He didn't have to say any more. Dave knew immediately that the man he was talking about was Jonas Taggert.

The sheriff said quietly, "Jonas Taggert. He must have come back to this section when Coaley did." He jerked a nod toward the form under the slicker. Dave was visualizing

Coaley's older brother, a stranger to him except by sight.

"I don't want any trouble with Jonas," Dave said.

The sheriff nodded. "That's my idea."

"I don't want any more trouble with anybody. This was enough."

"Esperson, this kind of trouble is always big trouble. When it comes to a man, he can't turn it on and off, like he'd be willing to. It has a way of festering out again."

"They told you what happened, didn't they?"

"Yeah. I'll say it now, Esperson, so you'll know—I say you did this thing you had to do. Now, what I'd like to do is to see that this ends here. Wonder would you mind riding on home and just keeping out of sight, sort of, for a few days?"

Dave said slowly, "I don't want to run, Sheriff. If that's what you mean."

For the first time Birdwell's voice went harsh. "Now, you're calling it 'run'—I'm not. Nobody said anything about running. Damn it, Esperson, don't be like so many of them are, don't get in a shape like this and all at once think about your pride or how nobody is going to scare you from off'n Main Street. Stuff like that. I just want you to avoid Jonas and any friends Coaley might have had. Don't start building it up inside you that stickin' around your home place awhile makes it look you're scared or anything like that. You've killed one man, and me or nobody doubts you could kill another if you had to, so they ain't no call for you to try to prove something."

Dave nodded, believing he understood what the sheriff was talking about. Still, the fact hung heavy before him that nobody could guarantee what Jonas would do.

As if mind reading, Birdwell said, "I'll have a talk with Jonas. I want him out of town. He's a sorry cuss, being a Taggert. But he's not as bad as Coaley was. Coaley just didn't have any sense to his meanness."

"There wasn't any sense to what he did a while ago," Dave said. "I didn't even know he was anywhere in the country till he rode up here and started on me. We were working the cattle and minding our own business, then all at once there he was." Suddenly he wanted to talk about it, to tell this quiet and understanding older man of those unreal minutes, to let it surge out of his mind and give him relief.

"First he looked at the steers and said by God he believed I'd worked my brand over

85

somebody else's stock. You know how he could start something like that, mean right off and with no excuse. Talking loud. Trying to pick trouble. I tried to pay no attention and one of the others told him to go away, that we were busy."

The sheriff held Dave's gaze, as if inviting him to get this off his chest. Dave fumbled over the next part of it, trying to reconstruct it.

"Then is when he mentioned Louise. I—I guess you already know they were married once. Just a little while."

"I know," Birdwell said. "He had a kind of reckless attraction to a young girl then, I expect. She soon saw her mistake. Wasn't more than eighteen or nineteen, your wife wasn't. And they were divorced in less than three months. I remember."

"Well, that was all long ago and forgotten." Bitterly he realized that this thing, this afternoon, would open it all up again. That was one reason he hated it so, felt so dirtied up over killing Taggert.

"Well, he said then—" Dave felt the hot red flush come to his face. "He said, 'Esperson, how you liking your second-hand—'"

"They told me," Birdwell cut in quickly. "They all heard it. Coaley never earned an

86

honest dollar in his life nor had a decent thought. So this ain't surprising."

"He was standing there, talking loud and braggy, and then he said—other things like that. And I got blind mad. All I had in mind was to hit him."

"That's when he took his gun out and told you to start running."

"Yes. He dangled the gun around, slack in his hand, and said, 'Esperson, I've heard you were a pretty fast man. Let's see how quick you can make it to town.' He said he'd give me a few bullets around the feet to help me along."

"He's done things like that before," Birdwell said quietly. "He thought it'd make a big show, that ever'body would think it made Coaley Taggert a big card, shooting at the feet of the man that had married Louise, and running him to town. That's the way his mind worked."

"Well, I'd taken my gun belt off while we were working, and it was hanging right back of me on the fence." Dave knuckled the sweat beads off his upper lip. This was the part that was all blurred.

"I turned and pulled the gun out. He already had his in his hand. I don't know how I got in the first shot."

"You did it fast and unexpected," Birdwell said. "They told me. And Coaley wasn't ready for that. You're not the type, son, that ordinarily fights back like that. What I mean," he amended, "you just ain't the caliber that Coaley'd expect would contest him to that extreme."

"He was trying to bring his gun up. It went off right to the second with mine, I guess. Just one loud noise, but his bullet must have gone straight to the ground. Then there he was. Dead."

The sheriff stood up and squinted toward town.

"You ought to get along home now, Esperson."

Dave looked and saw the distant spot of dust, too. It could be Jonas Taggert. Or anybody.

He did not know what to do. A killing is a big thing, almost bigger than a man could carry, making parts of it drag weight on a man's mind because it was too unwieldy to get sorted all at once. But the fact that he had killed would always be there. *Dave Esperson had killed a man.*

The sheriff said, "I'd suggest that you get home and tell Louise. Before somebody else does. Tell her just like it was, like you told me. That's just a suggestion."

The idea of that formed in his mind, something specific to be done.

He got his gun belt, noting that somebody had stuck the gun back in the holster. He untied his horse and mounted. Just for a second, his eyes were drawn to the tree shade where Taggert's boots stuck out from under a yellow slicker.

He lifted a hand to Birdwell, but the sheriff and the other men were looking at the horse dust approaching from town.

He rode east on the White Canyon trail, into the mesquite growth, over the route they had come only yesterday, the White Canyon men, driving their mixed herd. A different trail, now. Filled with shadows, silent, lonely as far ahead as he could see.

He told Louise, standing on the porch where she had come to greet him.

He told her like he had told Birdwell, even to the words, the things Taggert had said, words that ought never to be used about a woman in front of her husband. When he finished, she was holding to his arms with fingers locked stiff, looking up to him through the moisture in her eyes, trying to make him see her heart was pulled close to him.

"You did the only thing you could."

The night dragged by, and he did not sleep, and another day, with questions forming and expanding until they became all manner of grotesque worries. He busied himself about the corral, and rode to the creek pasture to look at some cattle, and back, and labored to make natural conversation when he was at the table with Louise, eating food that he did not taste.

What were people saying in town? Had they buried Coaley yet? What was Jonas saying? What about the court bond and grand jury and all that? He guessed Sheriff Birdwell would handle those things. Why hadn't anybody come to see him, some of the neighbors, the men he had been working with at the loading pen? Were they just staying away because they thought they wouldn't know what to say, how to act around him? What was Jonas Taggert going to *do?*

Sweat came out of him when these muddled thoughts milled around his mind, and it was hard to concentrate on the things he was trying to do.

Then, the second day, in midmorning, when he was in the barn, Louise came to the doorway, a cup towel still in her hand, and called to him.

"There's somebody riding up, Dave. From toward town."

He scanned the trail anxiously, then made out the dun horse of Tooley Webb, a herd hand who rode that way occasionally to and from the Colbert ranch. He was glad to see even Tooley, and urged him to get down and sit on the porch.

After small talk Dave asked quietly: "What's going on in town?"

Up to then Webb, a man of few words, had made no reference to the killing.

"Jonas Taggert is after you, Esperson. Reckon you know that."

"No, I haven't seen anybody since—in a couple of days. How you mean?"

Webb did not meet his eye. "I heard he was layin' for you. That he was set on squarin' it up, what happened to Coaley."

Webb left soon afterward. Dave could not be sure whether Louise, in the house, had heard through the open door what Webb had said. He concluded that she had, for her eyes were anxious when he came in to supper. But she asked no questions.

It's harder on her than anybody, he thought. He put an arm around her, in the old way, while she worked in the kitchen, and tried to grin and say genial, careless things. And she tried, too, but it was obviously pretense for both of them. The shadow was there, staying in the house, everywhere, as if it had moved in for good.

And the next day after breakfast he spoke the decision that had come to him through a restless night.

"I'm going to town this morning. We need a few things."

Her eyes were immediately fearful. She was young, but he was thinking how wise she was, too, with wisdom born of hardships, privations, and troubles.

"The sheriff—!" she almost whispered, her eyes appealing to him. "He told you, Dave—he said to stay away from town for a while."

He looked out the kitchen door to the prairie sweeps of his graze. "Louise, when a man gets thrown off a horse he's breaking, the first thing he ought to do is get up and get back on and ride that horse. It's not the horse he's got to master—it's his own opinion of himself. The horse that bucked him, it just represents something. He's got to do it then and there, not the next day or the next week. A man's got to get on top of his trouble or it'll get on top of him. I should have gone into town the first thing."

He hoped she knew what he was trying to say. It wasn't that Sheriff Birdwell hadn't meant well. It looked logical, to the sheriff, to try to avoid more trouble between Dave and a Taggert. But the sheriff wasn't the man who had killed. The man was Dave Esperson, and he had to handle this thing that gnawed at him in his own way, the way it spelled itself out to him, and not in somebody else's.

He was a man with fresh blood on his hands. He was not a killer, but he had killed. Now, from across the barrier that his mind had erected, the act was setting him off from his old world. He yearned, deeply and incessantly, for freedom to move, to go back and forth anywhere, any time, in the old way; to laugh and be carefree and have his mind loosed from these hobbles. To put the happiness back into Louise's eyes and into his own heart.

It couldn't be done, he had told himself through the long night, as he was trying to do. Maybe never at all. But he had to go into town, to move in his normal way, to meet men and talk with men. And if this involved coming face to face with Jonas Taggert, it would still have to be this way.

But what Louise said then came close to changing everything.

"I'm going with you."

The idea of that gave him racing chills along the spine, and she must have seen the quick negative forming on his tongue. Her eyes turned as determined as his own.

"I've got a stake in this, too, Dave. Had you thought of that? I'm the wife of the man that did the killing. I've got to go to town sometime, too, same as you, and meet people I know, and—and—get up and ride this buckin' horse that threw us!" She tried to smile, but her chin trembled and a film of tears went over her eyes.

He never could contest Louise when her eyes did that. And he made himself see her side, it sinking in that there were two of them, Louise and him, always. Not just one.

He got out the buggy and they rode in, talking little, and hitched on the main street under tree shade, and walked together down the plank walk in front of the stores.

The first person they met was Wilson, the hardware man, standing in the doorway of his store. He touched his hat and said, "Howdy-do, Mrs. Esperson, howdy, Dave."

Then chuckling, he said, "Heard you fellows expect to get thirty dollars a round for those steers, Dave. Sure would like to sell you a new buggy to replace that old relic you're drivin'."

Dave grinned, because Wilson had been trying to sell him a buggy for a year. And Louise said, "I'm working on him, Mr. Wilson."

In the general store the clerk who filled their grocery order talked casually about the range and the dry weather. When they started to the buggy, Dave carrying the box, somebody called his name loudly from across the street. It was Mid Owens, who angled over, stopping them in the middle of the street. He wanted to set a day for swapping help on building some fences. This done, Mid ambled off, after telling Louise straight-faced that the only reason he'd work on Dave's blasted fences was so he could eat some of her good cooking at dinnertime.

Ed Oliver bumped into them as they entered the post office.

Oliver beamed and thumped Dave on the chest and said, "Them cattle will be in Fort Worth tomorrow—just keep your fingers crossed that the market holds up."

There were a lot of things he wanted to

ask Oliver. But the man gave him no chance, rambling on about the cattle, the way he always did, and he was clomping off across the street before Dave got a word in.

It was like that all the way down the other side of the street, in the stores, and in front of the White Flat Hotel. And Dave felt good inside, because it was just like any other day, any other trip to town. Louise beside him, pretty as Indian paintbrush in the dress she was wearing, her eyes shining each time a man touched his hat and spoke neighborly to them.

It was just like any other day—on the outside. But it was all too pat. The people were doing their best, the way they saw it. Underneath, it settled nothing. What he suffered from, he knew, was like a sickness, and these things were just the medicine of relief, not the big cure he had to have.

They were near the end of the row of frame fronts, as far as the sidewalk went.

Louise's hand on his arm tightened.

"We're not going any farther, are we?"

He looked straight ahead. "Yes. All the way."

"Not past the saloon!"

But he kept walking.

Where the planks played out, there was a

step down to the hard-packed clay walk that ran in front of a long stretch of weedy vacant ground. And beyond that, where horses were tied to a hitch rail in front, was the wide flat-topped 'dobe building that housed the White Flat Saloon. It was the hangout, the last structure on the street. Off to itself, a meaningful symbol of the old and lawless days, away from the new part of town, with just the railroad right-of-way and the mesquite-studded prairie beyond. The sun was nearing high noon, and the log-pillared awning in front of the saloon made a dark shadow across the length of the packed caliche porch.

As they stepped down from the plank walk to the clay path a man was entering the White Flat's screen doors. He hesitated, a hand pulling the screen back, and looked at them, then went inside. When they were halfway across the vacant lots, another man came out.

This one walked slowly from the doorway, alone. He came down the earthen porch in the shadow. He stopped on the edge of the porch, facing them. He was in shirt-sleeves and black hat; not a big man, slightly stooped. He wore a gun.

"Dave!" Louise whispered. "Let's go back."

But he kept walking, with no feeling in his legs at all, nor any clear thought in his brain, except to keep walking toward Jonas Taggert.

Another half-dozen paces. Jonas's dark features began to come in focus, but not distinctly yet.

Dave said without turning his head, "You stay here."

But she kept the slow stride with him, not faltering.

"Dave, you'd better unbutton your coat now."

He told her, not even thinking, but speaking mechanically, watching Jonas's stance of feet wide parted:

"No use—I didn't bring the gun."

He heard, but it was a sound a thousand miles away, her low gasp.

Then he stopped and half turned, taking his eyes off Jonas and looking down at Louise.

"You really better stay here. I'd rather you would."

His eyes burned the meaning into her, and she understood. A man had to go the last distance alone. He saw in her eyes that she knew this, that this was the way he had to have the cleansing he craved, and he found time to marvel as he always did at the depth of her understanding. Because this was the moment to wash the blood off his mind, if it ever got washed off. He did not feel fear, but only a kind of tired resignation, as if he had checked the entire heavy load on to shoulders somewhere that were stronger than his own. It was the way he had to ride the big trouble, and have the whole town to walk in, not just the nice, neighborly part back where the plank sidewalks were.

From the tail of his eye he caught the front of the frame structure off toward the rails on the left, which was the temporary court-house, and the tall white-hatted figure who emerged to the gallery. Sheriff Birdwell. But that was a hundred yards away. As if he had already seen the distance was too great for him to make any difference, the sheriff had leaned against a post, just watching.

Dave walked on alone, not fast, not slow, holding sight on Jonas's face and hands, everything, and then to Jonas's tightened eyes when near enough to see them.

Now they were so close that words could be said without even raising a voice, had either spoken.

Close enough for the first deadly words, the opening movement, the prelude of hate and revenge before the gunplay.

And in that moment, with a calm intuition that came from out of nowhere, Dave felt a hundred pairs of eyes on his back in the enormous silence behind him. It was as if he walked for many people. That he was all the town, the neighbors, the essence of the new and civilized life out here. That somebody someday had to cross the weedy gap to the White Flat Saloon, and that this was the day and he was the one.

Jonas's eyes shifted.

Dave saw them change expression and work across to the right-hand side of the street, then beyond Dave's shoulders to the street behind him.

Maybe Jonas saw. The people who had emerged at store fronts. The men with guns on. The heads turned to watch, a town stopped in its tracks, and, across the street behind him, a man with a law badge and a courthouse.

Jonas's eyes came back to fasten no higher than Dave's chest. And when Dave would have to turn aside, or Jonas would have to move from his spread-legged stance, Jonas, at the last second, moved aside.

His mouth opened, as if he meant to say something, but no words came and Dave passed by, with not a yard to spare between his right shoulder and Jonas's chest.

In front of the screen doors Dave paused, and there was no sound at all from inside. He walked on, stepping off to the road at the far end of the saloon porch, and angled slowly on toward where Sheriff Birdwell still leaned motionlessly against a post.

Halfway across, Dave slowed his stride, stopped, and turned around.

Louise was walking toward the saloon porch.

He waited. He saw her small, unhurrying figure, the splash of colors in her cotton dress, and the people who were frozen dots beyond, along the distant streets and sidewalks.

She stepped from the path to the White Flat's shaded porch, coming in Dave's footsteps, and he saw Jonas Taggert, now pushed against the wall, clumsily raise his right hand and touch his hat brim as Louise passed him by.

As she came on to him he saw Jonas mount a horse at the hitch rail, look undecided right and left, then ride off slowly across the weedy lots, not looking back.

Together, they walked on to the path on the other side, toward the courthouse where Sheriff Birdwell still leaned against the post, while the town behind them picked up its usual sounds and motion again, with people going their various ways.

Norman A. Fox began writing stories about his home state of Montana for the pulp magazines just prior to World War II, and was soon a regular contributor to such top-of-the-line publications as Western Story *and* Dime Western. *His first novel,* Gun-Handy, *was published in 1941; over the next twenty years, until his tragic death in 1960, he wrote thirty-four more novels—among them such memorable titles as* Reckoning at Rimbow, Tall Man Riding, *and* Badlands Beyond. *The collections* The Valiant Ones *and the posthumously published* They Rode the Shining Hills *contain some of his best short stories, but none of them is better than the deceptively simple short-short that follows.*

The Makings

Norman A. Fox

They had a fire going behind the bluff overlooking Hibbs's place when Fremont came quartering up. He saw the shapes of men

103

and rifles black against it, and there was something else that interested him, too, something intangible in the starlight. There had to be a name for it. Coming down from his horse, he kept his head below the level of the bluff; this was instinct, but it gave him the word he sought: fear.

He stood, a tall, saddle-gaunted man grown gray at the temples. He said, "They told me in town."

Fitch Littlefield stirred among the assembled dozen. "So that's where you were! We combed the Rocking Chair fine for you."

It was there again, in Littlefield's voice, the fear.

Fremont touched his thumb to the circle of pasteboard dangling from his shirt pocket. "I run out of tobacco, Sheriff. It was closer to the crossroads than to the bunkhouse."

Barney Sands moved up. To his dim bulk Fremont gave a nod that held as much deference as a cow-country employer demanded. "You've got him cornered, Barney?"

"He's holding down Hibbs's shack. Alone."

Fremont looked around. "Ain't there enough of you?"

"More dead men won't bring the Dutchman back to life," Littlefield said.

"What kind of a man is Brokaw? Will he crumble if we rush him?"

"Barney could have told you," Fremont said. "We both went to work for Barney the same day."

"I never really knew him," Barney Sands said. "Maybe he was just hungry and edgy and the store looked soft to him, and the Dutchman made the wrong move. Maybe he's turned into a .45-caliber badman. He had the makings."

"To hell he did," somebody said and giggled. "I knew Curly when he rode this range. All his money went to poker and girls. Never met him but what the first thing he did was borrow my tobacco and papers."

Littlefield said, "What are we up against, Fremont?"

Fremont shook his head. Funny that when you hadn't seen a man for so long you'd forgot his face, you could still remember his smile. Funny it was always the little things that stuck. He said, "Curly and me lit out of Texas ten-twelve years ago. We trailed north. We had a lot of fun together. We went to work for Barney, but Brokaw didn't stick. He was fiddle-footed."

"But you knew him," Littlefield persisted. "You got him out of a few scrapes in those days. Will he crumble?"

"I don't think so. Let me go talk to him."

Sands said, "I don't want to lose a good man."

Fremont's voice turned cold. "He should have a chance to speak his piece."

Sands shrugged. "You always was a damn fool as far as he was concerned."

"We had a lot of fun together," Fremont said.

Littlefield scowled. "If there's trouble, crack a cap."

Fremont said, "He'll listen to me, Sheriff. Isn't that what you were thinking when you combed Rocking Chair fine?" He gave his gun belt a hitch and crawled to the crest of the bluff and cupped his hands to his mouth. He called, "Curly! It's me, Steve Fremont. I'm coming down there, Curly."

Below him lay the shack, tar paper silvered by starshine, this bleak homestead breaking an immensity of space. Fremont walked down the slant without haste, keeping his hands hanging straight down. He came to the fence, and his shirt was sticking under the arms, and he wondered then what counted with men, the things they did together at twenty, or what they had become at thirty. He thought, *Why did he have to come back to this range?* The yard was hard packed and gray with the emptying of much dishwater. The shack's door opened slightly, and Curly Brokaw said, "I don't like this, Fremont!"

Fremont said, "Let me in, Curly," making it friendly.

The one room was cluttered and odoriferous, and starlight came though the window. Brokaw said, when the door was closed, "There's a slew of them out there, eh?" and all the fear wasn't on the other side of the bluff.

Fremont said, "Too many for you, Curly. Will you walk back with me?"

The years had leaned down Brokaw, but they were still of a build. The floor creaked with the uneasy movement of Brokaw's body. He said, "You here as a friend, Steve?"

Fremont said, "The Dutchman wasn't much to me. But he had no harm in him. There don't need to be any more dead men."

"I didn't mean to shoot him." Brokaw's voice trembled. "I only wanted to fill a tow sack full of grub. Why did he crowd me?" He paused, and Fremont could feel the fear rising till it swirled in the darkness. "They'll hang me, Steve!"

"They let me come because they know we was friends," Fremont said. "I'm trying to make it easy for you."

Brokaw drew in a hard breath. "I should have known you came to help me. All you've got to do is stay here, partner. I'll walk out. They'll hold their fire, not being sure."

Fremont shook his head.

Brokaw smiled, and Fremont saw the smile in the starlight; it was the old smile, even with the fear in it. "You wouldn't want to be the one who leads me to the rope," Brokaw said. "Not after the times we had together. On a stack of Bibles, I never meant that store man harm. All I want is the chance to get through that door."

"To hit another store on another range?"

"I'll get me a new name and a job. So help me!"

There was the echo of Barney Sands's voice in this room saying, "You always was a damn fool as far as he was concerned."

"I've been ten years on this range," Fremont said slowly. "I won't have a friend."

"Ten years of being somebody's faithful dog. Ten years of growing on people. I can guess how you've stacked up, Steve. They'll

108

forgive you a heap. They'd do the same if they'd been as close as you and me."

There was an inevitability here that was too great for Fremont, and he wondered if this was what had brought him here, really. He said wearily, "I never was able to hold out against you. I'll give you your start. But you're a fool unless you keep that gun cased. A shot will fetch them running."

Brokaw let out a long-drawn sigh. "Another hour and I'd have busted down and took my chance. It's been plain hell, Steve. Not even a smoke. Have you got the makings?"

Fremont took out the new tobacco sack and tossed it to a table. Brokaw reached for it and made a cigarette, stepping beyond the window to light it. His face, stark in the matchlight, had grown more gaunt, but the old recklessness was there. He said, "Thanks. Mind if I keep this? You can get more. I had to light out of that store so fast I didn't even have time to lay my hands on tobacco." And he pocketed the sack and turned toward the door.

There was no thought in Fremont, only a stirring in his stomach. He said, "I've changed my mind, Curly. I'm not letting you go."

A hard sucking at the cigarette revealed Brokaw. His face was an animal's. He said, "I was afraid of that."

Fremont tried for his gun then, but Brokaw was faster. He'd always been faster. Sound filled the shack, and fire was in it, and pain, and Fremont went to the floor, numbed and voiceless, his right arm of no use to him. He went down with the sound of the door slamming; he heard the beat of boots across the yard and the shouts and the rifle fire and the thud of a tall man falling.

He lay there waiting for them to come to him, and he was remembering the man who had made a joke about the makings. Funny how it was always the little things that stuck. Yet it was true: Brokaw had never had the price of tobacco. Some men worked for their needings, and some men leaned on the ones who worked, and in a little thing like that you could see the pattern of a man's living. And the way Curly's pattern ran, sooner or later there'd be another dead man on another range. So—But Fremont was still remembering Curly's smile, and he was very sick. . . .

No one writes consistently top-notch Western fiction better than Henry W. Allen. Under his pseudonyms, Clay Fisher and Will Henry, he has won wide critical acclaim and four Spur Awards, two for Best Novel and two for Best Short Story; and it is not by accident that he has contributed more fine stories to the Best of the West series—"The Streets of Laredo" is the seventh—than any other writer. Others can be found in such Clay Fisher collections as The Oldest Maiden Lady in New Mexico and Other Stories *and* Nine Lives West. *Standouts among his novels include* Who Rides with Wyatt, Where the Sun Now Stands, *and* Alias Butch Cassidy *(as by Will Henry), and* Red Blizzard *and* The Brass Command *(as by Fisher).*

The Streets of Laredo

Clay Fisher

Call him McComas. Drifter, cowboy, card-sharp, killer. A man already on the road back from nowhere. Texas of the time was full of him and his kind. And sick with the fullness.

McComas had never been in Laredo. But his shadows, many of them, had been there before him. He knew what to expect from the townsfolk when they saw him coming on, black and weedy and beardgrown, against the late afternoon sun. They would not want him in their town, and McComas could not blame them. Yet he was tired, very tired, and had come a long, tense way that day.

He steeled himself to take their looks and to turn them away as best he might. What he wanted was a clean bed, a tub bath, a hotel meal, and a short night's sleep. No women, no cards, no whisky. Just six hours with the shades drawn and no one knocking at the door. Then, God willing, he would be up in the blackness before the dawn. Up and long gone and safe over the border in Nueva Leon, Old Mexico, when that Encinal sheriff showed up to begin asking questions of the law in Laredo. The very last thing he wanted in Texas was trouble. But that was the very last thing he had ever wanted in any place, and the very first he had always gotten. In Laredo it started as it always started, everywhere, with a woman.

112

Still, this time it was different. This time it was like no trouble that had ever come to him before. Somehow, he knew it. He sensed it before his trim gelding, Coaldust, set hoof in the streets of Laredo.

Those border towns were all laid out alike. Flat as a dropped flapjack. One wide street down the middle, running from sagebrush on one end to the river on the other. Some frame shacks and adobes flung around in the mesquite and catclaw, out where the decent people did not have to look at them. Then, the false fronts lining the main street. And, feeding off that, half a dozen dirt alleys lying in two lines on either side like pigs suckling a sow asleep in the sun. After these, there were only the church, school, and cemetery. It was the latter place, clinging on the dry-hill flanks of the town, where the land was even too poor for the Mexican shacks, that McComas and Coaly were presently coming to.

It lay to their left, and there was a burying party moving out from town, as they moved in. McComas had to pull Coaly off the road to let the procession pass. For some reason he felt strange, and hung there to watch the little party. It was then he saw the girl.

She was young and slim, with a black

Spanish *reboza* covering her head. As the buggy in which she was riding with the frock-coated parson drew abreast of McComas, she turned and stared directly at him. But the late sun was in his eyes and he could not see her features. Then, they were gone on, leaving McComas with a peculiar, unpleasant feeling. He shook as to a chill. Then, steadied himself. It was no mystery that the sight had unsettled him. It was a funeral, and he had never liked funerals.

They always made him wonder though.

Who was it in the coffin? Was it a man or woman? Had they died peaceful or violent? What had they done wrong, or right? Would he, or she, be missed by friends, mourned by family, made over in the local newspaper, maybe even mentioned in the San Antonio and Austin City papers?

No, he decided. Not this one. There were no family and friends here. That girl riding in the preacher's rig wasn't anybody's sister. She just didn't have the look. And the two roughly dressed Mexican laborers sitting on the coffin in the wagon ahead of the buggy were certainly not kith or kin of the deceased. Neither was the seedy driver. As for the square-built man on the sorrel mare heading up the procession, he did not need the pewter star pinned on his vest to tag him for McComas. The latter could tell a deputy sheriff as far as he could see one, late sun in the eyes, or not.

The deputy could tell McComas, too. And he gave him a hard looking over as he rode by. They exchanged the usual nods, careful and correct, and the deputy rode on, as any wise deputy would.

Directly, he led the buggy and the wagon into the weed-grown gate of the cemetery, and creaking up the rise to a plot on the crown of the hill. There, the drivers halted their horses, let down their cargoes. Still, McComas watched from below.

The two Mexicans strained with the coffin. It was a long coffin, and heavy. A man, McComas thought. A young man, and standing tall. One who had been taken quick, with no warning, and not long ago. No, this was no honored citizen they were putting under. Honored citizens do not come to boothill in the late afternoon with the town deputy riding shotgun over the ceremony. Nor with only a lantern-jawed, poor-bones preacher and a leggy young girl in a black Mexican shawl for mourners. Not by considerable.

McComas might even know the man in that coffin. If he did not, he could describe him perilously close. All he had to do was find the nearest mirror and look into it.

Again, he shivered. And again controlled himself.

He was only tired and worn down. It was only the way he felt about funerals. He always felt dark in his mind when he saw a body going by. And who didn't, if they would be honest enough to admit it? Nobody likes to look at a coffin, even empty. When there is somebody in it and being hauled dead-march slow with the wagon sounding creaky and the people not talking and the cemetery gates waiting rusty and half-sagged just down the road, a man does not need to be on the dodge and nearly drunk from want of sleep to take a chill and to turn away and ride on feeling sad and afraid inside.

In town, McComas followed his usual line. He took a room at the best hotel, knowing that the first place the local law will look for a man is in the second-and third-rate fleatraps where the average fugitive will hole up. Laredo was a chancey place. A funnel through which poured the scum of bad ones down into Old Mexico. If a man did not care to be skimmed off with the others of that outlaw dross, he had to play it differently than they did. He didn't skulk. He rode in bold as brass and bought the best. Like McComas and Coaly and the Border Star Hotel.

But, once safely in his room, McComas could not rest. He only paced the floor and peeked continually past the drawn shade down into the sun haze of the main street.

It was perhaps half an hour after signing the register, that he gave it up and went downstairs for just one drink. Twenty minutes more and he was elbows-down on the bar of the Ben Hur Saloon with the girl.

Well, she was not a girl, really. Not any longer.

Young, yes. And nicely shaped. But how long did a girl stay a girl at the Laredo prices? She was like McComas. Short on the calendar count, long on the lines at mouth and eye corners. If he had been there and back, she had made the trip ahead of him.

Pretty? Not actually. Yet that face would haunt a man. McComas knew the kind. He had seen them in every town. Sometimes going by in the young dusk on the arm of an overdressed swell—through a dusty train window at the depot—passing, perfume-close, in the darkened hall of a cheap hotel. Not pretty. No, not ever pretty. But always exciting, sensuous, female, and available;

yours for the night, if you could beat the other fellow to them.

Billie Blossom was that kind.

Her real name? McComas did not care. She accepted McComas, he did not argue Billie Blossom.

She came swinging up to him at the bar, out of the nowhere of blue cigar smoke that hid the poker tables and the dance floor and the doleful piano player with his two-fingered, tinkly, sad chorus of "Jeannie with the Light Brown Hair." She held his eyes a long slow moment, then smiled.

"Hello, cowboy, you want to buy me a drink before you swim the river?"

And he stared back at her an equal long slow moment, and said, "Lady, for a smile like that I might even get an honest job and go to work."

That was the start of it.

They got a bottle and glasses from the barman, moved off through the smoke, McComas following her. She had her own table, a good one, in a rear corner with no windows and facing the street doors. They sat down, McComas pouring. She put her fingers on his hand when he had gotten her glass no more than damp. And, again, there was that smile shaking him to his boottops.

"A short drink for a long road, cowboy," she said.

He glanced at her with quick suspicion, but she had meant nothing by it.

"Yes," he nodded, "I reckon that's right," and poured his own drink to match hers. "Here's to us," he said, lifting the glass. "Been everywhere but hell, and not wanting to rush that."

She smiled and they drank the whisky, neither of them reacting to its raw bite. They sat there, then, McComas looking at her.

She was an ash blonde with smoky gray eyes. She had high cheekbones, a wide mouth, wore entirely too much paint and powder. But always there was that half curve of a smile to soften everything. Everything except the cough. McComas knew that hollow sound. The girl had consumption, and badly. He could see where the sickness had cut the flesh from her, leaving its pale hollows where the lush curves had been. Yet, despite the pallor and the wasted form, she seemed lovely to McComas.

He did not think to touch her, nor to invite her to go upstairs, and she thanked him with her eyes. They were like a young boy and girl; he not seeing her, she not seeing him, but each seeing what used to be, or might have been, or, luck willing, still might be.

McComas would not have believed that it could happen. Not to him. But it did. To him and Billie Blossom in the Ben Hur Saloon in Laredo, Texas. They had the bottle and they had the sheltered corner and they were both weary of dodging and turning away and of not being able to look straight back at honest men and women nor to close their eyes and sleep nights when they lay down and tried to do so. No-name McComas and faded Billie Blossom. Outlawed killer, dancehall trollop. In love at first sight and trying desperately hard to find the words to tell each other so. Two hunted people locking tired eyes and trembling hands over a bareboard table and two unwashed whisky tumblers in a flyblown cantina at sundown of a hell's hot summer day, two miles and then minutes easy lope from freedom and safety and a second beckoning chance in Old Mexico, across the shallow Rio Grande.

Fools they were, and lost sheep.

But, oh! that stolen hour at sunset in that smoke-filled, evil-smelling room. What things they said, what vows they made, what wild sweet promises they swore!

It was not the whisky. After the first, small

drink, the second went untasted. McComas and Billie Blossom talked on, not heeding the noise and coarseness about them, forgetting who they were, and where. Others, telling of their loves, might remember scented dark parlors. Or a gilding of moonlight on flowered verandas. Or the fragrance of new-mown hay by the riverside. Or the fireflies in the loamy stardust of the summer lane. For McComas and Billie Blossom it was the rank odor of charcoal whisky, the choke of stogie cigars, the reek of bathless men and perspiring, sacheted women.

McComas did not begrudge the lack. He had Billie's eyes for his starry lane, her smile for his summer night. He needed no dark parlors, no willow-shaded streams. He and Billie had each other. And they had their plans.

The piano played on. It was the same tune about Jeannie and her light brown hair. McComas feared for a moment that he might show a tear or a tremble in his voice. The song was that beautiful, and that close, to what he and Billie were feeling, that neither could speak, but only sit with their hands clasped across that old beer-stained table in the Ben Hur Saloon making their silence count more than any words. Then, McComas found his voice. As he talked, Billie nodded, yes, to everything he said, the tears glistening beneath the long black lashes that swept so low and thickly curled across her slanted cheekbones. She was crying because of her happiness, McComas knew, and his words rushed on, deeply, recklessly excited.

He did not remember all that he told her, only the salient, pressing features of it: that they would meet beyond the river when darkness fell; that they would go down into Nueva Leon, to a place McComas knew, where the grass grew long and the water ran sweet and a man could raise the finest cattle in all Mexico; that there they would find their journey's end, rearing a family of honest, God-fearing children to give the ranch over to when McComas was too aged and saddlebent to run it himself, and when he and Billie Blossom had earned their wicker chairs and quiet hours in the cool shadows of the ranchhouse *galeria*, "somewhere down there in Nueva Leon."

It went like that, so swift and tumbling and stirring to the imagination, that McComas began to wonder if it were not all a dream. If he would not awaken on that uneasy bed upstairs in the Border Star Hotel. Awaken with the sound of the sheriff's step in the hallway outside. And his voice calling low and urgent through the door, "Open up, McComas; it's me, and I've come for you at last."

But it was no dream.

Billie proved that to McComas when she led him from the table and pulled him in under the shadows of the stairwell and gave him the longest, hardest kiss he had ever been given in his life. And when she whispered to him, "Hurry and get the horses, McComas; I will pack and meet you in the alley out back."

McComas pushed across the crowded room, the happiest he had been in his lifetime memory. But he did not allow the new feeling to narrow the sweep of his restless eyes. Nor slow his crouching, wolflike step. Nor let his right hand stray too far from the worn wooden grip of his .44. He still knew his name was McComas, and that he was worth $500, alive or dead, to the Encinal sheriff and his La Salle County posse. It was the price of staying alive in his profession, this unthinking wariness, this perpetual attitude of *qui vive*. Especially in a strange town at sundown. With the hanging tree waiting in the next county north. And a long life and new love beckoning from across the river, from two miles south, from ten minutes away.

He went out of the batwing saloon doors, glidingly, silently, as he always went out of strange doors, anywhere.

He saw Anson Starett a half instant before the latter saw him. He could have killed him then, and he ought to have. But men like McComas did not dry-gulch men like Anson Starett. Not even when they wear the pewter star and come up on your heels hungry and hard-eyed and far too swiftly for your mind to realize and to grasp and to believe that they have cut you off at last. You do not let them live because they are gallant and tough and full of cold nerve. You do it for a far simpler reason. And a deadlier one. You do it for blind, stupid pride. You do it because you will not have it said that McComas need-ed the edge on any man. And while you do not, ever, willingly, give that edge away, nei-ther do you use it to blindside a brave man like Sheriff Anson Starett of Encinal.

What you do, instead, is to keep just enough of the edge to be safe. And to give just enough of it away to be legally and mor-ally absolved of murder. It was a fine line, but very clear to McComas. It wasn't being noble. Just practical. Every man is his own jury when he wears a gun for money. No man wants to judge himself a coward. All that has been gone through when he put on the gun to begin with. Perhaps, it was even what made him put on the gun to begin with. What did it matter now? Little, oh, very, very little. Almost nothing at all.

"*Over here, Anse,*" said McComas quietly, and the guns went off.

McComas was late. Only a little, but he was late. He knew and damned himself, even as he spun to the drive of Starett's bullet, back against the front wall of the Ben Hur, then sliding down it to the boardwalk at its base.

But he had gotten Starett. He knew that. The Encinal sheriff was still standing, swaying out there in the street, but McComas had gotten him. And, he told himself, he would get him again—now—just to make sure.

It took all his will to force himself up from the rough boards beneath him. He saw the great pool of blood, where he had fallen, but it did not frighten him. Blood and the terrible shock of gunshot wounds were a part of his trade. Somehow, it was different this time, though. This time he felt extremely light and queer in the head. It was a feeling he had never had before. It was as though he were watching himself. As though he were standing to one side saying, "Come on, McComas, get up; get up and put the rest of your shots into him before he falls; drive them into him while he is still anchored by the shock of that first hit. . . ."

But McComas knew that he had him. He knew, as he steadied himself and emptied the .44 into Starett, that he had him and that everything was still all right. But he would have to hurry. He could not stay there to wait for Starett to go down. He had to get out of there while there was yet time. Before the scared sheep in the saloon got their nerve back and came pouring out into the street. Before the sound of the gunfire brought the local law running up the street to help out the sheriff from Encinal.

He thought of Billie Blossom. . . . The good Lord knew he did. But she couldn't do anything for him now. . . . It was too late for Billie Blossom and gunfighter McComas. . . . They had waited and talked too long. . . . Now he must get out. . . . He must not let the girl see him hurt and bleeding. . . . She must not know. . . . He had to get to his horse at the hitching rail. . . . Had to find Coaly and swing up on him and give him his sleek black head and let him go away up the main street and out of Laredo. . . . Yes, he must find Coaly at the rail . . . find him and get up on him and run! run! run! for the river . . . just he and Coaly, all alone and through the gathering dusk. . . .

He could not find Coaly, then. When he turned to the hitching rail in front of the Ben Hur, his trim black racer was not there. He was not where he had left him, all saddled and loose-tied and ready to run. McComas was feeling light and queer again. Yet he knew he was not feeling that queer. Somebody had moved his horse. Somebody had untied him and taken him, while McComas was on the boardwalk from Starett's bullet. Somebody had stolen Coaly and McComas was trapped. Trapped and very badly hurt. And left all alone to fight or die on the streets of Laredo.

It was then that he heard the whisper. Then, that he whirled, whitefaced, and saw her standing at the corner of the saloon, in the alley leading to the back. Standing there with a black Mexican *reboza* drawn tightly over her ash blond hair, shadowing and hiding her hollow cheeks and great gray eyes. McComas could not distinctly see her face. Not under the twilight masking of that dark shawl. But he knew it was her. And he went

127

running and stumbling toward her, her soft voice beckoning as though from some distant hill, yet clear as the still air of sundown—*"Here, McComas, here! Come to my arms, come to my heart, come with me—!"*

He lunged on. Stumbled once. Went down. Staggered back up and made it to her side before the first of the murmuring crowd surged out of the Ben Hur to halt and stare at the great stain of blood spreading from the front wall of the saloon. The moment her white, cool hands touched him, took hold of him and held him up, he felt the strength flow into him again. The strength flow in and the queer cold feeling disappear from his belly and the cottony mist dissolve from before his straining eyes. Now he was all right.

He remembered clearly, as she helped him along the side of the cantina, looking down at his shirtfront and seeing the pump of the blood jumping, with each pulse, from the big hole torn midway between breastbone and navel. He remembered thinking clearly, "Dear Lord, he got me dead center! How could it have missed the heart?" Yet, he remembered, even as he heard his thought-voice ask the question, that these crazy things did happen with gun wounds. A shot could miss a vital by half a hair-width, and do no more harm than a fleshy scrape. There was only the shock and the weakness of the first smash, and no real danger at all unless the bleeding did not stop. And McComas knew that it would stop. It was already slowing. All he had to worry about was staying with Billie Blossom until she could get him to a horse. Then he would be able to make it away. He could ride. He had ridden with worse holes through him. He would make it. He would get across the river and he and Billie would still meet on the far side.

She had a horse waiting for him. He ought to have known she would, a girl like that, old to the ways of Texas strays and their traffic through the border towns. He should even have known that it would be his own horse, saddled and rested and ready to run through the night and for the river.

Yes, she had slipped out of the Ben Hur before the others. She had seen how it was with McComas and Anson Starett. And she had untied Coaly and led him down the alley, to the back, where McComas could swing up on him, now, and sweep away to the river and over it to the life that waited beyond. To the life that he and Billie Blossom had planned and that Anson Starett had thought he could stop with one bullet from his swift gun. Ah, no! Anson Starett! Not today. Not this day. Not with one bullet. Not McComas.

There was no kiss at Coaly's side, and no time for one.

But McComas was all right again. Feeling strong as a yearling bull. Smiling, even laughing, as he leaned down from the saddle to take her pale hand and promise her that he would be waiting beyond the river.

Yet, strangely, when he said it, she was not made happy.

She shook her head quickly, looking white and frightened and talking hurriedly and low, as she pressed his hand and held it to her wasted cheek. And the tears that washed down over McComas' hand were not warm, they were cold as the lifeless clay, and McComas heard her speak with a sudden chill that went through him like an icy knife.

"No, McComas, no! Not the river! Not while there is yet daylight. You cannot cross the river until the night is down. Go back, McComas. Go back the other way. The way that you came in this afternoon, McComas. Do you remember? Back toward the cemetery on the hill. You will be safe there, McComas. No one will think to look for you there. Do you hear me, McComas? Wait there for me. High on the hill, where you saw the open grave. You can watch the Laredo road from there. You can see the river. You can see the sheriff and his posse ride out. You can see when they are gone and when it is safe for you to ride out. Then we can go, McComas. I will meet you there, on the hill, by that new grave. We will go over the river together, when it is dark and quiet and all is at peace and we know no fear. Do you understand, McComas? Oh, dear God, do you hear and understand what I am telling you, my love—?"

McComas laughed again, trying to reassure her, and to reassure himself. Of course, he understood her, he said. And she was thinking smart. A sight smarter than McComas had been thinking since Starett's bullet had smashed him into that front wall and down onto the boardwalk. He got her calmed and quieted, he thought, before he spurred away. He was absolutely sure of it. And when he left her, turning in the saddle to look back as Coaly took him out and away from the filthy hovels of Laredo into the clean sweet smell of the mesquite and cat-claw chapparal, he could still see her smiling and waving to him, slender and graceful as a willow wand moving against the long purple shadows of the sunset.

It was only a few minutes to the cemetery. McComas cut back into the main road and followed along it, unafraid. He was only a mile beyond the town but in some way he knew he would not be seen. And he was not. Two cowboys came along, loping toward Laredo, and did not give him a second glance. They did not even nod or touch their hat brims going by, and McComas smiled and told himself that it always paid to wear dark clothes and ride a black horse in his hard business—especially just at sundown in a strange town.

The rusted gates of the cemetery loomed ahead.

Just short of them, McComas decided he would take cover for a moment. There was no use abusing good luck.

Down the hill, from the new grave on the rise, were coming some familiar figures. They were the long-jawed preacher and square-built deputy sheriff he had passed earlier, on his way into Laredo. They might remember him, where two passing cowboys had shown no interest.

Up on the rise, itself, beyond the deputy and the parson's lurching buggy, McComas could see the two Mexican gravediggers putting in the last shovelfuls of flinty earth to fill the fresh hole where they had lowered the long black coffin from the flatbed wagon. And he could see, up there, standing alone and slightly apart, the weeping figure of the young girl in the black *reboza*.

McComas thought that was a kind, loyal thing for her to do. To stay to say goodbye to her lover. To wait until the preacher and the deputy and the gravediggers and the wagon driver had gone away, so that she might be alone with him. Just herself and God and the dead boy up there on that lonely, rocky rise.

Then, McComas shivered. It was the same shiver he had experienced on this same road, in this same place, earlier that afternoon. Angered, he forced himself to be calm. It was crazy to think that he knew this girl. That he had seen her before. He knew it was crazy. And, yet—

The deputy and the preacher were drawing near. McComas pulled Coaly deeper into the roadside brush, beyond the sagging gates. The deputy kneed his mount into a trot. He appeared nervous. Behind him, the preacher whipped up his bony plug. The rattle of the buggy wheels on the hard ruts of

133

the road clattered past McComas, and were gone. The latter turned his eyes once more toward the hilltop and the head-bowed girl.

He did not want to disturb her in her grief, but she was standing by the very grave where Billie Blossom had told him to meet her. And it was growing dark and Billie had wanted him to be up there so that he could see her coming from town to be with him.

He left Coaly tied in the brush and went up the hill on foot. He went quietly and carefully, so as not to bother the girl, not to violate her faithful sorrow. Fortunately, he was able to succeed. There was another grave nearby. It had a rough boulder for a head-stone, and a small square of sunbleached pickets around it. McComas got up to this other plot without being seen by the girl. He hid behind its rugged marker and tottering fence, watching to be sure the slender mourner had not marked his ascent.

Satisfied that she had not, he was about to turn and search the Laredo road for Billie Blossom, when he was again taken with the strange, unsettling chill of recognition for the girl in the black *reboza*. This time, the chill froze his glance. He could not remove his eyes from her. And, as he stared at her, she reached into a traveling bag, which sat

134

upon the ground beside her. The bag was packed, as though for a hurried journey, its contents disordered and piled in without consideration. From among them, as McComas continued to watch, fascinated, the girl drew out a heavy Colt .41 caliber derringer. Before McComas could move, or even cry out, she raised the weapon to her temple.

He leaped up, then, and ran toward her. But he was too late. The derringer discharged once, the blast of its orange flame searing the *reboza*. McComas knew, from the delayed, hesitating straightness with which she stood before she fell, that it had been a death-shot. When he got to her, she had slumped across the newly mounded grave, her white arms reaching out from beneath the shroud of the *reboza* in a futile effort to reach and embrace the plain pine headboard of the grave. McComas gave the headboard but a swift side glance. It was a weathered, knotty, poor piece of wood, whipsawed in careless haste. The barn paint used to dab the deceased's name upon it had not even set dry yet. McComas did not give it a second look.

He was down on the ground beside the fallen girl, holding her gently to his breast so that he might not harm her should life, by any glad chance, be in her still.

But it was not.

McComas felt that in the limp, soft way that she lay in his arms. Then, even in the moment of touching her, the chill was in him again. He *did* know this girl. He knew her well. And more. He knew for whom she mourned; and he knew whose name was on that headboard.

It was then he shifted her slim form and slowly pulled the black *reboza* away from the wasted oval face. The gray eyes were closed, thick lashes downswept. The ash blond hair lay in a soft wave over the bruised hole in the pale temple. It was she. Billie Blossom. The girl from the streets of Laredo.

McComas came to his feet. He did not want to look at that weathered headboard. But he had to.

There was only a single word upon it. No first name. No birth date. No line of love or sad farewell.

Just the one word:

"McComas"

He went down the hill, stumbling in his haste. He took Coaly out of the brush and swung up on him and sent him outward through the night and toward the river. It was a quiet night, with an infinite field of gleaming stars and a sweet warm rush of prairie wind to still his nameless fears. He had never known Coaly to fly with such a fleet, sure gait. Yet, swiftly as he went, and clearly as the starlight revealed the silvered current of the river ahead, they did not draw up to the crossing. He frowned and spoke to Coaly, and the black whickered softly in reply and sprang forward silently and with coursing, endless speed through the summer night.

That was the way that McComas remembered it.

The blackness and the silence and the stars and the rush of the warm, sweetly scented wind over the darkened prairie.

He forgot if they ever came to the river.

*One of the most popular of contemporary West-
ern writers, Lewis B. Patten published more
than one hundred novels between 1952 and
1980. Two of them were recipients of WWA
Best Novel Spurs:* The Red Sabbath *(1969)
and* A Killing in Kiowa *(1973). He received
another Spur in 1970 for Best Juvenile Novel—*The Meeker Massacre, *in collaboration
with Wayne D. Overholser—and in 1979 was
presented with WWA's highest award of merit,
the Golden Saddleman Award. A number of
his books and short stories were adapted for films
and TV, most notably* Death of a Gunfighter,
*which became a well-received theatrical movie
featuring Richard Widmark and Lena Horne.
"Too Good With a Gun," which appeared in*
Zane Grey's Western Magazine *in 1950, was
his first published story.*

Too Good with a Gun

Lewis B. Patten

They rode through the thin warmth of this

bright winter's day, a man and a girl, together on the bouncing seat of the grayed and weathered buckboard, very conscious of one another each time their bodies touched, laughing and red of face by turns.

Behind rode the boy, Claude, jogging gently in the rising dust. Suddenly he tugged at his sorrel's reins and as the horse fell behind, called to Russ Baker, "I'll catch up later," his fifteen-year-old mind dimly shocked by the man's antics.

Shaking out his rope, he dropped an experimental loop over a nearby clump of greasewood, rearing back in the saddle to tighten it as the blocky mustang braced to a stop.

He slid off the horse, running as he hit the ground. Grinning triumphantly, he reached the end of the tightened lariat in a matter of seconds. Pulling slack into the rope, he loosened the loop and slipped it off the spiny brush, then tensed abruptly and fell into a half-crouch. Easily, still crouching, he turned and his slim brown hand dropped swiftly. His gun cleared its holster and racketed across the wide valley as it bucked in his hand. A rock across the road shot off dust and Claude grinned, widely now as he holstered the gun.

The horse, startled, was moving away trailing the lariat in the dust. Claude broke into a run, caught the end of the rope and, jerking on it, yelled, "Whoa. Steady now."

The horse turned to face him obediently, backing gently as slack came into the rope. Again the boy let the grin cross his narrow, smooth face and he tipped his hat back on his head and swaggered to the horse, coiling the rope as he went. He mounted, kicked the horse into a run, and with a yell took after the buckboard.

He had meant to ride up behind the buckboard, shooting and yelling as a badman might, attacking a stage, but the sight of Russ Baker, blushing and grinning foolishly beside Claude's sister Edie, changed his mind and brought a look of disgust to his face. He felt ashamed for Russ and the shame touched him, too, so great was his liking and respect for the man. That this slim, taciturn rider should let a slip of a girl change him so was beyond belief.

He came up behind, not noticing the dust, and let his horse trot, its muzzle a foot from the rear of the buckboard. His head dropped onto his chest in an attitude of bored relaxation, but the eyes were alive and bright in their blackness and occasionally the full lips moved, tightening or twisting. Once he snarled under his breath, "Draw, you dirty sidewinder," his hand hanging clawlike over the holstered grip of his gun and his body growing tense.

The town of Four-Mile came into sight and Russ slowed the team. Edie brushed the dust carefully from her clothes and took on a prim expression and sat in the far corner of the seat, away from Russ.

Claude never paid much attention to Edie, but as she got down in front of Hatfield's store and walked across the board sidewalk, he noticed how pretty she was. Maybe it was the soft expression on her face or the way she moved her body, feeling Russ Baker's eyes upon her.

Claude was dismounting, eyeing the green batwing doors of the saloon, and he wondered how long it would be before he could drum up enough nerve to walk down there and go on through them. Russ tied the team to the rail and Claude climbed up in the seat beside him. Russ looked at the boy, grinning with the hard, tight muscles of his face.

"Jist as well take it easy, Claude. She'll be a while."

Claude looked at this man, seeing him now as he had always been, without the change on him that came when he was with Edie. He said, "I busted a rock back there, drawin' an' whirlin' at the same time," unconscious of the pride in his voice, his eyes waiting for the man's approbation. Instead he saw the uneasiness and the regret coming into Russ's face and the man spoke softly.

"Your pa an' ma feel pretty strong about gun-fightin'. They give you that gun for varmints, not men. They jumped all over me for teachin' you as much as I have. You'd best forget it. I reckon a man gets along better in this world if he don't use a gun too good."

He stopped and the feeling that he was talking too much was plain on him, but he still had something on his mind, something that rankled within him. "Your pa thinks, an' mebbe he's right, that I'm too good with my gun to be good for Edie."

Claude thought about that, thought about how right Pa was most of the time, thought about how much he liked this lanky puncher. He wished Pa could see Russ like he did. He saw the brightness of Edie's dress through the open door of the store, saw the heavy shape of Mr. Hatfield beside her. He took his eyes away, letting them drift on down the street again toward the saloon and

142

he felt the helplessness in him because of his age.

He said with a surly impatience, "A man ought to know how to use a gun."

A horseman came down the street and dismounted behind the buckboard, tying his horse beside Claude's at the hitchrail. He grinned at Claude and came over, a friendly man, well liked and universally respected. He wore a gun, as most men did, but it was rusty.

Arnold Hoffman put a big calloused hand on Claude's shoulder and said, "How are you, boy? How's your pa an' ma?" but then Russ turned and the man forgot Claude and said, "I'll buy you a drink, Russ."

Russ started to move and then, looking at the doorway of the store, shook his head. "Another time. I'm waiting for Edie."

Claude felt his throat tightening and he wanted to say, "I'll drink with you," but he couldn't make his voice come out. In a moment it was too late and Arnold was striding away. Now the boy made his lips move: *I'll drink with you,* silently, and after clearing his throat, again: "I'll drink with you," his face consciously without expression.

Russ turned. "What did you say?" But

Claude only got hot and red of face. He muttered, "Nothin'."

Old man Hatfield's voice droned on inside the store and after a while another man came from the hotel and stopped on his way to the saloon to stand in front of the buckboard and stare hard at Russ.

His voice had a soft, sibilant sound to it. "Russ Baker! I'll be damned. You're a long ways from home."

Claude felt the tightening and the straightening up of the man in the seat beside him. He heard a voice, but it did not sound like Russ's usual, easy drawl.

Russ said, "Hello, Slick," and the silence grew heavy as the two men stared, warily and with obvious dislike of one another. Then the other man, thin and sardonic of face, went on by and entered the saloon. There was something about him that lingered behind, making Claude feel uneasy without knowing why.

He asked, strongly curious, "You know him, Russ? He's a stranger here."

"Knew him in Texas. Slick Everitt."

Claude whistled. "The gunfighter?" and when Russ nodded, a boy's awe came into Claude's face. He had not seen anything prepossessing about Everitt, but the man had a

144

reputation that was well known. He said, "Gee, I hope I get to be as good as him someday."

Russ laughed, a harsh, bitter laugh. "No. Not 'as good as him,' boy, because there ain't no 'good' in him. He's a human rattlesnake and there ain't a bit more feelin' in him than in a snake."

The minutes ran on, dragged into an hour, but Everitt had left something behind with the two on the buckboard seat. They could not take their minds from him. Edie came out once, smiling at them, and put some packages into the buckboard.

When she saw their faces she said, "Don't look so grim. It won't be long now."

After a while over the stillness of the street, Claude heard a table crash to the floor in the saloon and afterward an angry shout. Then he heard the low murmur of a man's voice, steadily cursing. An uneasiness touched him and he felt Russ straightening up beside him.

The batwings of the saloon swung open and Arnold Hoffman and the gunfighter, Everitt, came out together, propelled by Big Nick Bidwell, the saloonman, who had a huge, powerful hand grasping each of their arms. The steady cursing came from Everitt,

145

bubbling from his thin lips in a revolting stream. Hoffman wore an angry flush on his ordinarily open and friendly face.

Big Nick growled, "I had that back-bar mirror freighted from Salt Lake. I'll not have it broken now."

Everitt left off his cursing long enough to say, "I'll settle you when I'm through with this one."

Big Nick gave a little shove and the man staggered across the walk, nearly falling as he went into the street. He swung, crouching, the bright eyes resting on Big Nick for a moment and then going to Hoffman.

Russ Baker was moving next to Claude. He was down off the buckboard and around in front of the horses before Claude was scarcely aware of his movement. Everitt had his pale eyes on Arnold Hoffman and he stood there in an easy way, but tense and sure.

He said, "You want to tangle with me and you got a gun. Use it." As he watched Arnold, his eyes betrayed a hot and vicious pleasure.

Claude could see surprise and sudden knowledge of how this argument must end in Arnold's face. Arnold knew he was up against a gunfighter and he knew that he would die. Claude watched the play of expression on the man's face, felt a little sickened as he saw it go gray with fear, felt the man's shame with him for a moment, and then saw the hopeless courage come into the eyes. He moved his glance to Everitt and saw the evil there in the predatory, waiting stance, in the pale eyes. He thought of a rattler and saw no more pity here than he would in a striking snake.

He felt a little sick, knowing that Arnold would die, but then Russ called out, "Slick. Turn around this way."

Slick Everitt spoke without turning. "This ain't none of your business, Baker. Keep out of it."

Russ's voice had a slow, deep quality. "No. This ain't my business. Somethin' else is. I told you once that there wasn't a town big enough for the both of us. Reckon you forgot. You won't again."

Some of the sureness went out of Everitt as he faced Russ. The surprise that came to his face as Russ spoke puzzled Claude as did his words, never finished, "You're a liar. You never—"

Russ cut him short: "All right. All right. You've said enough."

Arnold's relief and gratitude were naked

things, unconcealed as his face trembled in the extremity of his emotion. Russ kept his eyes steadily on Slick. Claude had felt proud and less afraid as Russ called to the killer, but now his fear came back tenfold, fear for his friend.

He saw a bright movement behind Russ in the door of the store and Edie came out onto the walk. Russ said irritably, "Edie, get back in the store," but Edie just stood there, uncomprehending, until Hoffman caught her arm and pulled her in.

Claude's thoughts cried out, *Why'd you do it, Russ? Why'd you step into Arnold's fight? Now it's you that's—*

Things happened fast then. Claude's last impression was of the pitiless evil in the gunfighter's eyes and of surprise that Russ did not show more change. Then the guns came out and spoke across the narrow distance between the two, Russ's a shade faster, Everitt's so close afterward that the two reports nearly mingled. But the shock of Russ's bullet spoiled the other's aim. The evil and the life went out of Everitt's eyes and was replaced by a blankness. He grunted softly and then limply collapsed into the dust.

Russ shoved his gun back into its holster and stood there looking at the lifeless body before him until Edie spoke behind him: "Russ! Oh no!" her young face stricken.

After that there was a crowd and confusion and Edie went back into the store with another woman, weeping brokenly, and Russ did not want to talk to Claude or to anyone. Excitement was so strong in the boy that he hopped up and down from the ground to the seat of the buckboard and back again.

Edie came out, her face red and a little mottled, not looking at Russ, and Arnold went around to her and said, "I know how you folks feel about gunfightin', but he done it for me, Edie."

Russ's face was pale and completely without expression as he climbed up into the buckboard. Edie sat far in the corner of the seat, looking straight ahead. Claude tied his horse behind as soon as the buckboard had been backed out and got up between them. The ride home was a misery, with them both strangers to him and to each other.

After he had unhitched the team and put them away, Claude stood in the quiet dimness of the barn and automatically his hand fell to his gun, practicing, but he lifted it away again, shaking his head a little, the cold smoothness of the gun feeling strange and unfamiliar.

Mack Duncan came in and looked at his son and he was puzzled and wondering whether to be angry or not. He asked, "What in the devil is the matter with Edie and Russ? What'd Russ do to her?"

"Russ kilt Slick Everitt. Everitt was about to kill Arnold Hoffman over an argument an' Russ stepped in an' kilt him. Say, Pa, Russ knowed Everitt. But all he was aimin' to do was git Arnold out of it."

He saw Pa's face harden and saw him tighten his jaw. "I knew it'd come out in him. It's good it came out now before him an' Edie—"

Pa swung around and went out of the barn. Claude had to hurry to catch up.

He cried, "Pa, don't send him away: he ain't no killer. He done it for Arnold."

Mack Duncan stopped and put a hand on the boy's shoulder. "You see why I don't like you foolin' with a gun all the time? It changes a man. He always has to wonder if he can beat somebody else. I don't want you to be like that."

Claude began, "But, Pa," wanting to explain the difference between the killer, Everitt, and Russ, but he didn't have the words.

Mack Duncan said sharply, "Don't you argue now. Git some wood for your ma."

It took three loads to fill the woodbox. As he was gathering up the last armful he saw Russ go to his little room in the shed that huddled in the shelter of the barn.

Edie was helping Ma in the kitchen, her eyes red, and as Claude came in she was saying, "He looked so calm standing there, like Pa would shooting a snake or a squirrel. But it was a man he shot. Oh Ma, I guess I don't know him at all."

Pa came in and Russ followed behind and they sat down at the long table, except for Edie, who had gone to her room. Pa prayed, not quick and sloughing the words but slow, like he meant it. Then Ma put the food on the table and they set to.

Claude was ashamed for his ma and pa because they were so silent and still. He was opening his mouth to speak when Russ said, "Reckon I'll jist stay this month an' then go on back to Texas."

Ma looked relieved and Pa spoke, showing his shame and regret, but meeting Russ's eyes. "You been a good hand, Russ, but mebbe it's just as well." Russ knew what he meant, and so did Claude.

Claude burst out, "You ain't treatin' Russ right. He ain't done nothin' bad."

Pa glared and snapped out, "Claude!" but

Claude wasn't finished. He was scared but he felt reckless, too. He saw Russ shaking his head, but he went on: "He saved Arnold from havin' to pull that rusty old gun an' gittin' kilt doin' it. He ain't done nothin' worse than killin' a rattler."

Mack Duncan half rose in his chair and caught Claude by his shirt front across the table. "Git up an' go to your room."

Claude left, but as he did, he saw Russ wiping his mouth and rising. Ma and Pa were left alone at the table.

Instead of going to his own room, Claude went to Edie's. She looked up as he came in, wiping tears from her eyes.

Claude said, "Pa's wrong this time. Russ is goin' away. I hope you're satisfied." Bitterness was in his voice.

He went to the window and looked out. Russ was cantering out of the yard and his saddle and bedroll made a lumped shape on the ground beside the barn. Dusk lay over the yard, soft and heavy, and in a moment Russ was only a dark, blurred figure, growing smaller.

Claude told Edie bitterly, "Russ is leavin'. His saddle an' bedroll are there by the barn an' he's goin' after his pinto."

He heard Edie's small gasp of dismay almost lost in the squeak of the window as he forced it open. He said, "I'm goin' with him. He's no killer. I know him an' he's my friend."

He was on the ground then, outside the house, moving carefully so as not to be seen. He got his saddle and bedroll from the barn and caught a horse out of the corral. When he heard the thundering of Russ's driven horse and, farther back, the one he rode, he was saddled, wearing his heavy coat and ready.

The pinto thundered into the corral and Russ swung down and shut the gate. Claude clambered over the corral fence and approached. Sudden shyness gripped him. He knew what he wanted to say, but did not know how to say it.

He called, "Russ!" and went over to the waiting man. "I want to go with you," and after a pause, "Kin I?"

He could not see Russ's face, but he thought Russ was angry. The man's voice sounded strained.

"No. You belong here, helpin' your pa." Russ's hand laid on Claude's shoulder and gripped it. "You go with me an' you'll wind up driftin' from place to place with nothin' but a twenty-dollar horse to call your own.

Stay, an' you'll be a cowman like your pa an' Arnold Hoffman. You could do worse. Your pa's a fine man."

"But I don't want to be like Pa an' Arnold. I want to be like you."

Russ's voice hardened and the boy knew he was really angry now. He rasped, "Or like Slick Everitt maybe? No. Anyhow, what would I do with a kid taggin' along? Go on up to the house now an' let me be."

Somehow Claude could not argue with Russ like he could with Pa. He turned and went out of the corral, a smarting behind his eyes. He saw another shape running from the house and ducked into the shadow of the barn. He heard Edie's timid, breathless voice, "Russ," and the clanking of Russ's spurs as he crossed to her.

Claude could just see the dim shapes of the two of them, Russ so tall and still, Edie small beside him. He knew he had no business listening, but he couldn't make his feet move. Edie's voice came so softly that Claude could scarcely hear.

"Russ, I'm sorry. I was wrong." Claude heard her sudden sobbing and saw the two figures merge. Edie cried, "I'll go with you if you want me."

He never heard Russ's answer if there was

one. A dozen men came riding into the yard, kicking up dust that swirled before the streak of light from the open door of the house. Claude saw Pa's big shape there, and Ma's smaller, stout one.

A man called out, "Where's Russ? We come to see Russ." It was Arnold's voice.

Pa's voice was big and rough like himself. "You'll likely find him out to the barn. Come on in an' I'll send Claude after him."

Russ and Edie came away from the corral and passed Claude there in the shadows without seeing him. They were talking softly.

The men were dismounting and two of them led the horses away toward the corral. Russ and Edie followed into the house and Claude tagged behind.

Arnold was talking to Pa and he said, "There's been too much trouble in town an' we've got together to ask Russ to be the marshal. Bein' easy with a gun is a trick a marshal has to have, an' with a man like Russ on the job there won't be much shootin'."

He saw Russ then, standing in the kitchen doorway. "How about it, Russ?"

Russ looked at Edie and Edie at Russ. Pa saw the look that was passing between the two. He shrugged only lightly and then he swallowed a couple of times, looking at the floor. When he looked up he was beginning to smile.

He said, "'Pears like you'll have to ask both of them, Arnold. Looks like it might be that way now."

He laughed and Claude, who knew Pa and his way of oblique apology, grinned suddenly, letting his eyes go from Pa's face to Russ's and back again, feeling good. Edie ran to Pa, crying and laughing at the same time.

Pa said, "Reckon I couldn't see Russ fer lookin' at that gun hangin' at his side."

Born in England, L. L. Foreman settled in the United States after serving in the British Army in World War I. He began writing for the Western pulps in the 1930s and produced hundreds of popular stories, both before and after he turned to novels with Don Desperado *in 1941. Many of his best stories and such books as* The Silver Flame *and* Rogue's Legacy *feature a black-garbed gambler and troubleshooter named Rogue Bishop, one of Western fiction's most unusual heroes. "Gunman," the tense story of John Card, a gunfighter who "played his talent as an artist," is Foreman at his most evocative.*

Gunman

L. L. Foreman

The horse wasn't much good any more, nor the saddle. The rider, John Card, still looked like a good man, but the girl must have sensed something wrong about him.

"You saw Bob killed?" she asked. "Are you sure? Were you with him?"

Her smooth young face was so stiff, her eyes so bitter, she reminded Card of her brother the moment before his death. Such a look masked a wrenching passion. These fair, slender people owned as much violent blood as anybody.

"Were you his friend, then?" she demanded. "Wasn't there anything you could do to help him?"

"Now, Grace," her father reproved her. "Not a doubt Mr. Card did what he could for Bob."

Card said carefully, "He hired out for trouble, like the rest of us. The showdown came fast. We were all pretty busy."

Speaking of it, he saw again the Brasada riot, the hot sun on the dust, men running, dodging, faces savagely wincing against the harsh reports of exploding cartridges. And the aftermath. The pay-off and the scatter. The long riding, money dwindling with every town passed, every saloon entered. None of it was much different from the others, yet it remained as clear as though it were the only fight he had ever been in.

Was it the drinking, he wondered, that caught into the girl's perceptions? But there had been none of that, the last few days since his money ran out. No, most likely it was the vague uneasiness that folks of her kind sometimes showed in the presence of folks of his kind.

He must handle her with care. She could influence her father, for or against him. Card sized up Haverill as a man of dull instincts but sound business sense, a cattleman who made money. This was a feeder ranch, fenced and run like a farm.

Come on down, Card, was the message McHaggert had sent from Mexico. Mac had got hold of a good thing down there. Something to do with a mining syndicate that was having trouble with its neighbors. High pay for the right men. But to get there Card needed a fresh horse and a cash stake.

He and Haverill watched the girl leave the room. They heard her walk quickly through the ranch house and close a door in the rear. Haverill then brought out a bottle and two glasses, poured two small drinks, and put the bottle back.

"They were pretty close, she and her brother Bob," he said. "We heard what happened, of course, but I don't think she quite believed it till now. Didn't want to, I guess, and she just can't thank you for telling her. Gunfighters don't get thanked much anywhere, come to that, eh?"

Card liked him for that, at least. He thought of himself as a gunfighter, not a gunman. A gunman plied his trade for pay and the lust of killing. A gunfighter played his talent as an artist.

Haverill said, "We never knew where Bob went when he left. He was restless. He liked guns. Liked 'em too much. Wish I could've kept him home. Did he kill anybody over there?"

Card hesitated only an instant for the right reply. "No. He made some trade for the doctor, but didn't kill anybody."

"H'm. Well, that's all right, I guess." Haverill got up. He put the glasses away. "You'll want to rest awhile before you push on up to Wyoming, eh? Lot of Texas outfits moving there, I hear. Not a doubt you'll catch a job there. See me before you go."

It was dismissal, tempered with ordinary hospitality and a meager hint that he might expect to be set up for travel any time he was ready to leave. Card murmured casual thanks and went out to the bunkhouse. He thought it probable that Haverill's generosity would have been larger if his daughter hadn't shown such hostility. It could yet shrink smaller, under her influence.

He would have to set about winning over

160

that girl. The necessity irritated him. But in his fix, broke, with a worn-out horse and saddle, he couldn't afford to waste a chance. It was mostly chance that had brought him to the Haverill ranch, and cold reason said he'd have to make something of it. Mac was expecting him down in Mexico.

Before he was able to make any headway he spent three days patching up his riding gear and idling around the horse corrals. He was in what Haverill called the hospital pen, giving his horse a grooming, when Grace Haverill came down from the house.

"Mr. Card," she said hurriedly, "I—I want to beg your pardon."

Well, of all damn things, he thought, straightening up with the curry comb in one hand and the brush in the other. Then he reminded himself that women often were swayed as strongly by reactions as by their prejudices. He had forgotten to take that into account, and had stationed himself to lie in wait for her, armed with a few words calculated to take her off guard.

In the bunkhouse he had learned that she had a sick colt in the hospital pen. Miss Grace, they said, gravely affectionate, was foolish about that skinny little colt. Dave

161

Petersen was doing all he could for it, but the runt had made up its mind to die. Dave Petersen was foreman—range boss, they would have called him in a Texas outfit.

She wore a flowered dress today, perhaps for courage and with the intent of giving the occasion a shelter of formality. She was quite lovely, unable to control a rising color and some shyness.

As far as he could recall, Card had never before received an apology from anybody like her. To overcome his confusion he briskly scraped the brush with the curry comb.

"*Por nada*," he said, from habit using the Mexican response. "What's your opinion of this horse, Miss Haverill?"

It was the question he had prepared for her, knowing that she was bound to look at the horse, see the shape it was in, and give some kind of reply that would afford him an opening for further talk. The blunt irrelevance of it now immediately struck him. Yet, glancing quickly at her, he saw that he could hardly have done better.

She was grateful to be relieved so promptly of her apology. She was glad to talk about a horse, as they all were at any time, these folks who lived on fenced range and thought forty miles was a good day's ride.

"He's been a good horse," she judged critically, running a serious inspection over it. "But ridden too much, I'm afraid."

Card put a meditative quality into his nod. Anybody could see at a glance that the brute had been overridden.

"You know horses," he told her, and wondered when she'd get around to noticing the improvement in her sick colt. These corn-fed folks were none too observant.

She was looking at him, not at the colt in the pen. He was considerably less than handsome, but about him hung a slightly rakish and alien air of elegance, now hard-worn. Broke and shabby as he was, he still had it, like a battered lance with scarred shaft smoothed by much use and ragged pennant faded.

When she did give her attention to the colt it was because Dave Petersen rode in and commented on it. "Little feller seems to be perking up at last, Grace," he said pleasedly. "Don't know why he went off his feed, but I'd say we've got him back on again."

"Sore spot on his jaw," Card remarked. "Parotid gland, maybe. I've been feeding him some soft mash I got the cook to fix for him. He can swallow that. You better get a vet on the jaw."

Dave Petersen was young and big, new to authority and not hard to embarrass. He flushed crimson. After clearing his throat several times he unsaddled and tended to his horse and walked up to the house alone.

Card hid a smile. The uneasy suspicion was gone from the girl, and her regret for her hostile manner was sincere now, not merely polite. There was a deep change in her eyes and voice. In all likelihood she entertained some notion that any man who took the trouble to nurse a sick animal was incapable of real sin.

The thought amused him. He had known badmen and killers who would feed a starving mongrel and go into a cold rage over an abused burro. The practice of violence was a matter of trained talent. And talent, whether for powdersmoke or the pulpit, was trained by the head, not the heart.

He sat on the porch of the house that evening with her, ignoring Dave Petersen's obvious resentment and Haverill's disapproving glances. Because Card occupied the chair beside Grace, Petersen refused to sit anywhere. He stood on the steps, talking with Haverill.

"Fence has been cut again." Trying for a casual tone, Petersen overdid it clumsily. "Tim Simms found it this morning. Spotted it where it was mended. I rode out and looked at it. He's right. That mend isn't our work."

The tip of Haverill's cigar glowed abruptly. "Where this time?"

"Just east of the hills this side of the scarp. That gravelly piece. No tracks."

Card studied Grace Haverill by the light of the lamp in the window behind them. The yellow lamplight softened her hair, and her face, in shadow, was a pale mist, motionless. She was listening to Petersen and her father. She caught Card's long glance and moved her head slightly, self-consciously. But almost in the same instant she met his eyes again, and as she turned away he saw the pale mist of her face growing warm.

Without conscious thought from him and without regard for impossibilities, his planned intentions broke and reformed. He went on gazing at her, astounded at the ambitious impudence of the visions flooding his mind. There was this girl and this ranch; and Haverill had no son left—

The visions collapsed and left him staring into bleak recollections. He found that his fingers were knotted hard together, and he looked swiftly to see if she had noticed. She was listening again to the two men, or pretending to.

Haverill said harshly, "That's close to the old *parada*. How about those calves we put out along there?"

Petersen answered with reluctance. "Well—Tim's hunting 'em."

"He won't find 'em! Dammit, you know he won't and so does he!"

Haverill reared up out of his rocking chair as if charging to battle, and Card knew then why Petersen had edged so cautiously into the subject. The man had a blazing temper, for all his slow ways.

"Damn thieving Parrons, I'll sheriff 'em this time! I'll run 'em out the country! I'll—"

"Dad!" his daughter called.

"No evidence to go on," Petersen pointed out worriedly.

"Evidence or no, I'll swear out warrants! High time that paper-back sheriff quit stepping out of their way!" Haverill's voice blared theirs to silence. "High time somebody made up his mind for him! If I can't do it, then I'll pay my own call on the Parrons!"

"Dad!"

166

"Damn stock thieves and gunmen! A blight anywhere, all their breed!"

Card froze. He watched Haverill stamp into the house, watched Dave Petersen walk slowly off, and he asked Grace quietly, "Who're the Parrons? I know that name."

"Ed and Ryal Parron," she said. "They moved onto the old Bausor homestead last year, east of our line. There's another man with them that they call Sidney. They raise no stock, but they sell calves under unregistered brands and everybody knows they're never without guns. I hope Dad doesn't call on them."

Card nodded. Ed and Ryal Parron. Second-rate gunmen, but full of tricks. Sidney he didn't know so well. Last he'd heard, Sidney was stealing sheep in New Mexico after going in with a band of stolen horses.

Stock thieves and gunmen. A blight anywhere, all their breed. And that, he guessed, included him. It was pretty hopeless to expect a fresh horse and a cash stake from Haverill, in his raging mood. The Parrons had queered that chance, blast them.

Lying in the bunkhouse in the dark, it grew easy to recall the look in Grace Haverill's eyes. It grew easy to examine plans broken and reformed. The impudent, ambitious visions came flooding back, and Card contemplated them and before he fell asleep they centered only on Grace Haverill.

While he sat splicing a worn bridle rein late next morning, Dave Petersen rode in alone after going out early with the hands. Petersen pulled up and asked stiffly, "Did Mr. Haverill start for town yet, d'you know?"

"Hours back, right after breakfast. Anything wrong?"

Petersen started to turn his horse, and stopped. "We didn't find those calves. Tim Simms went through the fence this morning and found their tracks on the Parron side."

"Not surprised, are you?"

"No. But I'm worried about Mr. Haverill. They've sold the calves somewhere, and they've gone into town. On a drunk on the money, I guess."

"How d'you know?"

"Tim saw all three of them, the Parrons and Sidney, riding toward town," Petersen said. "They wouldn't leave the place if there was stolen stock on it. They never all go in together except when they've got money."

"It's a small town. They're bound to meet. And the Old Man"—Card used the title from Texas habit—"is on the prod. So we better go in."

"Shall I go get some of the fellows?"

Card shook his head. "They might get excited." Those solemn young workers on horseback. They were the kind, big-fisted and willing, who sparked trouble and got in the way and left their names on the toll of the dear departed. "I doubt I need you, either."

"Thanks, but I happen to be foreman here!"

"Yeah, but I don't happen to work here!"

Mended bridle and reins in hand, Card went for his horse. If Haverill had got himself into a jam he'd have to favor any man who got him out of it. As he saddled up he saw Grace come out to the porch and beckon to Petersen. By the time he reached the house he knew from her face that she had got Petersen to talk.

"Please hurry!" she said.

"Sure. Come on, Petersen!"

Riding out of the yard, Petersen said, "The Parrons won't stand for anybody putting the sheriff on 'em. They've said so."

Card considered it. "How much do they have to worry about the sheriff?"

"He's scared of 'em, as long as everybody else is. But if folks would back him up he'd go after 'em. He's like that. The Parrons know it."

"Well, maybe we better hurry, at that," Card commented carelessly. He was hardly touched yet by any sense of urgency. He cared too little for Haverill. And that other sense, that blinding thing that memory evaded, still slept.

Such a quietness lay on the town, the thump of their horses' hoofs in the thick dust of the main street sounded drum-loud. The town, a farm and cattle town, had never been wild, never known the invasion of racketing trail hands on a spree. Its half-dozen store-fronts, unpainted, had taken on peacefully the grayish-tan hue of the clay soil, bright in the sun, drab in the shade.

Three horses drooped at the hitch-rack of the only saloon in town, and another stood outside the shack that was the sheriff's office.

"That's the boss's horse," Petersen told Card, and they drew in alongside it.

A boy appeared at the door, shaking his head, saying his father had just left. The boy was wide-eyed from nervous excitement. His father, the sheriff, had been having a beer in the barroom, he said, and Haverill walked in and demanded the arrest of the Parrons.

"Pop tried to cool him down, but he was shoutin' mad. I heard him from here, easy. Then the Parrons an' Sidney turned up. They musta heard him, too. Couldn't help. They talked soft an' tied their horses there an' went on in. After Pop came out—"

"Did he leave Haverill in there?" Petersen interrupted, and Card put in:

"Most likely he thought Haverill would follow him out like a sensible man." It wasn't right to make a boy suspect his father of cowardice. "Go on, kid."

"Pop hung around here a long time, waitin' for Mr. Haverill to come out. But he didn't. He's there yet. Then Pop said, hell, that ol' rooster's too proud to come out. Pop said he better go get some help. He just left, Pop did. You just missed him. Pop said the Parrons an' Sidney, they never said a word when they went in. They just looked at Mr. Haverill. Just looked, he said."

Card turned to cross the street. Petersen exclaimed, "Wait, now! Let's figure this out."

Card paused impatiently. "Figure what? The Parrons are crowded. Haverill's barked for the law and they've got to stop that. The sheriff's out of the way. Time he gets back

171

they'll have Haverill gunned and a self-defense case rigged. It's all they can do!"

He wondered, watching Petersen stalk on to the saloon, why he couldn't simply stand back and let him and Haverill make their mistakes and pay for them. It would be so easy to wait for the crash of the Parrons' gunfire, and then ride back to the ranch. And stay there. Better than joining Mac down in Mexico.

His high boot heels puffed the dust of the street. He walked across and entered the barroom. He didn't yet know why, in reason. An urgent and eager thrust steered him dominantly, requiring no reason.

It was low-roofed and the squatty half-curtained windows filtered the daylight down to a cool gloom. There was the dark and dully shining length of the bar backed with milky mirrors, and the chipped tables, chairs, bare floor, and the familiar blend of strong odors. He walked past Haverill and Petersen without looking at them.

Haverill, seated, sent him an uncertain nod. He wasn't drinking and he sat straight and unrelaxed like a man in court waiting to hear his name called. His face now reflected more hard strain than temper. Petersen had stopped at his boss's table, but remained standing.

At the bar Card said, "Whisky." When he got it he remembered that he couldn't pay for it. He drew his hand from his pocket, empty, and was aware of the bartender's sharp regard. He drank the whisky and motioned for another. Then he turned and glanced around, as any man might in a strange barroom after his eyes got adjusted to the low light.

The Parrons and Sidney occupied a table in the corner nearest the windows. They had their eyes on him.

He nodded across to them. "Hi."

"Hi," they said.

They were trying to figure out the set-up between him and Haverill. They were puzzled, Sidney especially. In the Brasada trouble Sidney had hired out to the other side for a while, long enough to look the horses over and make off with the pick of them during the final confusion. He was a smiling, talkative thief, gaunt and fair as a Swede settler. Card, seeing that fight again, swallowed his second drink and tapped the glass on the bar.

The bartender held onto the bottle. "Four bits a shot."

173

At his table Haverill said, "That's on me, Frank."

The eyes of the three men in the corner shuttled back and forth.

As Card picked up his third drink, Sidney remarked loudly to the Parrons: "Y'know, I ain't been round so much I can't learn something new. But this beats me!" He put his elbows on the table, wide apart, hands dangling over the edge. "Here's the story. The one I'm talking about, he's so thick with a certain cowman, he don't even have to pay for his drinks. An' yet he's the same jigger who—"

Card said, "Hey, feller, you make too much noise!" He leaned sidewise against the bar, the drink in his left hand.

Sidney smiled slyly. "If you don't like to hear the story, you can leave, can't you? We won't feel hurt!" He paused, waiting, and ran his light eyes over Haverill and Petersen. "It's a free country an' this is a public place. It suited us till you came in."

"I'm staying." Card gazed intently into his glass. But anywhere he looked he kept seeing a pair of bitter eyes in a stiff face that let a wrenching passion break through before it blurred over. He felt his skin grow cold and prickly.

Sidney shrugged. "All right." He glanced at Ed and Ryal Parron, one on each side of him at the table. He was the kind of untamed man who could sense danger miles off in the open, and fail to detect it ten steps away when under a roof. "As I was saying, this jigger, he's the one who—"

"Shut down!" Card said. He set his glass on the bar and looked at it a second longer. "You mouthy, Injun-robbing sheep thief! Shut down or I'll shut you!"

He chose the words deliberately and spoke them in a matter-of-fact tone, knowing that they were more than the man could take. The challenge was as intolerable as he could make it. He took note of the instant tensing of Sidney's hands, and gave his attention next to the Parrons.

The Parrons were dark men. Ed, the eldest, was generally taken to be the more dangerous of the two, but he wasn't. His black beard and fierce eyes often won him his way. Ryal, the fat one who liked pink silk shirts, didn't need tough looks. They were staring at him, in a narrow margin of indecision, not yet quite sure of their own intentions.

He said, "That includes any stock thieves and gunmen who might feel like taking up for you!"

In the brief and savage burst of gunfire, it seemed to him that anybody could detect and wreck the pattern of their play—Ed lunging up tall and flaring tough, while fat Ryal slid from his chair shooting and Sidney staged a fast, weaving detour around the table and half around the barroom. Such a stale pattern. The man who simply stood and took his time, took that fraction of a second necessary to sight his shots and know where they went, was the master of such jumping, sliding, dancing fools. Such targets, all three of them.

He fired three times.

In the crackling silence he eyed the three men. He would remember them exactly as they looked as they fell, as they lay. He picked his glass of whisky off the bar, stared into it intently, and smiled because he was free of the bitter eyes and the stiff face. He couldn't even see the Brasada fight any more.

"Pay for three shots, Haverill," he said, and emptied the glass and walked out past Haverill and Petersen without looking at them.

Petersen caught up with him on the western road when the evening was red in the sky and dark on earth. "Pull up, will you?" Petersen asked. "She told me to come after you. So did Mr. Haverill. The sheriff won't make trouble."

He pulled up. "Tell her you couldn't find me, you damn fool!"

"But the sheriff won't—"

"Shut down! Don't you know what Sidney was going to tell?" He nudged his horse on, and called back harshly, "Bob Haverill was on the other side in that Brasada scrap. He scored me in the ribs and I went after him. I'm the gunman who got him!"

He rode on alone. There was Wyoming and the Texas outfits that had moved up there since the Spanish fever. Easy to catch a job there. A riding, working job. His own words kept repeating in his ears, an echo refusing to die: *I'm the gunman—the gunman—gunman—*

He could see them, the three men falling, lying on the floor. He could see them, and the saloon. It was all as clear as though it were the only fight he had ever been in.

At the first fork in the road he turned south. It was a tough trek ahead. He needed a fresh horse and a cash stake. But he'd make it somehow. Mac was expecting him down there in Mexico.

*One of the most popular of contemporary West-
ern writers, Wayne D. Overholser published his
first short story in 1936 and was a frequent
contributor to all the major Western pulp magazines over the next two decades. His first novel,*
Buckaroo's Code, *appeared in 1947; of his
ninety-nine subsequent titles, two were recipients
of WWA Best Novel Spurs—*The Lawman,
as by Lee Leighton, 1953, and The Violent
Land *in 1954. A number of Overholser's short
stories feature youngsters as protagonists;
"Mean Men Are Big," a good-humored tale
about a boy named Tuck and his experiences
with a couple of gunfighters, is among the best
of these.*

Mean Men Are Big

Wayne D. Overholser

My sister's name is First Merrybelle Dorcas. I'll bet you think that's the funniest
name you ever heard. I think so, too. She
wasn't really the first Merrybelle. Mamma

178

was. Her name is Laura Merrybelle Dorcas, so my sister should be named Second, but she wasn't because we happened to move to Antioch just when we did.

Papa's name is James Finley Dorcas and he was a famous peace officer in a Kansas trail town. That was before I was born, but people have told me about it. I forgot to say I'm Tuck. That's a nickname. Mamma named me James Finley Dorcas, but I hate being called Junior.

I guess it all started in that Kansas town when Papa was standing on the street talking to a big cattle buyer. Mamma was riding along in her buggy when a cowboy let out a yell and fired a gun and Mamma's horse ran away. Papa jumped into the street and stopped the horse and that's how she turned out to be my mamma.

Papa had to put his guns away and give up his job before Mamma would marry him. She said he had to have a respectable business. That's why they moved to Denver, where Papa bought a hardware store. That satisfied Mamma, so I guess it was respectable.

I was born in Denver but I don't remember it. I don't remember anything about Denver except that Aunt Minnie came to keep house when Mamma got sick. Aunt Minnie is Grandpa's sister and keeps house for him in St. Louis, but she isn't like Grandpa. She has a mustache like he does, but she doesn't have a beard.

Aunt Minnie has the biggest chest I ever saw. She wears a gold watch on one side. Her eyeglasses hang down on the other side. Papa says she has a "sea chest." When I asked him why he called it that, he said, "Why, when you see Aunt Minnie, you can't help seeing her chest."

Mamma said, "Jim, you ought to be ashamed to talk that way."

Papa said, "Well, its the truth."

What Papa said made sense all right. When you see Aunt Minnie, you sure can't help seeing her chest.

We moved to Pueblo, and Aunt Minnie went back to St. Louis. Papa bought another hardware store but he wasn't happy. He'd walk the floor and say, "A man can't get ahead in a town like this. The course of empire is westward."

He'd fling a hand out toward the mountains. "That's where fortunes are being made. Gold is being discovered. Railroads are being built. Towns are being born. Here

I am, missing opportunities because we're held down by a hostage to fortune."

"I won't go where there aren't any schools or doctors," Mamma said. "Aunt Minnie says we should have stayed in Denver."

"Hang Aunt Minnie," Papa said, sounding pretty mad. "I wish I could. We had to leave Denver to get rid of her."

"I'm still not going to some terrible old mining camp where there aren't any schools or doctors," Mamma said.

"Our little hostage looks mighty healthy to me," Papa said, "and you were a schoolteacher before I saved you from being an old maid."

"Being healthy won't keep him from taking smallpox or scarlet fever," Mamma said, "and just teaching doesn't take the place of a school." Her mouth was a long white line. "I won't go."

Her mouth didn't get that way very often, but when it did, Mamma looked a lot like Aunt Minnie. In the face, I mean. She didn't really look like Aunt Minnie because she didn't have Aunt Minnie's sea chest. Anyhow, Papa always quit talking when she got that Aunt Minnie look on her mouth. He'd just walk out of the house.

After we lived in Pueblo for quite a while,

Papa left on the train and was gone for a long time. I asked Mamma where he'd gone, and she said, "He took a lot of mining machinery over the mountains." Then she hugged me. "We miss him when he's gone, don't we, darling?"

I said, "He'll be back pretty soon, won't he?"

Mamma cried a little then and said, "Yes, I think so."

When Papa got back, his mustache just kind of bristled. He laughed and hugged Mamma and joked a lot. Then he said, "I found the right place, honey. There's a school and a doctor and fortunes are being made overnight. It's the opportunity of a lifetime, and you know what they say. Opportunity only knocks once on a man's door."

Mamma asked, "What's the name of this great town?"

"Antioch," Papa said.

"Never heard of it," Mamma said.

"You will, honey. You will. It's going to be a big place."

Mamma folded her hands and put them on her lap. She stared down at them as she said, "Jim, we're going to have another hostage to fortune."

Papa just stood there looking at her and the funniest thing happened. His mustache didn't bristle anymore. It kind of wilted. He said, in a low voice, "Not . . . another one?"

"Yes," Mamma said. "Another one," and she began to cry.

Papa got down on his knees and kissed her. "That's wonderful, honey."

Mamma kept on crying. "All right, Jim," she said. "I'll go. Living with you like this is like living with a hungry lion in a cage. You've just got to go and try it."

Papa's mustache got bristly again right away. He said, "That's my girl, Laura. That's my girl."

After that there was a lot of bustling around. Mamma felt puny but she got things packed up. Papa sold his store and the house and we took the longest train ride. It was a little train. Papa said it was a narrow gauge. It wound around through the mountains and it tooted its whistle. We traveled awfully fast. I guess we were going twenty miles an hour.

We slept on the train and it was about noon the next day when we got to Antioch. It was the funniest-looking town I ever saw. Not like Pueblo at all. It was down in the bottom of a canyon with a creek running along one side. All the buildings were kind of brown like an old leaf. But the funniest part of it was that right in the middle of Main Street there was an open spot.

"Two vacant lots," Papa said. "They haven't found out who to give them to yet."

Maybe they were vacant lots. Papa ought to know, but it looked to me like my upper teeth where the two front ones were gone.

We went to the hotel and had dinner. Mamma got mad at me because I dumped all the little crackers into my soup. She made me eat every bite, and then I was so full I couldn't eat anything else.

Just about the time Papa finished his pie, a man with a long white beard came to our table. Papa introduced us. He said his name was Uncle Luke Mattingly. I thought that if he was my uncle, he must be married to Aunt Minnie, so I asked him if he was.

He laughed and slapped his leg. "No, son, I ain't."

Papa said, "That's the luckiest thing that ever happened to you. Since you discovered the Yankee Doodle, that is."

Mamma said, "James!"

"It's the truth," Papa said. "There's just two ways of looking at Aunt Minnie. Front or back, and sideways. You can't miss her either way, but I'd like to."

"What do you think of our town?" Uncle Luke asked Mamma. "I'm the town daddy, you know. Started it twenty years ago when I discovered the Sweetheart Mine, then we lost the vein and the town died. I stayed right here and kept looking. Folks said I was crazy, but they changed their tune when I struck the vein again." He pointed at the hill across the creek. "Up yonder on that there ridge. This time I called it the Yankee Doodle."

"I never saw a town like it," Mamma said. "Do you have a doctor in town?"

"You bet we do," Uncle Luke said. "Doc Pettybone. He's the best doggone pill roller in all the San Juan. Just one thing wrong. He's treated broken bones and taken out more bullets than you can shake a stick at, but he ain't brought a baby into the world since he came to this camp. It sure grieves all of us. I figured I'd take care of it when I reserved them two lots for the first baby born in Antioch, but it's been twenty year and it ain't worked yet."

"Give us time, Luke," Papa said. "Just give us time."

When we got upstairs to our room, Mamma began to cry. She said, "Jim, I've got to have a doctor, and all there is in this awful wilderness is a pill roller."

"He's a doctor," Papa said.

But Mamma kept on crying. "Pills won't do me any good when my time comes, and I don't care how he rolls them."

Papa got up and went out. Pretty soon he came back with a tall man who had a little mustache and a goatee and carried a black bag. He was wearing a boiled shirt and a string tie and a long-tailed coat. I guess he was just about the most handsome man I ever saw, and Mamma quit crying the minute she saw him.

Papa said he was Doc Pettybone. Mamma said, "I'm happy to know you."

"And I'm happy to know you, Mrs. Dorcas," he said. "You're going to have the best of care it's possible for me to give you. I practiced in Durango before I came to Antioch and I delivered lots of babies."

For some reason that made Mamma happy. Doc Pettybone sat down and held her hand for a while, then he opened his bag and took out a little silver-looking thing and put it into her mouth. He pulled it out after about a minute and looked at it and nodded.

"You're strong and healthy, Mrs. Dorcas," he said. "I'm sure you won't have a bit of trouble."

"Unless you're taking a bullet out of some man or putting broken bones together," Mamma said.

"The biggest thing that ever happened in this camp will be the birth of the first baby," Doc Pettybone said. "You'll come ahead of everything else. Believe me." He put the little silver thing into the black bag and closed it. "How long will it be, Mrs. Dorcas?"

"Six months," Mamma said.

He nodded. "That's going to be real fine. It will all be over with before cold weather starts. Now any time you don't feel good, you come and see me. Or send for me."

After Doc Pettybone left, Papa said, "He's a good doctor, Laura. Everything's going to be all right just like I told you."

Mamma looked happier than I'd seen her since we'd left Pueblo. She said, "Yes, I think it will. As soon as we get settled, I'll send for Aunt Minnie and she can take care of you and Tuck."

Papa threw up his hands and started to say a bad word. Then he choked and coughed and said, "By the great horned toad, you

187

won't do any such thing. We'll find some-body right here in Antioch."

Mamma's mouth turned into a long white line again. She said, "I'll feel better with Aunt Minnie here."

Papa walked out. I don't know when he got back. I was asleep.

The next day Papa bought a house and we moved into it that afternoon. It was on the creek clear up above town and you could see a long ways down the canyon. It was two stories and had a long bannister beside the stairs. I slid down it until Mamma made me stop. Then I went outside and turned the doorbell until Mamma told me to stop doing that, too. She said it made her nervous.

After that I went inside and shut the front door. It had one big glass pane and a bunch of little colored panes all around it, blue and red and yellow. I'd shut one eye and put the other one up close to a colored pane and look through it. Then the funniest thing hap-pened. The whole world turned blue or red or yellow, depending on which pane I looked through.

Mamma and Papa got along pretty well after that. He went to work for Uncle Luke Mattingly, and Mamma got bigger and big-ger. She said that was what always happened when a woman had a baby. That's all she'd tell me, but I asked Uncle Luke about it one day and he said he didn't know why that was, either. He said babies came out of a cabbage patch.

I hunted all over town for a cabbage patch but I couldn't find one. Uncle Luke took me fishing the next day and I told him I didn't think there was a cabbage patch anywhere in Antioch. He got red in the face and his mustache and beard kind of quivered. Then he said, "I didn't tell you all of it, Tuck. You see, it don't make much difference where the cabbage patch is. I seen some real nice ones the last time I was in Durango." He choked up and wiped his eyes. Then he said, "Tuck, you ain't getting no bites today. Let's go to the store and see if they've got any licorice."

That was what we did, but I kind of hated to get licorice. It made my face dirty and Mamma always scolded me. I decided I could wash my face in the creek, so I walked along with Uncle Luke. The more I thought about the cabbage business, the more I wondered about it. It seemed to me there had to be some way to get the baby from the cabbage patch in Durango to Antioch.

When we left the store, I had a stick of licorice in my mouth. I was going to ask

Uncle Luke about the baby business when a man called, "Mattingly."

He turned around, and there was the biggest man I ever saw. He had the biggest mustache I ever saw, too. It was red and went way out on the sides of his face and hung down on both ends. He had a beard, too. It was short and seemed to stick out and point right at Uncle Luke.

"What do you want, Dunbar?" Uncle Luke asked.

"You know what I want," the man said. "You've pussyfooted around long enough."

Uncle Luke looked like he wished he was somewhere else. He sucked in a long breath and stood on one foot and then the other one. Finally, he said, "Doak, this here boy is Jim Dorcas's son. Tuck, I want you to meet Doak Dunbar."

I guess the big man hadn't even seen me until then. He stared at me when I said, "How do you do, Mr. Dunbar." He growled kind of like the dog I used to have in Pueblo did when he had a bone and I tried to take it away from him.

I didn't know Dunbar was a mean man until he turned his head and looked at Uncle Luke. He said, "So this is the Dorcas brat.

Now you're figuring on another one, ain't you? You're cute, Mattingly. Mighty cute."

Nobody had ever called me a brat before. I hadn't done anything to him. I'd been just as polite as I could. I said, "I'm not a brat and you don't have any reason to call me one."

"He's right," Uncle Luke said. "Just as right as rain. When I tell Jim about it, you'd better hunt for cover."

Dunbar laughed and said a bad word. He pulled his coat to one side and I saw he had a gun in a leather holster. Nobody in Antioch carried a gun except Pete Jones, the marshal, and he didn't carry his except on Saturday night.

"There was a time when I'd have believed that," Dunbar said. "They say when he was in Kansas he was a tough hand, but he ain't no more. Don't even pack his iron, and I've given him plenty of excuses."

Uncle Luke didn't say anything to that. He turned around, and we started off down the street. Dunbar said another bad word and grabbed Uncle Luke by the arm and whirled him around.

"I'm giving you till tomorrow night, Mattingly," Dunbar said. "Then I'm going to run you and Dorcas out of town if you don't sell me them lots."

He raised a thumb to his hat and shoved it back on his head, and I saw that his hair was just as red as his beard and mustache. "Use your noggin, man. I'm offering you five thousand dollars for them lots and I'm promising I'll build the best saloon and gambling place on the western slope. You owe that much to the men in this camp and they know it."

He let Uncle Luke's arm go and turned around and walked off. Uncle Luke said, "You run home, Tuck."

So I didn't get to ask him any more about the cabbage patch being in Durango. When I got home, Mamma said he was coming for supper, so I thought I'd get another chance, but I didn't because as soon as we started eating, Mamma said, "Jim, Aunt Minnie will be here tomorrow on the train. You be sure to meet her."

Papa didn't say a word, but he looked just like he did the time he hit his thumb a hard whack with the hammer and started to say some bad words and Mamma yelled, "Stop that. Little pitchers have big ears." After that he just swelled up and got purple in the face and I thought he'd bust.

192

When Mamma went into the kitchen to do the dishes, Uncle Luke said, "I want to talk to you."

Papa said, "I know what about, too. The Lord doesn't do it halfway when He sets out to punish a man. It ought to be enough for Him to send Aunt Minnie."

"I should think you'd be thankful to have her here to take care of Laura," Uncle Luke said.

"Thankful?" Papa looked surprised. "Do you thank the Lord when he sends a blizzard? Or a snow slide? Or an earthquake?"

They got up and went into the parlor. I crawled behind a big chair to play with my blocks. I thought they'd talk about the cabbage patch, but instead they talked about that Doak Dunbar.

"He's been after me for weeks to sell him those lots," Uncle Luke said. "Now he's telling everybody it's a put-up job. You're working for me and your wife's about to have a baby and that's why you came to Antioch."

"That's true as far as it goes," Papa said. "I expect to build a hardware store as soon as the baby comes and I get a deed to those lots. You knew that all the time. If you sell them to Doak Dunbar. . . ."

"I know how you feel," Uncle Luke said,

"but we've got to be practical. Dunbar's got the reputation of being a killer. He says he'll run both of us out of town if I don't sell to him. Of course if you'd take your guns and. . . ."

"I've told you before how it is," Papa said. "I promised Laura."

"Then I'll have to do it," Uncle Luke said.

Mamma called me to bed, so I didn't get to hear any more. I thought about it before I went to sleep. I wondered who Papa thought was worse, Doak Dunbar or Aunt Minnie. I decided he was scared of Aunt Minnie, but I know he wasn't scared of Dunbar.

I'd seen Papa's guns lots of times when I got into the trunk in the attic. In the morning soon as I finished breakfast I went upstairs and looked in the trunk. The guns were gone, but I didn't tell Mamma.

I went with Papa to meet the train. Aunt Minnie was on it, all right, with her sea chest and everything. She kissed me and hugged me till I couldn't get my breath. She said, "Sakes alive, Tuck, how are you going to eat an apple with those front teeth gone?" Then she looked at Papa and kind of grunted. "Well, James, you haven't changed any."

"Neither have you," Papa said.

He put her valises in the bed of the buckboard, and I heard him say under his breath, "Looks like it's going to be a long hard winter."

Aunt Minnie hugged and kissed Mamma when we got home, then she said, "Laura, you wrote me you were eight months along."

"I am," Mamma said.

"Then I guess you can't count," Aunt Minnie said. "You're nine months. I can tell just by looking at you. You're not well, either. I can tell that, too. James, you stay home. You hear me?"

"I'll stay home when I'm needed," Papa said.

He walked out. Aunt Minnie said, "Laura, I told you that you were making a horrible mistake when you married that man. When are you going to get enough sense to leave him and come home to me and your father?"

"I'll never get that kind of sense," Mamma said. "Jim's my husband, and I love him."

Then Aunt Minnie saw me and made me go outside. I got a stick of wood and whittled with the new knife Uncle Luke had bought me. I cut my hand and it bled like everything, but I didn't go in and tell Mamma. I guess I was like Papa. I was afraid of Aunt Minnie.

That afternoon Mamma went to bed. She said she didn't feel good. When Papa got home for supper, Aunt Minnie said, "Laura's going to have your baby tonight. You stay here and you'd better get the doctor."

Papa didn't say anything. He didn't say anything when Aunt Minnie brought the big dish of dumplings to the table, either. If there was anything he hated, it was dumplings. I tried to eat one, but it was big and doughy and tasted awful. Papa excused himself and went into Mamma's bedroom. He stayed until it was dark and then he left without saying a word to Aunt Minnie.

I had to sit there until I finished my dumpling. Then Aunt Minnie said I looked bilious, and I went out on the front porch and sat down. I stayed there quite a while, getting sicker all the time until I heard some shooting downtown. I forgot about being sick when I remembered that Papa's guns were gone from the trunk. I got up to go find out about the shooting when Aunt Minnie ran out of the house.

"Your mamma's got to have the doctor right away," she said. "You go get him.

Fetch your papa, too. Just wait till I get my hands on that man."

Something in her voice scared me, and I ran. Doc Pettybone wasn't in his office, and there wasn't anybody on the street. Then when I got to the Antioch Bar I looked in and saw a crowd of men. Doc was in the middle of the room bending over someone laid out on a billiard table.

I squirmed between men's legs until I got to the table. Doc was leaning over Uncle Luke. He had his sleeves rolled up, and Uncle Luke had his shirt and undershirt off and was lying awful still. There was a round hole in his chest.

I grabbed at Doc's pants legs and started to yank on it and tell him Mamma needed him when somebody grabbed me and put a hand over my mouth. I kicked and tried to get free, then I saw it was Papa who was holding me.

Just then Doc straightened up and held something between his fingers. "There's the bullet," he said. "Didn't hit anything vital. I think he's going to be all right."

Papa took his hand off my mouth and I yelled, "Mamma's sick. She needs you right away."

Doc looked at Papa. "I can't go now."

"You promised," I said. "The first night we were in Antioch. You said Mamma came first. You said broken bones and bullets could wait."

"The boy's right," Uncle Luke said. His face was white as anything, just as white as his beard. "You take care of her first."

Doc grabbed his black bag and went out of there on the run, Papa a jump or two behind him. I tried to keep up but I couldn't. When I got home, Doc came tearing out of the house, still holding his black bag and headed back downtown.

I went inside but I didn't go into the bedroom. The door was open and I heard Papa say, "I'm sorry I had to break my promise to you but I never should have made it. You wouldn't have asked me to if it hadn't been for Aunt Minnie. She tried to bust us up in Denver and she's trying it again, scaring you into going to bed and sending for the doc and maybe causing Luke to die because Doc had to leave him."

I peeked through the door. Mamma was in bed and she was crying. I jerked back real quick because Papa had hold of Aunt Minnie's shoulders and was pushing her toward the door. They didn't see me. Aunt

198

Minnie was too scared and Papa was too mad.

When they got out into the parlor, Papa said, "I've put up with your cussedness because of Laura but I'm done. You're leaving on the midnight train. You're a mean old woman who never had a man and so you think there's something wrong with Laura loving me and me loving her. The only thing wrong is you. Now you pack up and get out of here."

Aunt Minnie climbed the stairs to her room real fast. Papa went back into the bedroom and got down on his knees beside the bed. I peeked through the door again and heard him say, "I love you, Laura. All I want is to have our home away from your father and Aunt Minnie. I'm not the only one that loves you here in Antioch. Luke told Doc to come to you. Maybe he's bled to death by now but he wouldn't have cared. You came first to him just like you did to me and Doc. To everybody, I guess." He kind of choked up, then he said, "You wouldn't have been scared of having babies if it wasn't for your Aunt Minnie. You've got to stop it. Lots of women have babies."

Papa leaned over and kissed her. "You

199

don't really care about me? I mean, you aren't mad because I had to kill a man?"

"No, Jim," Mamma said. "You go find out how Luke is. I guess I can be as brave as he was tonight."

Well, Aunt Minnie left and Uncle Luke got well and Mamma had the baby a month later. That's how my sister happened to be named First Merrybelle Dorcas. She was the first baby born in Antioch, you see, so Papa got those lots and he built a big, fine hardware store on them.

It was a whole year before I found out there wasn't anything to that cabbage-patch business. That was when Mamma had another baby. She named him Luke Mattingly Dorcas and Mamma wasn't scared any more. She didn't even worry, Papa said, and I guess he was just about the happiest man in the whole camp. He's going to build another room on the back of the house. This one's going to be a girl, he says, to keep First Merrybelle company.

Before turning to television work in the mid-1950s (he regularly contributed scripts to "Bonanza" and later became the show's associate producer), Thomas Thompson was a top hand at Western fiction. He published thirteen uniformly excellent novels between 1949 and 1960, among them Shadow of the Butte, Trouble Rider, *and* Brand of a Man. *(A new novel,* Outlaw Valley, *his first since a 1966 "Bonanza" novelization, is scheduled for a 1987 publication date.) Two of his short stories, "Blood on the Sun" and "Gun Job," received Spur Awards; these and other fine tales can be found in his collections* They Brought Their Guns *and* Moment of Glory. *"Killer in Town" is one of his best about gunmen in the Old West.*

Killer in Town

Thomas Thompson

He rode purposefully into the town, a tall, lean man with serious blue eyes and a wealth of wavy blond hair that grew low on his neck.

201

He had shaved away the drooping mustache that he had worn to make him look older, but the steady aging of those in his profession had left its mark on him. Leading his pack horse, he passed the well-chewed watering trough where two barefoot boys pulled horsetail hairs from under splinters and put them into the water, hoping for them to turn to wriggling snakes. They glanced up and saw him, recognizing him as a stranger, and when he had ridden on, the boys stood there staring after him, saying nothing, not knowing what thing it was that had suddenly made them quiet.

He turned left into the rutted but well-used street that led to the livery stable, following the directions in the letter Jim Collingwood had sent him. He had memorized the letter, then destroyed it. There was a quickening within him now, an eagerness to see Collingwood mixed with a growing dread of the meeting. He hadn't seen his old friend in ten years, and nothing would be the same. A man couldn't go back in time and a gun marshal couldn't plan on tomorrow. He felt that growing sense of being trapped between the past and the future, a man squeezed in a tiny pocket of today, and that pocket always a trouble spot.

Coming to the livery stable, he rode directly through the door, ducking his head, tugging his pack animal behind him. There were four men there, discussing their own business. They glanced up, not knowing that this was Reb Lefton, the gun marshal. The secret of his coming here had been well guarded. Four horses, still saddled, stood in the shade of the barn. Reb Lefton made out the Anvil brand on their left hips and he looked at the four men with renewed interest, knowing he would see them again. One of the men said, "The old man will be along in a minute."

"I got time," Reb Lefton said. He cocked a leg around his saddle horn and looked through the door toward Jim Collingwood's town, a small place of no importance. He thought of how a few years back Collingwood could have handled the trouble in ten towns this size. But now Collingwood had sent for help. It was a compliment to his own ability, Reb Lefton knew, and once it would have flattered him. It didn't now. He made a cigarette, keeping his hands busy. That was the best when the first nervousness built its vacantness inside. Jim Collingwood had taught Reb Lefton that a long time back in a place a long way from here.

He finished the cigarette and touched a match to it, breaking the match in his fingers and rubbing out the fire and dropping the two pieces of the match in his shirt pocket in the way of a man who has lived long in dry country. Unoccupied, his hands were uncertain, and he calmed himself by drawing smoke deep into his lungs, letting it out with a gusty sigh. This was the bad part, this first waiting. Whether it was waiting for a man to reach for a gun or waiting to see a great man who had outlived his time, it was a bad thing. He heard the shuffling gait and he saw Jim Collingwood coming toward him.

Reb Lefton had prepared himself. He knew that Jim would be older; he knew that Jim was crippled. He had told himself he would ignore both outward signs, because the man inside the shell would be the same, a fighting man—but, rarer than that, a man who had been able to pass his talent along to another. Jim Collingwood was the greatest gun marshal of them all. Now Reb saw him, the man who had been his teacher and his friend, and Reb forced the casual grin he had practiced for a month. "This a good barn you got here?" Reb said.

Jim Collingwood had been a strongly built man, and the strength was still there in a heavy chest and broad shoulders, and it was in his eyes, eyes that were bright with pleased recognition as they momentarily masked the pain in a shattered body. Collingwood leaned his weight on the single-shaft, homemade crutch. His left leg twisted around the shaft of the crutch; his right hand, the famous right hand, was a nearly useless claw. He looked up at Reb Lefton, a quick look of defiance on his face now, as he guarded against the pity he hated. He spit at the toe of his good foot as if to remind himself he had that much; then he squinted his left eye in that old way he had and his voice was the same soft drawl Reb remembered. "Mister," Jim Collingwood said, "it don't have to be a good barn, seeing as how it's the only one within fifty miles of here."

"Then I'll have to make it do," Reb said. He swung down from his saddle, the stiffness of a prolonged ride in him. His eyes drifted to the four Anvil riders and then back to Collingwood, asking their question. He caught Collingwood's unspoken warning to guard his identity and he knew that this was not the time and these were not the important ones. "A hotel, then," Reb said. "You got a good hotel in this place?"

"Not a good one," Jim Collingwood said.

"Ask me about a saloon. You've got a choice there."

"A man don't need much choice when it comes to whisky or women," Reb said.

"A young man don't need a choice," Jim Collingwood said. "Me, now, I favor Pat Kelly's place, left side of the main street, six doors down from the corner. Clayt Brunson and Fred Mallory both say it's the best, so that makes it so." He had a way of turning, using his crutch for a pivot. "Ain't that right, boys?" he said to the Anvil riders.

"You're getting smart, old man," one answered, and Reb felt the sting of the man's tone rip through Jim Collingwood. Forty-five years old, Reb calculated swiftly. Eighteen years older than Reb himself. A broken shell who had sent for help because there was trouble in this place, trouble that had to be stopped because this place was all there was left for Jim Collingwood. Someday it will happen to me, Reb thought to himself, and aloud he said, "I'll try Pat Kelly's, then. I'll be back later for my possibles."

He stepped out into the brilliant sunshine, feeling each shaft of heat strike through him like an arrow, feeling each bullet that had struck through Jim Collingwood's flesh, leaving him what he was today. He walked swiftly to the corner, his boots striking the ground solidly, trying to take him away from the past. He remembered a sailor he had known once, the only seafaring man he had ever met. The sailor had a quarter section in the center of Kansas and when Reb asked him how he came to be there the seafaring man had laced his fingers across a contented stomach and said, "I left New Orleans with a pair of oars across my shoulder. Yonder by that cottonwood I met a man who asked me what was those things I was carrying. I made a fire with them oars and settled down."

There was a thin line of perspiration on Reb Lefton's bare upper lip. He, too, had come to the time where he was looking for a place where someone would fail to recognize his oars when he saw them, Reb knew. He hadn't found it yet, and maybe he never would. He wanted to quit, and the feeling was stronger on him now than it had been before. A man didn't win in this business. If his arms and legs didn't wind up crippled, something inside him might, and that was worse.

He turned down the main street toward Kelly's saloon, knowing he had to hurry before he changed his mind. "You don't shuffle when you're walkin' toward trouble,

Reb," Jim Collingwood used to tell him. "You hurry up and get to it and then it's over faster. Trouble ain't somethin' you think about; trouble's somethin' you face." It was good advice and true advice and Reb Lefton had used it often. But now he was facing trouble belonging to a man who could no longer handle his personal chores. He felt a sharp dislike for himself and knew it was because of that thought. He came to the saloon and shouldered open the door.

It was a small saloon, but the beginning was here. Six men were here, an ordinary-looking lot, working cowboys, young. People had the idea that a man who needed killing looked different from other men. It wasn't so. Reb covered the room with his swift glance and found the leader, and this was his man, a man no different from the others except that he had red hair and a grin on his face. The talk grew a little louder when they recognized Reb as a stranger.

The bartender, a thick, tubby Irishman with a moonlike face and a bulbous red nose turned his new-customer grin on Reb. "Howdy," the bartender said, giving the bar an extra wipe. "My name's Pat Kelly. Ain't seen you before, have I?"

Six men and a bartender waited for an

answer. Fred Mallory, the man with the red hair, yawned prodigiously and squinted up at the cobwebs on the ceiling.

"Not unless you got mighty good eyes," Reb said, answering the bartender's question. "I been quite a piece from here." He tossed out a silver dollar. "Whisky."

"Best order by brand, stranger," Fred Mallory said. "I saw Pat's old woman makin' soap yesterday and Pat ain't one to waste the lye water."

"I'll buy you a drink for the advice," Reb said.

Fred Mallory turned, and his green eyes were grave and thoughtful behind his smile. "Save your money, cowboy," he said. "She's makin' up for a hot summer." There was nothing personal in the refusal; there was a cool alertness in Fred Mallory's glance as he recognized in Reb one of his own kind. He'll be fast and he'll enjoy the killing, Reb Lefton thought, but he won't come up behind a man. He's got himself a reputation around here, and his pride will make him meet a man head on.

"Lookin' for work?" the bartender said. He poured a free drink and did his best with his practiced smile.

"Will be, when my belly tells me it's

time," Reb said. He emptied his glass and sighed. "Not lye water, that," he said.

Fred Mallory leaned against the bar, eyes half closed, the dark pinpoints of his pupils following the course of a fly on the opposite wall. "This is a one-outfit country," he said unexpectedly. "Either a man works for Anvil or he don't work at all."

"I've heard of such places," Reb said. He lifted his glass to his lips and through the window he saw the man and the girl coming down the sidewalk. The man held the girl's arm possessively. Reb set his glass down hard, finished here for the moment, and he took his change from the bar and dropped it into his vest pocket.

"Figgerin' on stayin' around here?" Fred Mallory said. He turned then, meeting Reb's gaze, making his question direct and plain, asking for a direct answer.

"Depends," Reb Lefton said quietly. "I'll let you know." He turned abruptly and walked to the door and there he paused briefly, timing himself. When the man and the girl were directly opposite, he pushed roughly through the door and collided solidly with them.

He reached out and gripped the girl's arms, holding her off, seeing the slow, uncertain recognition in her eyes. It had been ten years since he had seen Tess Collingwood—she had been fourteen then; he had been seventeen. The years had made a difference. The man laid a hand on Reb's shoulder and twisted him around, and now Reb was face to face with Clayt Brunson, the owner of Anvil. "Apologize," Clayt Brunson said.

Brunson was young—not more than thirty. Reb would have recognized him anyplace, he realized now, just from Jim Collingwood's description. He was well dressed, as Jim had said he would be, but it was more than that. It was the arrogance and sureness of a man with money. There was a stain of ready anger in his cheeks, spreading from a deeper anger in his brooding, dark eyes. Reb released his grip on Tess Collingwood's arms, seeing the color drain slowly from her cheeks as she recognized the trouble that was coming and knew her father's part in it. "I beg your pardon, miss," Reb said. He touched the brim of his hat with the side of his forefinger.

Clayt Brunson appraised Reb swiftly and found nothing to fear in the deceiving grin, the ready acceptance of his order. He reached out and shoved Reb slightly. "Watch your clumsy feet, then," he said.

"The man said he was sorry, Clayt," the girl said quickly.

Reb looked at the girl and the smile on his lips was broad and it was in his eyes. "But I said it to you, lady," he said.

"You'll say it to me, too," Clayt Brunson said hotly. "Loud. I'm not in the habit of letting drunks bump into me on a public sidewalk."

Reb turned and surveyed the man carefully, seeing the full pattern of the trouble here. This was the man who threatened to drive the small ranchers from the valley. This was the man Jim Collingwood could not handle. Clayt Brunson was a cattle king—a young one who had inherited his wealth and didn't deserve it. He was a man who had been thrust into a position he wasn't big enough to fill, so he had surrounded himself with gun help and resorted to force to build his ego. Reb felt the old, slow anger, the confidence of knowing that he had been asked to do a job, the confidence of knowing he would do that job.

"Mister," Reb said softly, "when I'm drunk you'll know it. Until I'm drunk, don't get sassy with me or I'm right apt to pull that hat of yours down around your ears." He gave the girl his deep smile, trying to reassure her, but failing. He touched the brim of his hat again and sauntered across toward the hotel, deeply affected by what he had seen in Tess Collingwood's eyes. Women didn't like gunfighters. Not even gunfighters who came to save a woman's father's peace of mind.

He registered for a room at the hotel, signing his own name, no longer concerned about concealing his identity. *You have to run straight at trouble*, he told himself. That was the way Jim Collingwood had taught him. This was Jim Collingwood's fight and he would do it Jim Collingwood's way. A memory of Tess, Jim's daughter, crossed his mind and lingered there and found its own little pocket where it would remain for eternity. She was a beautiful girl, and the memory of her reminded him of things he would never have. Peace, security, a home, a woman to share his worries and his thoughts. He went back outside without looking at his room and he went toward the livery stable. Jim Collingwood was leaning against the door, his broken body twisted as if it were reaching out for every bit of the sun, not wanting to waste a ray of it.

Reb saw two of the men who had been in the saloon. They looked at him with renewed interest, a curbed hostility in their glances. Reb crossed the street and Jim Collingwood said, "You meet a thing head on, Reb."

"It's the way you taught me," Reb said. "What's next?"

"A meeting at my house," Collingwood said. "Soon's it's dark. There's six men from the valley. They've all been pushed around by Clayt Brunson's gun crew and they're spoiling for a fight. But they need a leader, Reb. Someone with know-how."

"You told me that in your letter," Reb said impatiently.

Jim Collingwood studied the younger man intently. "Anything you've seen so far bother you?"

"Tess," Reb said bluntly. "Clayt Brunson acts like he owns her."

"He acts that way about everything," Collingwood said.

"Does Tess object?"

"Tess don't like a fight, Reb," Collingwood said quietly. "Tess would do 'most anything to prevent a fight."

Reb saw the hurt, the real worry in Collingwood's eyes. Jim Collingwood, too, was feeling that tremendous press between the past and the future, the tiny pocket of today. Jim Collingwood was responsible for his daughter's frame of mind. She saw the broken, bullet-riddled body of her father and she hated the fighting that had caused it, seeing only cause and effect because she was young. So she would do anything to prevent a fight. How much? That was the question that was plaguing Jim Collingwood. How far would she go?

"Tonight, then," Reb said. He went to his pack saddles and got a change of clothes and his possibles sack. For a long time he looked thoughtfully at the gun belt and the holstered sixshooter that was there. He hadn't worn it into town, purposely, for he wanted time to look around, but he had left the carbine in the saddle boot and he could have reached it any time.

It angered him to realize how conscious he had become of his gun. Other men could wear a gun and think nothing of it, but when a gun was your business you felt self-conscious about it. It was like a man off duty wearing a uniform that clearly proclaimed his occupation. Reb Lefton couldn't wear a gun unless he intended to use it. Neither could Jim Collingwood, in the old days. And neither could Fred Mallory, the red-haired foreman of Anvil. Reb had seen that in the man.

He folded the gun belt in his clothes—this was still not the time—and he went swiftly outside without speaking to Collingwood. The fading sun was blood-red against his bronze skin and the ache inside him was deep and penetrating when he thought of Tess Collingwood and Clayt Brunson.

He came onto the opposite sidewalk, paying little attention to the two men who were lounging there against the wall. One of them stepped forward suddenly and deliberately bumped him, pushing him off the sidewalk. Reb turned quickly and saw that it was Fred Mallory, the Anvil foreman. "What's the matter, man?" Reb said, holding back his anger. "That whisky of Kelly's give you the blind staggers?"

"I hear tell you go around bumpin' people," Fred Mallory said. "I thought maybe it was a game you like to play."

Reb took time to study Fred Mallory carefully. Fred wasn't tall, but he gave the impression of size. His shoulders were broad, his chest thick. He was built like a wedge, tapering down to small feet. His red, curly hair was fiery in the late sun. There was humor in the man, but it was an angry humor, nursed by the love of a fight. He was a man who had gained his position of leadership by taking it away from others. Now it was nearly the time, and it was all right to let Fred Mallory see that Reb knew him.

"Being foreman of Anvil means a lot of different chores, don't it, Fred?" Reb Lefton said quietly.

"That could be so," Mallory said, and if he felt surprise, he hid it. He hitched at his beltless pants. He wore no gun. "Why don't you try staying off the sidewalks for a day or so? Might learn you some manners."

Reb stood there grinning. He thumbed back his hat and in that casual movement he was able to glance up and down the street. He saw that the entire Anvil crew was outside, leaning against the buildings in groups of twos and threes, watching this, waiting for Reb to put his cards on the table. The old pattern of trouble was as familiar to Reb as the back of his hand.

He walked up to the board sidewalk. He took off his hat and dusted off a place and carefully laid his bundle in the cleaned-off spot. "Well, Fred," he said, almost wearily. "I wouldn't want you neglecting your chores." He straightened up. His left hand shot out and pulled Mallory's hat down over his eyes. His right fist drove savagely into Mallory's stomach.

217

It was an old trick and not a particularly clever one, a trick Reb had used on fifty or more fractious drunks. It needed only an element of surprise and a little speed. He was almost sorry that Fred Mallory had fallen for it. Once a fight started there was a thing that grew inside Reb Lefton, an eagerness that made him welcome violence. Sometimes a man needed a fight, and Reb needed one now.

The breath exploded from Mallory's lungs in a gusty sigh. He took two steps forward, still bent over, and Reb's right fist cracked solidly against the butt of the man's jaw. Mallory's knees buckled and he fell grotesquely, falling across the sidewalk, his feet and hips still on the walk, his torso and face in the dust of the street. The man who had been with Mallory stood there, doing nothing. Reb walked toward him. For a long second the man waited, staring at Reb; then he turned and moved down the sidewalk, and Reb, looking that way, saw Clayt Brunson and Tess Collingwood standing there.

The blood had drained from the girl's cheeks and her hands were clenched tightly at her sides. Clayt Brunson was a man swollen with anger, a man who was not used to being crossed. Reb walked steadily toward

218

the man and the girl. When he was close he said, "About that hat, Brunson." He reached out and jerked Brunson's hat savagely down, partially ripping the brim from the crown. That done, he looked at the girl soberly, trying to reach her. "It's best, Tess," he murmured. He walked away before she could see the swelling anger inside him, before she could see the thing that troubled him most, the anger that grew to where it would be easy to kill a man and enjoy the killing. She had seen too much of that in her time; he didn't want her to see it in him.

He stopped and picked up his bundle from the sidewalk and went to the hotel, feeling an awkwardness in his walk that wasn't there, knowing the girl's eyes were on his back.

In his hotel room he sat on the edge of the bed a long time, his face in his hands. He felt the tired helplessness that came to him more and more often when he was alone, and his banter and the quickness of his temper, he saw, were walls he had constructed to keep people from seeing his inner self. More than anything, he wanted peace, a chance to settle down and live his life.

But there was always something in the way, just as now. When he thought of a future at all he thought of it as a vast, even plain, unobstructed by trouble. That was what the seafaring man had been looking for when he came to the place where he could burn his oars; that was the thing Reb Lefton wanted most. And to find peace like that a man would have to refuse to fight, for as long as a man fought, there would be other fights ahead.

He thought of cabins that would be burned if he didn't fight now, cabins out there in the valley, burned by Clayt Brunson's men, by Clayt Brunson's orders. He had seen such cabins before, black remnants of a dream, and he remembered the twisted bedframes and knew that men and women had lain upon those beds, staring up into the dark recesses of smoky rafters, dreaming their dreams and making their plans. That was the big thing—the looking into the future. That was the only thing, and a troubled man didn't have that thing, for he moved only from one trouble to another and the next day might be the last day. It wasn't fear for self that made a man want to quit. Rather it was the gradual realization that man's only heritage was hope for tomorrow, and that hope was denied a gunman.

Reb unwrapped the clothing bundle and took up his gun belt. He slid the weapon from his holster and tested its weight in his hand, feeling the familiar slickness of the gun butt, feeling the satisfaction of knowing that he was an expert with that gun and just as surely feeling the tired drag of knowing that it was a negative accomplishment. He heard the light rap on the door and he hesitated, then strapped on the gun belt. He stepped to the door, keeping to one side out of old habit. "Yes?" he said.

"It's Tess," the voice said. "I have to talk to you."

He had known he would have to face her, but now that the time was here he dreaded it and he felt a rebellion that made him want to tell her it was none of her business. He opened the door and she came inside the room, and when he closed the door behind her he stood there for a moment seeing her as a grown woman with a grown woman's thoughts, the full maturity of her bringing a constriction to his throat. He could not brush her aside, he knew, for she was Jim Collingwood's daughter, and she was a lot like Jim in that she would have to have her own convictions and those convictions would have to be expressed.

"You've grown up, Tess," he said. "You're a beautiful woman."

"Go back where you came from, Reb," she said. She met his eyes and held them, and he thought of the ten years since he had seen her, remembering swiftly.

"Remember when we were kids in Kansas?" he said, grinning now. "I must have been a blind fool, not to know you'd grow up someday."

"Your being here can't do any good, Reb," she said. "There's two sides to everything, Reb. There has to be. Mr. Brunson has had a lot of trouble with the small outfits." She searched for a stronger argument, found none, and said helplessly, "Clayt hasn't killed anyone and he doesn't intend to."

"You always had a rag around your toe," he said. "I never saw a girl could stub her toe so often."

"You start this thing and Dad will be into it," she said, anger in her now. "Hasn't he earned the right to live out his life in peace?"

"A long time ago," Reb Lefton said. "Too long."

"Reb," she said, and now she moved forward and put her hands against his chest as if she could push him out of his decision. "Clayt Brunson will be fair. He only wants the valley. There's plenty of land for those who want to work for it."

He reached out suddenly and gripped her shoulders and pulled her toward him, remembering the things he had missed, remembering the things he could not claim. And suddenly the old pattern of a man grabbing land, bit by bit, and other men resisting and failing or winning—all that was of little importance. There were bigger things in life. His fingers closed tightly on her arms. "Do you love Clayt Brunson?" he asked quietly.

For a long moment she stood there close to him, her eyes on his eyes, a strange, wondering bewilderment on her face as she saw this man for the first time. Then she pushed away from him and turned her back. "Yes," she said. "I love Clayt Brunson. I plan to marry him."

"All right, Tess," he said. "All right."

He waited then until the darkness came and then he buckled on his gun belt and went downstairs, asking the clerk for directions to Jim Collingwood's place. He walked down the street with the gathering darkness unfriendly around him and turned in at the white gate in the picket fence. The yard was full of flowers, and he remembered Jim's wife, always planting things, always wanting something with roots in the ground. He rapped lightly on the door and it opened immediately. Mrs. Collingwood said, "Reb Lefton." She stood on tiptoe and kissed his cheek and he took his hat and stood there, looking at the circle of expectant faces.

Jim Collingwood was the leader here, but he was a leader who could make decisions only. He couldn't act. Jim introduced the men in the room. "We got to get it out in the open, Reb," Jim said. "We got to meet Clayt Brunson and Fred Mallory head on and stop 'em before they start. There's no other way."

Reb saw the strained faces, the faces of men who had spent a lifetime planning on a piece of earth that would be their tomorrow, a place they could call their own. These men had wives at home, wives who shared the dream and looked to the future, and suddenly he was remembering Tess and of how she had told him of her plan to marry Clayt Brunson. The land, then, wasn't important; the dream of the future was. And Tess Collingwood had a right to her dream, too, and no man with a gun had a right to kill that dream.

"You ain't said how much you'll pay me," Reb Lefton said.

He saw the shocked surprise in Jim Collingwood's eyes. He felt the sudden dryness that had come into the mouths of these men who had waited for a famous man to come to lead them in their fight. Jim Collingwood had sent for him as a friend, not as a hired gun.

"Pay?" Jim Collingwood said. An anger was growing in him, an anger intensified by his inability to put it into physical action.

"A man learns better than to work for nothing," Reb Lefton said. "If there's no pay I reckon I'll be going now."

He left the room hurriedly, feeling the shocked surprise running into pained disappointment, turning finally to whipped despair. At the door Mrs. Collingwood took his arm and gripped it strongly. "Why, Reb?" she whispered. "Why?"

"I told you," he said. "I don't kill for nothing." He pulled away from her grip and hastened outside, and now it was full dark and every shrub and every tree along the street was a shadow. He heard his name, softly, and he stopped and waited, and he felt the nearness of Tess before she touched him.

"You turned them down?" she said.

"That's right."

"Thank you, Reb." She raised on tiptoe and put her arms around his neck and drew his head down, and in that second all the old longing was in him and he held her and met her lips and he could no longer hold back his dreams.

He felt a response as violent as his own, and he felt something more—something stronger—something more real. There was a barrier here, a waiting and an expectancy, and this girl's emotions were straining against that barrier, waiting for fulfillment. He knew then that she had waited for him even while she told herself she did not want him, and he knew that she had never really loved another man, and he could feel the intenseness inside her, locked away from him, a protecting wall around her emotions. She didn't love Clayt Brunson, and he knew it as plainly as if she had said so. He held her, the wonder of it strong on him, and then he let her go. "I made a mistake, Tess," he said. He hurried down the walk, and she took two steps to follow him and then caught herself and stood there with her hand reaching toward him, and she started to cry.

He went to the hotel, the uncertainty thick in him now, and there tied to the porch rail he saw his pack horse and his saddle, ready.

He crossed the porch and went inside, and Fred Mallory was slumped deep in a chair, his eyes bright and alert, and Reb's extra clothes and his possibles bag were there in the middle of the floor. "So you're Reb Lefton," Mallory said. "I've heard of you." He pushed himself out of the chair and stood up. "Your horses are outside, ready," he said.

Now was the time and this was the decision. The time always came, and a man fought or he ran. "You sure I'm ready to go, Mallory?" Reb said.

"I heard you were smart, Lefton," Fred Mallory said. "We do things a certain way around here. You might not fit that way. So long, Lefton."

Reb stood there looking at Fred Mallory, feeling a calmness now, able to see clearly. Tess Collingwood had wanted a future and he had been willing to give it to her, respecting her desires. But you couldn't buy a future by selling yourself. Jim Collingwood knew that. All Jim wanted was a quiet town, a place to soak his aches in the sun—but, more than that, a place where he would be wanted and respected. And that, Reb saw, was the biggest thing of all, and Tess Collingwood would never have it if she gave herself to Clayt Brunson.

"I reckon you made a mistake, Mallory," Reb said quietly.

Fred Mallory stiffened, a wild smile on his face, the strain and tension and eagerness of a gunfighter in that smile. Reb saw Fred Mallory take the challenge. He saw Mallory's weight shift and Reb's hand dropped to his holster and flashed up. Two shots rolled into one, both wide of their mark, and now boots were pounding and a woman screamed and Fred Mallory's gun was bucking against his hand and the orange stabs of death were slanting toward the floor, pointing at the torn white splinters of wood in the planking. Reb Lefton emptied his gun, knowing too late that the last two shots were not needed, knowing he had won again, and the reaction of having killed and the emptiness of his victory was a deep-seated pain inside him.

Men rushed across the sidewalk and paused at the door of the hotel, seeing Fred Mallory's upturned face, seeing Reb Lefton standing there with a gun in his hand, not taking time to realize that the gun was empty, and they fell back against each other, not wanting to face him. Reb Lefton felt the empty gun and he thought suddenly, *This is*

228

what you have, Jim Collingwood. An empty gun, and still it has strength, because you never backed down from making a stand for what you thought was right. Reb Lefton moved forward and he saw the men moving back, dry-lipped men now, and he saw Clayt Brunson.

He heard Brunson's thin cry, "Rush him, men! He's only one!" and in that cry he saw the real nature of Brunson, a man who would not make a stand, even with a loaded gun, but would leave it to others to fight for him. He felt a welling anger as he realized that Brunson had even tried to use Tess Collingwood, making her say she loved him, even believing it. And Tess had said the words Clayt Brunson wanted to hear because she thought she could buy peace for her father. In time she would have realized what an empty bargain she had made, but by then it would have been too late. When he had kissed her Reb Lefton had known that would be so.

"Is there more to this, Brunson?" Reb Lefton said.

Fear was a phlegm in Clayt Brunson's throat. He looked wildly at the gun crew he had hired and saw no response in them. They folded their arms and stood and waited, their glances heavy on him, their way telling him that now it was either his fight or no fight at all, waiting for him to become a leader. This was Brunson's decision, and the whole town saw him make it. "There never was anything we couldn't work out," he said weakly.

The men had come up from Collingwood's place. "That's right, Brunson," one of them said. "But we'll work it out our way."

Later, in the hotel, Reb Lefton sat alone, letting the shock run out of him. He heard the heavy, broken step loud on the stair and in time Jim Collingwood came into the room and sat with him there in the darkness. For a long time the two men didn't speak, knowing each other's thoughts.

"A man has to live with himself all his life," Jim Collingwood said presently.

"It's hard for a woman to see," Reb Lefton said.

He felt Jim Collingwood's smile in the darkness. "We've been happy, my wife and me," he said finally. "It wasn't always so, but it's lasted." He was thinking back, and his voice was soft with remembering. "I reckon a man does what he has to do and a woman loves him in spite of it or she don't love him at all."

Reb thought of Tess, knowing she was

somewhere crying, and he thought of how a woman had an advantage, being able to cry. She could wash away a decision that was a mistake and get a clearer look at what was right. Jim Collingwood moved his crutch and got to his feet, and the twisted right hand closed on Reb Lefton's shoulder. "Settling down ain't the same as quitting," he said quietly. "Sometimes when the snow is deep in the winter I get to thinking about how the sunsets will look next summer. That's a good thing, Reb, looking ahead to something. A man couldn't do it if he hadn't been honest with himself. He'd keep looking back."

Collingwood turned and left the room, and Reb looked after him, remembering this man and the way he was ten years ago, seeing now the broken body but feeling the spirit that was not broken and never would be. He closed his eyes and thought of Tess and of what might be. He had some money saved and there was land here for a man if he wanted it. A great sense of contentment claimed him, and he thought of the time ahead and of a woman whose kiss was an unfilled promise. "Tomorrow I'll look for a piece of land," he said silently. "Tomorrow will be a good day."

Elmore Leonard needs no introduction to modern readers. His recent crime novels such as Bandits *and* Glitz *have been bestsellers, and his Western fiction, in particular the novels* Hombre *and* Valdez Is Coming, *is regarded as among the finest penned over the past four decades. Leonard's terse, tense short stories have appeared in several previous anthologies in this series, and have also been adapted into such outstanding Western films as* 3:10 to Yuma *(from the story of the same title) and* The Tall T *(from "The Captives"). "Jugged" is less well known than most of his short fiction—undeservedly so, as the reader will no doubt agree.*

Jugged

Elmore Leonard

Stan Cass, his elbows leaning on the edge of the roll-top desk, glanced over his shoulder as he said, "Take a look how I made this one out."

Marshal John Boynton had just come in.

232

He was standing in the front door of the jail office, one finger absently stroking his full mustache. He looked at his regular deputy, Hanley Miller, who stood next to a chair where a young man sat leaning forward looking at his hands.

"What's the matter with him?" Boynton said, ignoring Stan Cass.

Hanley Miller put his hand on the back of the chair. "A combination of things, John. He's had too many, been beat up, and now he's tired."

"He looks tired," Boynton said, again glancing at the silent young man.

Stan Cass turned his head. "He looks like a smart-aleck kid."

Boynton walked over to Cass and picked up the record book from the desk. The last entry read:

Name: *Pete Given*
Description: *Nineteen. Medium height and build. Brown hair and eyes. Small scar under chin.*
Residence: *Dos Cabezas*
Occupation: *Mustanger*
Charge: *Drunk and disorderly*
Comments: *Has to pay a quarter share of the*

damages in the Continental Saloon whatever they are decided to be.

Boynton handed the record book to Cass. "You spelled nineteen wrong."

"Is that all?"

"How do you know he has to pay a quarter of the damages?"

"Being four of them," Cass said, mock-seriously, "I figured to myself: Now if they have to chip in for what's busted, how much would—"

"That's for the judge to say. What were they doing here?"

"They delivered a string to the stage line," Cass answered. He was a man in his early twenties, clean shaven, though his sideburns extended down to the curve of his jaw. He was smoking a cigarette and he spoke to Boynton as if he were bored.

"And they tried to spend all the profit in one night," Boynton said.

Cass shrugged indifferently. "I guess so."

Boynton's finger stroked his mustache and he was thinking: Somebody's going to bust his nose for him. He asked, civilly, "Where're the other three?"

Cass nodded to the door that led back to the first-floor cell. "Where else?"

Hanley Miller, the regular night deputy, a man in his late forties, said, "John, you know there's only room for three in there. I was wondering what to do with this boy." He tipped his head toward the quiet young man sitting in the chair.

"He'll have to go upstairs," Boynton said.

"With Obie Ward?"

"I guess he'll have to." Boynton nodded to the boy. "Pull him up."

Hanley Miller got the sleepy boy on his feet.

Cass shook his head watching them. "Obie Ward's got everybody buffaloed. I'll be a son of a gun if he ain't got everybody buffaloed."

Boynton's eyes dropped to Cass, but he did not say anything.

"I'm just saying that Obie Ward don't look so tough," Cass said.

"Act like you've got some sense once in a while," Boynton said now. He had hired Cass the week before as an extra night guard—the day they brought in Obie Ward—but he was certain now he would not keep Cass. Tomorrow he would look around for somebody else. Somebody who didn't talk so much and didn't have such a proud opinion of himself.

"All I'm saying is he don't look so tough to me," Cass repeated.

Boynton ignored him. He looked at the young man, Pete Given, standing next to Hanley now with his eyes closed, and he heard his deputy say, "The boy's asleep on his feet."

"He looks familiar," Boynton said.

"We had him here about three months ago."

"Same thing?"

Hanley nodded. "Delivered his horses then stopped off at the Continental. Remember, his wife come here looking for him. He was here five days because the judge was away and she got here court day. Pretty little thing with light-colored hair? Not more'n seventeen. Come all the way from Dos Cabezas by herself."

"Least he had sense enough to get a good woman," Boynton said. He seemed to hesitate. Then: "You and I'll take him up." He slipped his revolver from its holster and placed it on the desk. He took young Pete Given's arm then and raised it up over his shoulder, glancing at his deputy again. "Hanley, you come behind with your shotgun."

Cass watched them go through the door

236

and down the hall to the back of the jail to the outside stairway, and he was thinking: Won't even wear his gun up there he's so scared. That's some man to work for, won't even wear his gun when he goes in Ward's cell. He shook his head and said the name again, contemptuously. Obie Ward. He'd pull his tough act on me just once.

Pete Given opened his eyes. Lying on his right side his face was close to the wall and for a moment, seeing the chipped and peeling adobe and smelling the stale mildewed smell of the mattress, which did not have a cover on it, he did not know where he was. Then he remembered, and he closed his eyes again.

The sour taste of whisky coated his mouth and he lay very still waiting for the throbbing to start in his head. But it did not come. He raised his head and moved closer to the wall and felt the edge of the mattress cool and firm against his cheek. Still the throbbing did not come. There was a dull tight feeling at the base of his skull, but not the shooting sharp pain he had expected. That was good. He moved his toes and could feel his boots still on and there was no blanket covering him.

They just dumped you here, he thought. He made saliva in his mouth and kept swallowing until his mouth did not feel sticky and some of the sour taste went away. Well, what did you expect?

It's about all you deserve, buddy. No, it's more'n you deserve.

You'll learn, huh?

He thought of his wife, Mary Ellen, and his eyes closed tighter and for a moment he tried not to think of anything.

How do I do this? How do I get something good, then kick it away like it's not worth anything?

What'll you tell her this time?

"Mary Ellen, honest to gosh, we just went in to get one drink. We sold the horses and got something to eat and figured one drink before starting back. Then Art said one more. All right, just one, I told him. But, you know, we were relaxed—and laughing. That's hard work running a thirty-horse string for five days. Harry got in a blackjack game. The rest of us were just sitting relaxed. When you're sitting like that the time seems to go faster. We had a few drinks. Maybe four—five at the most. Like I said, we were laughing and Art was telling some stories. You know Art, he keeps talking—then there's a commotion over at the blackjack table and we see Harry haulin' off at this man. And—"

And Mary Ellen will say, "Just like the last time," not raising her voice or seeming mad, but she'll keep looking you right in the eye.

"Honey, those things just happen. I can't help it. And it wasn't just like last time."

"The result's the same," she'll say. "You work hard for three months to earn decent money then pay it all out in fines and damages."

"Not all of it."

"It might as well be all. We can't live on what's left."

"But I can't help it. Can't you see that? Harry got in a fight and we had to help him. It's just one of those things that happens. You can't help it."

"But it seems a little silly, doesn't it?"

"Mary Ellen, you don't understand."

"Doesn't throwing away three months' profit in one night seem silly to you?"

"You don't understand."

You can be married to a girl for almost a year and think you know her and you don't know her at all. That's it. You know how she talks, but you don't know what she's

239

thinking. That's a big difference. But there's some things you can't explain to a woman anyway.

He felt a little better. Facing her would not be pleasant—but it still wasn't his fault.

He rolled over, momentarily studying the ceiling, then he let his head roll on the mattress and he saw the man on the other bunk watching him. He was sitting hunched over, making a cigarette.

Pete Given closed his eyes and he could still see the man. He didn't seem big, but he had a stringy hard-boned look. Sharp cheekbones and dull-black hair that was cut short and brushed forward to his forehead. No mustache, but he needed a shave and it gave the appearance of an almost full-grown mustache.

He opened his eyes again. The man was drawing on the cigarette, still watching him.

"What time you think it is?" Given asked.

"About nine." The man's voice was clear though he barely moved his mouth.

Given said, "If you were one of them over to the Continental I'd just as soon shake hands this morning."

The man did not reply.

"You weren't there then?"

"No," he said now.

"What've they got you for?"

"They say I shot a man."

"Oh."

"Fact is, they say I shot two men, during the Grant stage holdup."

"Oh."

"When the judge comes tomorrow, he'll set a court date. Give the witnesses time to get here." He stood up saying this. He was tall above average, but not heavy.

"Are you"—Given hesitated—"Obie Ward?"

The man nodded, drawing on the cigarette.

"Somebody last night said you were here. I'd forgot about it." Given spoke louder, trying to make his voice sound natural, and now he raised himself on an elbow.

Obie Ward asked, "Were you drinking last night?"

"Some."

"And got in a fight."

Given sat up, swinging his legs off the bunk and resting his elbows on his knees. "One of my partners got in trouble and we had to help him."

"You don't look so good," Ward said.

"I feel O.K."

"No," Ward said. "You don't look so good."

"Well, maybe I just look worse'n I am."

"How's your stomach?"

"It's all right."

"You look sick to me."

"I could eat. Outside of that I got no complaint." Given stood up. He put his hands on the small of his back and stretched, feeling the stiffness in his body. Then he raised his arms straight up, stretching again, and yawned. That felt good. He saw Obie Ward coming toward him, and he lowered his arms.

Ward reached out, extending one finger, and poked it at Pete Given's stomach. "How's it feel right there?"

"Honest to gosh, it feels O.K." He smiled, looking at Ward to show that he was willing to go along with a joke, but he felt suddenly uneasy. Ward was standing too close to him and Given was thinking: What's the matter with him?—and the same moment he saw the beard-stubbled face tighten.

Ward went back a half step and came forward driving his left fist into Given's stomach. The boy started to fold, a gasp coming from his open mouth, and Ward followed with his right hand, bringing it up solidly

242

against the boy's jaw, sending him back, arms flung wide, over the bunk and hard against the wall. Given slumped on the mattress and did not move. For a moment Ward looked at him, then picked up his cigarette from the floor and went back to his bunk.

He was sitting on the edge of it when Given opened his eyes—smoking another cigarette, drawing on it and blowing the smoke out slowly.

"Are you sick now?"

Given moved his head, trying to lift it, and it was an effort to do this. "I think I am."

Ward started to rise. "Let's make sure."

"I'm sure."

Ward relaxed again. "I told you so, but you didn't believe me. I been watching you all morning and the more I watched, the more I thought to myself: Now there's a sick boy. Maybe you ought to even have a doctor."

Given said nothing. He stiffened as Ward rose and came toward him.

"What's the matter? I'm just going to see you're more comfortable." Ward leaned over, lifting the boy's legs one at a time and pulled his boots off, then pushed him, gently, flat on the bunk and covered him with a blanket that was folded at the foot of it. Given looked up, holding his body rigid, and saw Ward shake his head. "You're a mighty sick boy. We got to do something about that."

Ward crossed the cell to his bunk and standing at one end he lifted it a foot off the floor and let it drop. He did this three times, then went down to his hands and knees and, close to the floor, called, "Hey, Marshal!" He waited. "Marshal, we got a sick boy up here!" He rose, winking at Given, and sat down on his bunk.

Minutes later a door at the back end of the hallway opened and Boynton came toward the cell. A deputy with a shotgun, his day man, followed him.

"What's the matter?"

Ward nodded. "The boy's sick."

"He ought to be," Boynton said.

Ward shrugged. "Don't matter to me, but I got to listen to him moaning."

Boynton looked toward Given's bunk. "A man that don't know how to drink has got to expect that." He turned abruptly. Their steps moved down the hall and the door slammed closed.

"No sympathy," Ward said. He made another cigarette and when he had lit it he walked over to Given's bunk. "He'll come back in about two hours with our dinner.

You'll still be in bed, and this time you'll be moaning like you got belly cramps. You got that?"

Staring up at him, Given nodded his head stiffly.

At a quarter to twelve Boynton came up again. This time he ordered Ward to lie down flat on his bunk. He unlocked the door then and remained in the hall as the day man came in with the dinner tray and placed it in the middle of the floor.

"He still sick?" Boynton stood in the doorway holding a sawed-off shotgun.

Ward turned his head on the mattress. "Can't you hear him?"

"He'll get over it."

"I think it's something else," Ward said. "I never saw whisky hold on like that."

"You a doctor?"

"As much a one as you are."

Boynton looked toward the boy again. Given's eyes were closed and he was moaning faintly. "Tell him to eat something," Boynton said. "Maybe then he'll feel better."

"I'll do that," Ward said. He was smiling as Boynton and his deputy moved off down the hall.

Lying on his back, his head turned on the

mattress, Given watched Ward take a plate from the tray. It looked like stew.

"Can I have some?" Given said.

Chewing, Ward shook his head.

"Why not?"

Ward swallowed. "You're too sick."

"Can I ask you a question?"

"Go ahead."

"How come I'm sick?"

"You haven't figured it?"

"No."

"I'll give you a hint. We'll get our supper about six. Watch the two that bring it up."

"I don't see what they'd have to do with me."

"You don't have to see."

Given was silent for some time. He said then, "It's got to do with you busting out."

Obie Ward grinned. "You got a head on your shoulders."

Boynton came up a half hour later. He stood in the hall and when his deputy brought out the tray, his eyes went from it to Pete Given's bunk. "The boy didn't eat a bite," Boynton observed.

Ward raised up on his elbow. "Said he couldn't stand the smell of it." He watched Boynton look toward the boy, then sank down on the bunk again as Boynton walked away. When the door down the hall closed, Ward said, "Now he believes it."

It was quiet in the cell after that. Ward rolled over to face the wall and Pete Given, lying on his back, remained motionless, though his eyes were open and he was studying the ceiling.

He tried to understand Obie Ward's plan. He tried to see how his being sick could have anything to do with Ward's breaking out. And he thought: He means what he says, doesn't he? You can be sure of that much. He's going to bust out and you got a part in it and there ain't a damn thing you can do about it. It's that simple, isn't it?

Obie Ward was right. At what seemed close to six o'clock they heard the door open at the end of the hall and a moment later Stan Cass and Hanley Miller were standing in front of the cell. Hanley opened the door and stood holding a sawed-off shotgun as Cass came in with the tray.

Cass half turned to face Ward sitting on his bunk, then went down to one knee, lowering the tray to the floor, and he did not take his eyes from Ward. He rose then and turned as he heard groans from the other bunk.

"What's his trouble?"

Ward looked up. "Didn't your boss tell you?"

"He told me," Cass said, "but I believe what I see."

"Help yourself then."

Cass turned sharply. "You shut your mouth till I want to hear from you!"

"Yes, sir," Ward said. His dark face was expressionless.

Cass stared at him, his thumbs hooked in his gunbelt. "You think you're somethin', don't you?"

Ward's head moved from side to side. "Not me."

"I'd like to see you pull somethin'," Cass said. His right hand opened and closed, moving closer to his hip. "I'd just like to see you get off that bunk and pull somethin'."

Ward shook his head. "Somebody's been telling you stories."

"I think they have," Cass said. He hesitated, then walked out, slamming the door shut.

Ward called to him through the bars, "What about the boy?"

"You take care of him," Cass said, moving off. Hanley Miller followed, looking back over his shoulder.

Ward waited until the back door closed, then picked up a plate and began to eat and not until he was almost finished did he notice Given watching him.

"Did you see anything?"

Given came up on his elbow slowly. He looked at the tray on the floor, then at Ward. "Like what?"

"Like the way that deputy acted."

"He wanted you to try something."

"What else?"

Given pictured Cass again in his mind. "He was wearing a gun." Suddenly he seemed to understand and he said, "The marshal wasn't wearing any, but this one was!"

Ward grinned. "And he knows you're sick. First his boss told him, then he saw it with his own eyes." Ward put down the plate and he made a cigarette as he walked over to Given's bunk. "I'll tell you something else," he said, standing close to the bunk. "I've been here seven days. For seven days I watch. I see the marshal. He knows what he's doing and he don't wear a gun when he comes in here. A man out in the hall with a scatter-gun's enough. Then this other one they call Cass. He walks like he can feel his gun on his hip. He's not used to it, but it

249

feels good and he'd like an excuse to use it. He even wears it in here, though likely he's been told not to. What does that tell you? He's sure of himself, but he's not smart. He wants to see me try something—and he's sure he can get his gun out if I do. For seven days I see this and there's nothing I can do about it—until this morning."

Given nodded thoughtfully, but said nothing.

"This morning I saw you," Ward went on, "and you looked sick. There it was."

Given nodded again. "I guess I see."

"We let the marshal know about it. He tells Cass when he comes on duty. Cass comes up and sure enough, you're sick."

"Yeah?"

"Then Cass comes up the next time—understand it'll be dark outside by then: he brings supper up at six, but he must go out to eat after that because he don't come back for the tray till almost eight—and he's not surprised to see you even sicker."

"How does he see that?"

"You scream like your stomach's been pulled out and you roll off the bunk."

"Then what?"

"Then you don't have to do anything else."

Given's eyes held on Ward's face. He swallowed and said, as evenly as he could, "Why should I help you escape?" He saw it coming and he tried to roll away, but it was too late and Ward's fist came down against his face like a mallet.

He was dazed and there was a stinging throbbing over the entire side of his face, but he was conscious of Ward leaning close to him and he heard the words clearly. "I'll kill you. That reason enough?"

After that he was not conscious of time. His eyes were closed and for a while he dozed off. Then, when he opened his eyes, momentarily he could remember nothing and he was not even sure where he was, because he was thinking of nothing, only looking at the chipped and peeling adobe wall and feeling a strange numbness over the side of his face.

His hand was close to his face and his fingers moved to touch his cheekbone. The skin felt swollen hard and tight over the bone and just touching it was painful. He thought then: Are you afraid for your own neck? Of course I am!

But it was more than fear that was making his heart beat faster. There was an anger inside of him. Anger adding excitement to the fear and he realized this, though not coolly, for he was thinking of Ward and Mary Ellen and himself as they came into his mind, not as he called them there.

Ward said roll off the cot. All right.

He heard the back door open and instantly Ward muttered, "You awake?" He turned his head to see Ward sitting on the edge of the bunk, his hands at his sides gripping the mattress. He heard the footsteps coming up the hall.

"I'm awake."

"Soon as he opens the door," Ward said and his shoulders seemed to relax.

As soon as he opens the door.

He heard Cass saying something and a key rattled in the lock. The squeak of the door hinges—

He groaned, bringing his knees up. His heart was pounding and a heat was over his face and he kept his eyes squeezed closed. He groaned again, louder this time, and doing it he rolled to his side, hesitated at the edge of the mattress, then let himself fall heavily to the floor.

"What's the matter with him!"

Four steps on the plank floor vibrated in his ear. A hand took his shoulder and rolled him over. Opening his eyes, he saw Cass leaning over him.

Suddenly then, Cass started to rise, his eyes stretched open wide, and he twisted his body to turn. An arm came from behind hooking his throat, dragging him back, and a hand was jerking the revolver from its holster.

Hanley Miller tried to push away from the bars to bring up the shotgun. It clattered against the bars and on top of the sound came the deafening report of the revolver. Hanley doubled up and went to the floor clutching his thigh.

Cass's mouth was open and he was trying to scream as the revolver flashed over his head and came down. The next moment Ward was throwing Cass' limp weight aside. Ward stumbled, clattering over the tray in the middle of the floor, almost tripping.

Given saw Ward go through the wide-open door. He glanced then at Hanley Miller lying on the floor. Then looking at Ward's back, the thought stabbed suddenly, unexpectedly in his mind—

Get him!

He hesitated, though the hesitation was in his mind and it was part of a moment. Then he was on his feet, moving quickly, silently in his stocking feet, stooping to pick up the

253

sawed-off shotgun, turning and seeing Ward near the door. Now Given was running down the hallway, now swinging open the door that had just closed behind Ward.

Ward was on the back porch landing starting down the stairs and he wheeled bringing up the revolver as the door opened, as he saw Pete Given on the landing, as he saw the stubby shotgun barrels swinging savagely in the dimness.

Ward fired hurriedly, wildly, the same moment the double barrels slashed against the side of his head. He screamed as he lost his balance and went down the stairway. At the bottom he tried to rise, groping momentarily, feverishly for his gun. As he came to his feet, Pete Given was there—and again the shotgun cut viciously against his head. Ward went down, falling forward, and this time he did not move.

Given sat down on the bottom step, letting the shotgun slip from his fingers. A lantern was coming down the alley.

Boynton appeared in the circle of lantern light. He looked from Obie Ward to the boy, not speaking, but his eyes remained on Given until he stepped past him and went up the stairs.

A man stooped next to him, extending an

already rolled cigarette. "You look like you want a smoke."

Given shook his head. "I'd swallow it."

The man nodded toward Obie Ward. "You took him by yourself?"

"Yes sir."

"That must've been something to see."

"I don't know—it happened so fast." In the crowd he heard Obie Ward's name over and over—someone asking if he was dead, a man bending over him saying no . . . someone asking, "Who's that boy?" and someone answering, "I don't know, but he's got enough guts for everybody."

Boynton appeared on the landing and called for someone to get the doctor. He came down and Given stood up to let him pass.

The man who was holding the cigarette said, "John, this boy got Obie all by himself."

Boynton was looking at Ward. "I see that."

"More'n I would've done," the man said, shaking his head.

"More'n most anybody would've done," Boynton answered. He looked at Given then, studying him openly. He said then, "I'll recommend to the judge we drop the charges against you."

Given nodded. "That'd be fine."

"Anxious to get home to your wife?"

"Yes sir."

For a moment Boynton was silent. His expression was mild, but his eyes were fastened on Pete Given's face as if he were trying to read something there, some mark of character that would tell him about this boy.

"On second thought," Boynton said abruptly, "I'll tear your name right out of the record book, if you'll take a deputy job. You won't even have to put a foot in court."

Given looked up. "You mean that?"

"I got two jobs open," Boynton said. He hesitated before adding, "Look, it's up to you. Probably I'll tear your name out even if you don't take the job. Seeing the condition of Obie Ward, I wouldn't judge you're a man who's going to be pressured into anything."

Given's face showed surprise, but it was momentary, his mouth relaxing into a slow grin—almost as if the smile widened as Boynton's words sank into his mind—and he said, "I'll have to go to Dos Cabezas and get my wife."

Boynton nodded. "Will she be happy about this?"

Pete Given was still smiling. "Marshal, you and I probably couldn't realize how happy she'll be."

The son of Hal G. Evarts, Sr., an acclaimed Western and wildlife-fiction writer in the twenties and thirties, Hal Evarts, Jr. began writing quality Western fiction of his own in the years following World War II. His first novel, Renegade of Rainbow Basin, *appeared in 1953; he followed it with fourteen more over the next sixteen years. He has also produced a number of juvenile historical and mystery novels. "Portrait of a Gunfighter" is just one of his suspenseful Western short stories; others can be found in the paperback collection,* Fugitive's Canyon *(1955).*

Portrait of a Gunfighter

Hal G. Evarts, Jr.

The painting hangs behind the bar in my saloon. Strangers who know about such things tell me it shows real promise, and I've turned down cash offers more than once. I'll never sell that picture, not for any price. It's still too close.

Back in those days nearly every man packed a gun on his hip. The good ones, the real gunslingers, only carried one—never two. Like this fellow in this picture. Nothing fancy, a single-action .45 with a black grip swinging free and easy. Holster whanged down to his thigh like part of his body. That's how the fast ones wore their guns, and this gent was deadly fast. I know, because I saw him draw one night to kill.

It started the morning young Dave Chandler came into my place—the One Strike, same as now—only then my customers were mostly cowmen off the range. Dave didn't drink nor pack a gun. A tall gangly kid with blue eyes and a shock of yellow hair, he looked younger than his eighteen years—like he still belonged in school. The quiet kind, colt-shy, he ducked his head and turned pink when I asked if he wanted sarsaparilla or lemon soda.

"Thanks, Jake," he gave me that sheepish smile. "But not today. I—I'm drumming up trade."

"Trade?" I put down a glass and stared. Across the bar he smelled of turpentine and his bib overalls were speckled with paint. "What kind of trade?"

"Your sign out front. It's peeled pretty

259

bad. I'll paint you a new one for three dollars."

I ran the only saloon in fifty miles. I didn't need a sign. But I liked Dave Chandler, and his old man, too. "You in the sign painting business now?"

He nodded. "I paint anything. Barns, houses, chicken coops—you name it. Been working out in the country. Now I'm starting in town."

Ever since he was a button Dave had been dabbling with crayons or pencils, drawing pictures the way a kid will. Whenever you dropped by the Chandler house there'd be young Dave with his nose in a sketchbook. Polite, well mannered, but lost from this world. You'd never find him helling around with other boys his age. "So you picked me first?"

Dave grinned. "Figure you need me most."

Well, he had me there. The One Strike was a weatherbeat old false front I'd never bothered to fix up. It could stand a coat of paint, inside and out. But right then—I'll admit it—I got curious. "Fixing to stay in this business permanent?"

"Till the customers run out."

That wouldn't take long. Big Butte had

five other stores, maybe two dozen houses. Trouble is, this desert wind can scour the paint off a building in one good blow. "Then what?"

He blushed. "I got some plans."

"What's your Dad think about this?"

"I don't care what he thinks," Dave said. He said it nice, but firm, too, telling me to mind my own business.

"All right, Dave," I said. "You got yourself a job."

He pumped my hand and hurried out, saying he'd be back soon as he rounded up his gear. "One more thing," I called after him. "Tell your Dad I got some news for him. Might be important."

He kept right on up the walk, like maybe he hadn't heard. My news would keep. But I wondered, because he didn't catty-corner across the street toward the jail and the house behind where he lived with his father and brother.

Dave was hardly out of sight when Walt Chandler—Sheriff Chandler, that is—stepped out of his office. Right behind Walt stepped Dud, his older boy and deputy. They looked alike, those two, big solid men with twin stars pinned to their vests. From my front window I watched them tramp across the street. They walked like soldiers. And right then I got a feeling—hunch. That trouble was on the way.

They clomped inside, old Walt first and Dud a pace behind. That time of day the place was empty except for me. "What'd he want?" Walt demanded.

"Yeah, what'd he want?" Dud echoed.

"You mean Dave?"

Walt Chandler scowled and gave his shell belt a hitch. "I mean Dave."

Dud Chandler hitched his belt, too, and said, "Yeah, he means Dave."

Walt had been sheriff for so long he was sort of a fixture around town, like that wooden Injun in front of the mercantile. Most of his life he'd packed a gun and a law badge, back in the rough frontier days. He could chill you with his eyes. But today he looked like a grizzled old badger with a big paunch. Dave didn't favor him much, took after his mother more. She'd died years ago and Walt had raised both boys himself. That can age a man, too.

"He's going to paint my sign," I told Walt.

"Don't give him the job, Jake."

"But I already promised the boy."

"As a favor to me," Walt said.

"Yeah, as a favor—" Dud began, but Walt cut him short. "Keep outa this, Dud." Like he'd shush up a four-year-old.

For a fact Dud wasn't much older in his mind than four, though he stood six feet and could bend a horseshoe straight with bare hands. Some claim he'd been injured at birth. Dud was slow and easy-going, just not very bright. But nobody deviled him—he was Walt Chandler's son.

"Now look," I told Walt, "I gave my word and I can't back down. Not without you give me some reason."

"I got one," he growled. "Good one, too."

He was like that, close-mouthed, proud, and quick to bristle. But at heart I took him to be a kindly man. "Walt," I said, "this is between me an' Dave. Seems like he's big enough to make up his own mind."

Walt grunted and slacked his bulk into a chair. So I poured him a shot and broke out a bottle of strawberry pop for Dud. That's one way Dud never copied the old man. Walt wouldn't let either of his boys touch the hard stuff. Then I remembered my piece of news. "I hear a lot of gossip over this bar," I said. "One of the Bar-J riders was in here early. He ran into Chalk Kirby over at Pyramid yesterday."

263

Walt stared from under his shaggy brows. "So?"

"So you sent Kirby to the pen five years ago. He got out last week. Might be he'll turn up here."

"Chalk Kirby ain't got the guts to come back."

I wasn't so sure, but you didn't argue with Walt. I went on polishing glasses while Walt and Dud watched the street through my window. Maybe thirty minutes went by before Dave pulled up out front in his rickety wagon behind one swayback mare. They both got up as he pushed through the doors. Dave hesitated, then said in a real low voice, "Morning, Pop. Morning, Dud."

Walt's eyes softened a bit, then he stiffened when he saw the paint can and brush in Dave's hand. He said, "Get back over to the house, Dave."

Dave's smile died. His mouth set.

"You quit this foolishness," Walt said, "and we'll forget the rest."

"We talked it out last night," Dave said. "I'm not moving back."

Walt's face turned red. "You'll move back today, or you're never movin' back. That clear?"

"Pop, please—"

"A—a damn paint dauber!"

"Pop, will you listen—"

But Walt stormed past him through the doors, Dud trailing like a shadow.

There was a hurt look in Dave's eyes but he squared his shoulders and walked out to the wagon. After he'd mixed his colors he climbed up to the sign. He didn't look back across the street toward the sheriff's office. But I could see Walt peering out the window at him over there, face pressed against the pane. It might have been funny except that Walt was the stubbornest man in six counties.

During the day customers drifted in and out, most of them joshing Dave on his ladder. But he never let on and I didn't interfere. About suppertime he finished and I stepped out to inspect my sign. He'd done an A-one job, spruced up the whole saloon front. When I paid him off he thanked me and said, "How 'bout painting the inside tomorrow? Make you a good price."

"I don't reckon—"

"Jake, I need the money. Need it bad. And that back bar looks terrible."

It did. The One Strike's original owner must of purely loved gilt paint. He'd had gold slapped all over the back wall—cupids and angels and such. Artistic, if you got that turn of mind. Only now it looked downright scabby, the gilt had flaked off so. But mainly I was thinking of Walt Chandler.

"Pop won't make any more trouble," Dave said. "Not for you. I promise, Jake. How about it?"

"Well—" I hedged. He was a hard one to turn down. Stubborn like his Dad. "I'll sleep on it. See me in the morning."

He stowed his gear back in the wagon and drove off out of town. Soon as his dust settled I walked over to the sheriff's office. Walt was slumped in his cowhide chair, staring at the floor, Dud beside him, glum as a statue. "That Dave—" Walt began.

"Didn't come here to talk about Dave," I said. "You know your job, Walt. But Chalk Kirby's on the prod for sure."

Walt frowned, like he'd forgotten the name. "Chalk Kirby?"

"Three-four people saw him in Pyramid yesterday. Heard him brag. He's got it in for you."

Walt snorted.

"Walt," I said. Chalk Kirby had been a killer in his day, a professional gunhand, and five years behind bars is a big chunk of any man's life. But I might of been talking to a stump, for all the heed Walt paid. "Anyway, I warned you."

I turned back to the door. Walt said, "What's got into that kid, Jake?"

"Somebody's got to paint signs," I told him. "There's worse ways to earn a living."

"I ain't talking about signs. He wants to paint pictures. Kind you hang on a wall." Walt slammed a fist on his desk. "Dabs on a wall!"

"What's wrong with that?"

He gave me a pitying look. "Dave has it in his head to go East to some art school. Study for two years. That's why he's savin' every dime." Walt shook his head. "We had a row last night. Lost our tempers. He moved his stuff out. Camped down by the creek."

"Yeah," Dud said, "down by the creek."

Walt fished a nickel from his pocket and his voice turned gentle. "Step over to the mercantile, will you, Dud?" he said. "Buy yourself a bag of gumdrops."

Dud's eyes lit up. After he'd gone Walt leaned back and sighed. "I can't help Dud much. Keep him out of harm. Dud's the way the good Lord made him. But Dave—Dave could be anything. Only why in hell can't he be a man!"

267

There was genuine bafflement in Walt's voice and I knew how strong he felt, to be talking so free.

"I always figured he'd grow up and take my place here. I'm not getting any younger. This is where Dave belongs."

Walt's fingers, not quite steady, touched the badge on his vest. I realized then how old and tired and sick looking he was. It was a shock to see him with his guard down because for years he'd been the giant of our town, respected and feared, strong as a mountain. "Maybe Dave don't want to be sheriff," I said.

"Even that I wouldn't mind so much. If he'd take a job punching cows, or in the stamp mill. A man's job. But this—"

I put a hand on his shoulder. I felt sorry for Walt, but kind of put out, too. He was so bull-headed blind. "We been friends a long time," I said. "But a man's got to follow the way his stick floats. Or he's nothin'. You know that. You done it all your life. Dave's not a kid any longer. Why not give him his chance?"

"No, by Judas!" Walt's fist slammed the desk again. "No boy of mine's goin' to make a fool of himself, and me, too!"

"How'll you stop him? Tell me that."

"I dunno yet," Walt said bleakly. "But I will."

Next morning when I opened up, Dave was waiting. I gave him the job. I admired his grit. He set up his paint cans on a bench behind the bar and went to work on those cupids. You couldn't smell the whisky for the turpentine. Every now and then I peeked out at the sheriff's office, knowing Walt wouldn't back down. He never had in fifty years.

During the morning I picked up another piece of gossip about Chalk Kirby from the mail rider. According to him Kirby had left Pyramid, fifty miles down the line, and disappeared. I didn't know whether to be worried or relieved. But at dinnertime, when Dave cleaned off his brushes and came back from the wagon with a sandwich, I passed on the word. Dave looked over at Walt's office. "You want *me* to tell him?" he asked.

I nodded.

"He can look after himself."

"Maybe," I said. "But how long since he's had to tame a man like Kirby? A few payday drunks is about all Walt's bucked up against lately."

"He won't listen to me," Dave said bitterly. "He'd just get mad and chew my ears off."

I let it go. After a bit I noticed Dave hunched over one of my tables with a sketch-pad and pencil, sandwich in one hand, drawing with the other. He was so absorbed he forgot to eat. I come up behind and peered over his shoulder. Gave me quite a turn. He'd done a picture of me wiping the bar. Real as life—mustache and apron, sleeve garters and all. So doggone real I give out a grunt and Dave looked up, embarrassed.

"You just did that? Just setting there?"

He tore off the sheet and handed it to me. "Compliments of the artist," he said and laughed.

I'd never seen any of his pictures. Never bothered to look, I guess. "You got any more?"

"Whole trunk full." He shrugged. "Mostly chicken tracks like this."

I reached for his sketchpad. Dave turned pink, like Walt had caught him chawing out behind the barn, but let me have it. The first picture was a stud game in my place, five faces around a table, and every one a regular I could name by sight. There was a picture of old Felix, the sheepherder, with his goatskin wine bag, another of the professor at the piano. Mostly folks around Big Butte, they were—a couple of cowpokes, the blacksmith, a drummer in his derby. One of Walt Chandler, too, big and bushy-haired, head like a lion.

They all had a feel that made your skin prickle. With those little squiggles on a piece of paper Dave had caught us all. Not prettyfied—the way we really looked. I kept staring at those drawings until, grumbling, he reached for the pad. "They're not very good."

"Dave," I said, "no man who can draw like that needs to go to any school. There's nothing they can learn you."

He gave a funny little smile. "Pop's right. I'm just a dauber. Got to get away from here."

"I'm sure no critic but these look good to me."

He told me what was wrong—perspective, technique, anatomy—a lot of words I didn't rightly savvy. But one thing I knew: He was hellbent to leave Big Butte and go back East to New York, maybe even to Paris, France, which he said was the capital of the art world. Study the old masters and paint in oil. A five-hundred-dollar stake would get him started. He talked like a starved man at a feast and I let him ramble, watching that glow building up in his eyes.

Our schoolteacher had loaned him all her art books and borrowed more. He'd took some courses by mail—learn to draw in ten easy lessons. All the while Walt was hammering him to quit and take a steady job. Not that Dave was lazy. To earn his keep he hauled wood and dug wells, even loaded freight. But every spare minute, to hear him tell, he'd kept at his drawing until he'd drove old Walt half crazy.

When he finally ran down I said, "No hurry, Dave, you've got years to spare. Walt ain't got so many left. Couldn't you maybe put this off a bit?"

The glow faded. "He's got Dud," Dave said.

"Not the same," I told him. "Dud's the cross he has to bear. In his way Walt's proud of you."

"Of me?" Dave shook his head. "The only thing he's proud of is that office across the street, the badge he wears." His voice shook. "He's ashamed of me, Jake. It's why he wants me to quit."

I thought he was wrong, wrong as an eighteen-year-old can be, but I didn't say so. Because just then Walt himself walked in with Dud at his heels. Walt glanced at the half-finished cherubs behind my bar and sniffed. "Still trimmin' up the One Strike, I see," he said to Dave.

"Yes, sir."

"Got your license?"

"What license?"

"Had a meeting," Walt said, "with John Throop this morning." Throop was the only lawyer in Big Butte and doubled as county prosecutor whenever we had a trial. "Seems there's a statute on the books says any itinerant's got to have a license. That means peddlers."

"I'm no peddler."

"You got any fixed place of business? Then accordin' to the law you're a peddler."

Dave said weakly, "How much does a license cost?"

"Fifty dollars."

I stared at Walt, not believing he'd job his own son like that. "If you're short of cash," he went on, "you might borrow on your outfit, or sell that wagon."

"But I'd be out of business!"

Walt stood there like a fence post. "That's the law," he said, and Dud echoed, "Yeah, that's the law."

I walked over to my cash box, scooped out

a handful of silver, and slapped it down on the bar. "There's your money," I told Walt. "But damned if I'll count it for you."

Dave got up from the table and it looked like all the blood had drained out of him. "Thanks, Jake," he said. "But I'm not buying any license. I'll work somewhere else."

They stood there, Walt and Dave, squared off like two fighters. Walt's chin was trembling and I think he might of relented some then if Dave had given him any encouragement. But Dave was a chip off the old block—a block of solid granite.

Finally Walt said, "Not till you pay that fifty dollars."

"Don't do this to me, Pop."

"Hold on," I broke in. "Dave's got to finish up my bar. Can't walk out and leave it like this."

Walt gave me a bare half-inch nod. "I got some papers to serve out on South Fork, but I'll be back by suppertime. If you're still here, Dave, I'm going to impound your horse and wagon."

Maybe he expected Dave to slack off, offer some compromise, but Dave didn't budge, just kept staring. So Walt motioned Dud and they went out. For a minute it was so still you could hear the wall clock ticking. Then

Dave ripped his sketchpad in half, tossed it in the stove and without a word went back to work.

After a long while he said, "Pop raised us strict, Dud and me. He was always fair, up till now. Never gave us a licking unless we deserved it. But I won't take this."

A lot of thoughts ran through my head, but mostly how obstinate two proud men can be. Maybe you'd call it principle. But it seemed a crime to me. Because somebody was bound to get hurt. And Walt Chandler most of all.

That turned out to be the longest afternoon I ever spent. About four o'clock a couple of ranchers wandered in and began ragging Dave to paint some dimples on a cupid's behind. Dave joshed them back while I drew two beers. When I turned around I almost dropped the glasses. A third man was leaning against the bar. Slipped in so quiet we hadn't heard a board squeak.

"Howdy, Jake," he said, like he'd seen me only yesterday.

I swallowed. "Howdy, Chalk."

Chalk Kirby always had been yeasty-faced and jail hadn't improved his color. He looked a little older, gaunter, but I'd've known those eyes any place or time. Gray and cold as river pebbles, and with no more feeling. He stared around the saloon and said, "Gettin' mighty fancy."

"Passing through?" I said.

"Depends."

That's when I got a good look at his gun—a single-action .45 with a black butt, shoved down in a worn holster tied to his thigh. Before he'd gone away there used to be talk about how fast he was, how many men he'd shot. Maybe most of it was true. Personally I could swear to only one man he'd killed for sure. But I wished I had a sawed-off handy under the bar-top.

He slid into a chair easy and quiet as a snake. "What'll it be, Chalk?" I said. "On the house."

He shook his head. "Maybe later." His gaze fastened on Dave who was still busy up behind the bar. "What's your name, sonny?"

Dave turned slowly and wiped his hands on a rag. He'd been a kid when Walt wounded Kirby and brought him down from the hills on a murder charge. At the trial Kirby claimed that Walt had sneaked up in the dark and shot him from behind. Nobody who knew Walt believed it, including the jury. No kid could forget a thing like that about his father, but I don't think Dave had quite tagged Kirby yet. "Chandler," he said in a puzzled voice. "Dave Chandler."

Kirby sized him up. "You must be Walt's younger boy. Not the dummy."

Dave frowned. "You looking for him, mister?"

"I tried his office but it's locked. So I come over here."

"He'll be back directly."

"I know he will, sonny." Kirby picked up a deck of cards and laid out a game, his back to the street but with his eyes straying frequent to the mirror. He was cool, I'll give him that, the way he ran those cards like a black queen was the only worry on his mind. Maybe, I prayed, he won't brace Walt. But instinct told me different.

The two cowmen drunk up fast and left. I had to get Dave out of there, or anyway try. "Dave, you might as well finish up to-morrow. Light in here is fadin' fast."

Dave looked over at Kirby, a tight squint around his eyes. "I can see well enough," he said.

Hardly any time passed before two new customers sidled in. The first pair had spread the word. Times like that I wonder about all humankind. Man gets a whiff of

277

somebody else's trouble, it draws him like a cat to liver. Before long we had a dozen or so, Walt Chandler's friends and neighbors, itching to see what Walt would do. Nobody howdied Kirby or slapped him on the back. Behind that poker face of his he must of been despising us all.

What Dave was thinking I can't guess. Expect he knew by now who and what Kirby was, but he wasn't ducking out. He went on gilding those damn fool cherubs. Then I spotted a dust across the flats south of town.

I sneaked back into the washroom and out the rear door into the alley. It was three blocks to the livery but I ran all the way. Walt and Dud rode under the arch as I came panting up. Walt swung down and stepped back, staring at Dave's horse and wagon hitched in front of the One Strike. "Still there," Walt said. "By grab, I meant what I said."

"Never mind that," I snapped. "Chalk Kirby's in there! With a *gun!*"

Walt hauled out his watch. "Five o'clock. Go pick up his outfit, Dud."

"Walt!" I yelled. "Don't walk in there! He's waiting for you—Kirby!"

He didn't pay me no mind, not the thinking part of him. My sense didn't get through.

He shook his head and there was sadness in his eyes. "He's a good boy, Jake. Always minded. But he's gettin' too big for his britches."

"Walt, for God's sake—"

He walked up the street with that heavy stride, Dud close beside him.

And that's how we came back to the One Strike, pushing through the batwings three abreast. Walt took a step or two, gaze seeking out Dave, and froze. Chalk Kirby slapped down his cards and stood up. Every other man in that room went silent, holding his breath. Kirby, showing the faintest smile, said, "Been a long time, Walt."

Walt blinked. Until that moment he hadn't wanted to believe. He'd shut his mind up tight like you shut a door to keep out the dark. Now Kirby was here, grim and deadly and determined, with a gun on his hip. A nerve jumped in Walt's cheek. "How are you, Kirby?"

Kirby waited, neither moving nor speaking, his eyes fixed on Walt and his mouth still pinched in that hard half-smile. Finally Walt wet his lips. "So you came back after all?"

"I came back."

"For good?"

"I don't think so," Kirby said. "I never liked your town much, Walt. It hasn't changed. Neither've you."

A stain spread up from Walt's collar. Gruffly he said, "Your privilege."

"Haven't changed a bit, Walt. Still the same big empty blowhard you was five years ago. That's what I came back for—to tell you to your face."

A shudder ran over Walt's frame, but Kirby spoke on, like he had to get the words out before they choked him. "Look at you! Old and fat and soft as blubber. I could shoot you twice before you touched your gun. You're not sheriff. You're nothin' but a has-been hidin' behind a rep. You and that booby of a kid you call your dep'ty."

Dud looked from Walt to Kirby and let out a little whimpering noise. Sweat glistened on Walt's forehead. His hands were knotted at his sides. He wasn't afraid—not for himself. But he saw the truth now. Knew he was a tired, burnt-out old man. No match for Chalk Kirby. All of us saw it. If he tried for his gun he was dead.

Slow bitter thoughts moved across his face. Maybe he thought of Dud, who needed him so much. Or maybe of Dave, who didn't need him at all. I never felt sorrier for a man in my life, nor admired one more. Then his shoulders sagged.

Kirby had won. In seconds he'd cut Walt Chandler down, smashed him. But he couldn't leave it there, not Chalk Kirby. He had to rub Walt's nose in it. "Whyn't you quit this job while you're still alive?"

Walt stared.

Kirby took two quick strides, reached out and ripped the badge off Walt's vest, flinging it on the floor. "There's your pride, Walt."

"Kirby!"

Kirby spun. I'd forgotten Dave. But Dave was coming around the end of the bar, paint brush in hand, moving slow and quiet. Moving like Walt used to move, straight and sure of himself, eyes like blue ice. He looked as big as Walt ever had—man size.

"Kirby," he said, "pick that up off the floor."

Kirby laughed. "Get away from me, sonny."

The crowd squeezed back to let Dave through and he came up by Kirby's table. Walt growled in his throat, started forward. I caught his arm. "Kirby," Dave said, "pick up that badge."

Kirby measured him, tiny puzzle lines webbed around his eyes; and laughed again.

He stepped on the badge and ground it under his boot.

The rest happened so quick it's hard to tell. Dave slapped his paint brush in Kirby's face. Turpentine splashed. Kirby screamed, jabbed a hand at his eyes and drew with the other. His gun came out. His arm was just a blur but he shot blind and wild, the slug smashing my front window. Then Dave had his wrist, twisting the gun free, clubbing him with the barrel. Kirby dropped without a sound.

The gunshot was still roaring in my ears, but I heard Dave's deep wracking gasp. He was shaking when he turned to Dud. "Dud," he said, "take him over to the jail."

Dud's face brightened, like the sun sliding out from under clouds. "Yeah!" he said. "Yeah, I'll take him to jail." He got Kirby over one shoulder and carried him out.

Not a one of us moved while Dave picked up the badge. He straightened and slipped his arm through Walt's. "Come on, Pop," he said, in the gentlest voice I ever heard. "Let's go home."

Dave Chandler never left the Big Butte country. Never studied art back East or saw the museums in Paris, France. Stayed right here at home. Still draws and paints in his spare time a little. That's one picture he did, up behind the bar. The gunfighter, Chalk Kirby. The other one is Walt, back in his prime, the way I like to remember him.

Dave is packing the tin for us, now. Youngest sheriff we ever elected. And Dud's still packing the deputy's star.

A respected Western writer for more than thirty years, T.V. Olsen is perhaps best known as the author of two novels that were the basis for quality films: Arrow in the Sun, *filmed as* Soldier Blue, *and* Stalking Moon, *filmed under the same title. Other of his fine historical Westerns include* Blizzard Pass, Starbuck's Brand, Rattlesnake, *and the recent Fawcett original,* Lonesome Gun. *His short stories have appeared in two previous books in this series,* The Warriors *and* The Cattlemen, *and in the collection* Westward They Rode. *"The Man We Called Jones" is Olsen at the top of his form.*

The Man We Called Jones

T. V. Olsen

The gun? The .45 hanging over the mantel? Why, sure, look at it. Look at it, but don't handle the belt, son. It's old, over sixty years old. Leather's brittle, hasn't been worked. Like to fall apart.

284

Why do I keep it there? I can tell you a story about it if you want. Really a story about the man who owned it. The bravest and best man I ever knew. . . .

It was way back, the summer of 1890. This same valley. I was seventeen that year. You weren't yet a twinkle in your pappy's eye, so it'll take a sight of doing for you to see it as it was then. You made your way by team, by horseback, or walked. Roads were mud, mud, mud.

The valley was all big ranches, or rather most one big ranch. That'd be Kurt Gavin's Anchor. Gavin came into the country early after the last tide of gold-seekers was drifting out, drove his stakes deep and far, and being a little bigger and a little tougher than most others, he made it stick.

By '90 with the Cheyennes long pacified and the territory opened to homesteading, Gavin was the biggest man in the valley, nigh the biggest in the territory. Even his swelling herds couldn't graze the whole of the open range he laid claim to. Least, that's what the homestead farmers figured. Or sodbusters, as the cattlemen called 'em—the *damned* sodbusters who came in with their plows and chewed up the good graze.

Which is what we did in Gavin's eyes to

285

the range he called his, because Uncle Jace and me were among the first. We'd had strong ties back in Ohio, but my ma had been dead a good many years. Typhoid-pneumonia had taken Pa in '89. Uncle Jace and Pa had been mighty close brothers. They'd run the farm together for years, and the old home held too many memories for Uncle Jace. He hadn't any family or close kin left, 'cept for me, and nothing to hold him from pulling stakes for the West, which he'd always wanted.

A year after Pa's death saw me and Uncle Jace running a shoestring outfit on Gavin's east range. Gavin give word to his riders to hooraw us off, and I tell you the high-spirited lads made our lives some miserable what with cutting our barbed wire and riding shortcuts through our fields, or riding past the house of a midnight after a drunk in town, screeching, shooting at the sky.

You could call Uncle Jace a peaceable man, but he was that stubborn he wouldn't budge off what was his by law. And when Gavin's crew pulled down a whole section of fence by roping the posts and dragging it away with the ponies, Unc's temper busted. Him and me were out scouting boundary that morning when we found the fence down and some Anchor cows foraging in the young corn. They'd even left one rope on the fence to make their sign plain.

Unc was mad clean through, though not so's you could see it—, less you knew Unc. Me helping, he hazed the cows out cool as you please, and we got tools and repaired the fence, Uncle Jace giving brief, jerky orders in as few words as needed.

Afterward, grimy and soaked with sweat, he turned to me. "Get on your horse, Howie, I'm going to see Gavin."

We cut across the Anchor land on a beeline for the ranch headquarters, Uncle Jace riding ahead. He was a huge-framed man, though so leaned-down with hard work, the clothes hung on him like tattered cast-offs on a scarecrow. Even so, with the big back of him erect and high in his wrath, I could almost hear his rage crackle across the space between us.

Unc didn't pack a sidearm. He had his old Union issue Spencer .54 in the saddle boot under his leg, and I'd seen him drive nail-heads with it, and I was some squirrelly, I tell you.

It must have been ten minutes later when we sighted the little knot of horsemen off to our left, and Unc quartered his bronc around so we were heading for them. I caught his thought then—that these were the jiggers who pulled the fence down and ran that Anchor beef through the break.

Coming near up, we saw all five of them were mounted but not moving, and then we saw why. They were grouped under one of the big old ironwoods you don't see anymore, and there was a rope tied to a spreading bough. The end of the rope was noosed around the neck of one of them, a little fella with his hands tied at his back. They were all of them motionless, waiting on our approach.

The little one I'd never seen, but the other four were all Anchor crewmen I recognized—one of them Gavin's tough ramrod, Tod Carradine. He was a tall, pale-eyed Texan with ice in his smile, cocky, sure of himself. The others were ordinary punchers with the look of men ready for a dirty job they didn't relish but held to be necessary.

"Howdy, Tod," Uncle Jace said in a voice easy-neutral without being friendly. "Hemp cravat for the man?"

"Why yes, Devereux," said Carradine in a voice amused, also without being friendly. "You ever see this little man before?"

Unc shook his head no without taking his

eyes off Carradine. He wasn't worried about the others.

Carradine pointed lazily at the hip of the horse the little fella sat. It bore an Anchor brand. "We found him hypering off our range on this bronc." Carradine smiled, altogether pleasant. "Suit you, Devereux?" he then asked in a voice suggesting he didn't give a damn how Unc was suited.

It was open and shut, far as I could see. A stranger had been caught riding off Anchor range on an Anchor horse. The answer for that was one no Westerner would argue. That's why I was surprised when Uncle Jace's glance shuttled to the little fella.

"Friend," Unc said quietly, "speak out your say. It's your right. How'd it happen?"

The little man looked up slowly. His head had been bent and I hadn't seen his face full till now. It was shocking, pitiful, ravaged somehow in a way I couldn't explain. He gave a bare tilt of his head toward Carradine, murmured, "However he says," and looked down again.

Carradine smiled fully at Unc. He repeated: "Suit you, Devereux?"

"Not quite," Uncle Jace frowned, looking back at the Anchor foreman.

Carradine was still smiling, uncertainly. It

289

had only come to him then what this was building to. He was the only Anchor man packing a gun, and I saw the instant impulse chase through his mind.

Uncle Jace didn't waste time. He never wasted time, or words either. Somehow the old Spencer cavalry carbine was ready to his hand, and he laid it light across the pommel. "Don't even think about it, Tod," Unc advised mildly. "Howie, cut the gent loose. Give him a hand down. Tod, take what's yours and keep your dogs off my fence-line. Or I'll larrup you out of this valley at the end of a horsewhip."

Carradine's hands hung loosely, his eyes hot and wild—wicked. He said, "I'll mind this, Devereux!"

"Do that. I'd kind of deplore having to remind you," Unc said mildly.

We silently watched the four Anchor men out of sight. I found my voice. "Unc, we going to see Gavin?"

"We won't have to. He'll hear about this."

Uncle Jace got off his horse, only now taking a close look at the raggedy drifter, and his eyes went quick with a pitying kindness as his hand went out. "I'm Jace Devereux. My nephew, Howie. We homestead over east."

The little horse-thief looked at Unc in a grave, considering way. He said in a bass deep, startling in such an undersize man, "My name is Jones. I'd admire to work for you. For nothin'."

Unc looked at the hand in his own, seeing it crossed with rope-scars. "Well, now, as a cowman, ain't you afraid of some farm stink wearing off on you?"

"I'd admire to work for you," Jones repeated, adding, "for nothin'."

I knew a kind of warm surge for this runty, spooky-looking gent with his sad and faded eyes looking up from the shadow of his Stetson at Unc's great height. And glancing at Uncle Jace, I saw he felt the same.

He said in his rich big voice, "Come along, and hang up your hat, Jones."

That was the way of it, and Jones settled into the workaday routine of the farm, as natural a part of it as the buildings themselves, already dry and gray and weatherbeaten. Jones was all of those, too. He was that colorless he might have been anywhere from thirty-five to fifty-five. He fitted to the new work like an old hand, so quiet you'd hardly know he was there but for the new-improving ways the farm began to shape up.

He stayed, and we called him Jones, just

Jones. He never gave another name and we never asked. I reckoned Unc had been shamed into hiring him. Shamed by the little fella's offering his services for nothing, though the main reason he'd saved Jones was to retaliate on Anchor and show what he thought of all its power. Jones must have known that. How could life kick a man into such a corner he could be so beggar-grateful? It was as though no one'd done him even a half-intended kindness till now.

I saw him right off as a man a boy could tie to. He worked alongside Uncle Jace, who was twice his size and three times his power, and he let Unc set the pace. He'd be so tired he could barely stand, and never a whimper. Watching him hump alongside Uncle Jace in the fields, he cut a comical earnest figure that made you want to laugh and cry all at once. It might be that I'd laugh, and sometimes, if you laughed too hard, he had a way of looking at you that made you feel you'd need a ladder to reach a snake's belly.

But there was another special way he could look, a way that made you feel two feet taller, like the wry grin of him when I'd lick him in our nightly games in the kitchen. He was mighty proud of his checker game, was

Jones. It was the one little vanity he had, yet he was the best loser ever I saw.

We got close, the two of us. Mind, I was just seventeen, a hard time of growing up. You get that age, you'll know what I mean. A lot of things are confusing to a fellow. In the one month he was with us, it was Jones helped me see my way to the end of more than one bad time. He had a way of looking at things, of talking them out so they'd seem a lot clearer. Fact, he was as much pa as I ever knew after my own pa died. He sort of took up that empty place in one boy's life that Uncle Jace, for all he was as big a man inside him as outside, couldn't quite fill.

Jones would go into the settlement of Ogallala now and then to get supplies, and Gavin's riders hoorawed him every time, and sent him packing out of town. They never hazed him if Unc or I was along, so I never seen it. Heard plenty, though. Neighbors saw to that. Folks would snicker behind their hands watching Jace Devereux's new man go out of his way to walk around trouble. Never carried a gun, either. Not even a rifle on his saddle.

Never spoke of his past, did Jones. But he had one behind the face he showed the world. Remember, he'd come to us a reprieved horse-thief. And strange how Uncle Jace in taking him on hadn't thought, being a middling cautious man, that he might be getting a pig in a poke. But seemed like it hadn't even occurred to Unc.

Uncle Jace was right that Gavin had heard his warning to leave us be. His riders hauled off their war of nerves, at least on Unc and me and our fences and crops, and rode herd on the homesteaders—and, of course, Jones. Gavin had soft-pedaled on us, but we only wondered what he had up his sleeve.

We found out about a month after Jones came to the farm. Gavin himself, sided by Tod Carradine, came riding into the yard one night after supper, as Uncle Jace and Jones and me was sitting on the front steps, breaking in some new cob pipes.

Gavin's hardness was a legend in the territory, and it was easy to see that age hadn't softened him. He was a blocky, well-fed man in the slightly dust-soiled dignity of a black suit, and his habit of authority sat him like a heavy fist. There was even a touch of arrogance to the way he bent the hand holding his cigar.

Uncle Jace got off the step, knocking out his pipe. "Light down a spell, Gavin. You too, Tod."

"I'll speak my piece from here," Gavin said. "Your tracks are big, Devereux. Big enough so I respect 'em." He paused, and Unc didn't speak, wondering, like me, where this was leading to.

Gavin said it then: "I need men like you. Devereux. Sign on with me for double wages. The boy, too."

Unc said, "No," instantly, as I knew he would. We Devereuxs aren't that way we work for other people. And even if Unc was, it wouldn't be he'd work for the likes of Gavin.

The rancher didn't look mad, not even greatly concerned. He'd had his own way for too many years. There was only a faint irritation in his voice. "You go, Devereux. You go this week—or next week you'll crawl out of this valley on your belly." He turned his horse in a violent way and rode out of the yard.

Carradine's soft drawling chuckle slid into the quiet like a gliding rattler. "I always suspicioned you was a Sunday man, Devereux. Now we'll see."

"A Sunday man?"

"A man who's a man one day—when he talks big. I don't think you'll back up what you said when you saved that horse-stealer."

Carradine smiled with full insolence. "I don't think you can."

"You tell me that with Anchor behind you," Uncle Jace said, the snap of an icicle in his voice, "which by my lights makes you a yellow dog, Tod."

Carradine smiled, ever so gentle. "I'll be in town tomorrow afternoon—in front of Red Mike's. You be there, and we'll see if you're man enough to call me that again. Or send your big bad hired man . . ."

So the issue was in the open now.

When the sound of Carradine riding off had died on the still evening air, I turned to Unc. "He's a mean one, Uncle Jace. With a gun. There's stories followed him from Texas."

"And I offer there's something to 'em," Jones said softly, his voice startling us. He could kind of fade back so you forgot he was there. "It's why he needled you. I reckon you'd better not take him up, Jace."

"And I reckon I had," Unc said grimly.

Jones only nodded. "I figured so," he said, and walked around back. I wanted to say more to Uncle Jace, but a look in his face warned me, and in a minute I followed Jones around back where he was working with the ax on some stovewood. He had his shirt off against the heat, and the scrawny, knobbly upper body of him gleaming with sweat made him look like a plucked chicken.

Jones paused, leaned on the ax and mopped his face with his shirt. "Why has Gavin got his sights primed for your unc, Howie? There's other farmers squattin' on his land, and more comin'."

"Squatting" was the word a *cattleman* would use for a legal government homestead. It was Jones saying it, though, so I let it ride. You didn't get mad at Jones.

"The others got no heart to 'em," I said with contempt. "Unc's got more gall than a government mule, and the homesteaders know it as well as Gavin. If he can stampede Unc, the others'll follow suit."

"Hum," said Jones, and went back to his work. I got the other ax and helped. But a couple times I caught him leaning on his ax and looking off toward the hills with that air like a considerable thought was riling him.

I didn't sleep much that night, thinking about the next day, with Carradine waiting in front of Red Mike's bar and Unc dead set on meeting him. Uncle Jace was no gunman. He knew it, I knew it. Even Jones knew it.

So I was near relieved when about noon of the next day Jones came into the kitchen where I was fixing some grub and quietly told me that Uncle Jace's leg had got broken. They'd been heisting the massive ridgepole timber of the barn Unc had finally got to building, raising it into place, and it fell . . .

Between the two of us we splinted up Unc's leg and got him into bed. His face was white and drawn, and his eyes near starting from his head with the pain.

Jones said in his gentle voice, "I reckon this is in the way of a lifesaver for you, Jace."

"But won't they say Unc ran away from it?" I asked.

"They'll say more," Uncle Jace said bitterly between set teeth. "They'll say I got stove up a-purpose to get out of meeting Tod. And it'll be a spell before I can call any of 'em a liar and back it. By that time the farmers will be out, and Gavin'll swallow up their homesteads."

Jones and I looked at each other. Unc was right; he was the backbone of the homesteaders. With him broken, they'd cut and run.

"That leg'll need a sawbones," Jones said, unruffled. "I'm going into town, and I'll send one."

There was a note in Jones's voice that left me curious, and after a while, when Uncle Jace was resting more easy, I followed Jones out to the harness shed where he'd rigged his bunk. I came to stand in the doorway as I saw him, and I almost fell over. Jones didn't see me. He was facing a shard of mirror he had nailed on the wall over an old packing crate which held his possibles—and there was a gun in his hand.

For thirty seconds I stood and watched as he drew and fixed a mock bead on his own reflection, the hammer falling on an empty chamber each time. I tell you, he made that fine-balanced gun do tricks.

The truth all rushed down on me at once. I'd had it figured how Jones's hell-born past was that of any rabbity little gent who couldn't hold up his head in a world of big men. But the man who could make a cutter do his will like this one—why, he was head and shoulders over the biggest man.

It was the gun—that was the hell in Jones's life. That's why he'd never packed it, why he walked soft and gave Gavin's loud-mouths a wide berth. It wasn't them he was afraid of, it was himself. His own skill, his deadly skill. That was the real truth and tragedy of his backtrail. While the rest of us, rancher and homesteader, talked war and primed ourselves for it, Jones was already fighting his own private battle, a harder one than any of us would ever know.

Now he'd lost his war. Lost it in the way a real man would—by facing out the enemy of the only one who ever befriended him . . .

He'd loaded the gun while my thoughts raced. Like magic, that gun it was in the fine-tooled holster, and then he swung toward the door and saw me.

For a full five seconds he didn't speak. "I'm going to see Carradine, Howie. You won't try to stop me." There was the thinnest undercore of steel to his voice, and I wouldn't have tried even if I'd been of a mind to.

But I was going with him, and I said so. He didn't comment, and it was that way the whole ride. Neither of us spoke a word till we'd nearly reached Ogallala.

"Jones," I said. He grunted. "Jones, I wouldn't be surprised you let that beam slip on purpose to keep Uncle Jace from going out."

"You talk too much," he said mildly, and that was all. I didn't care, I was that sure he'd saved Unc's life.

Ogallala was drowsing in the westering sun. One horse stood hipshot at the tierail in front of Red Mike's: Carradine's blazeface sorrel.

Jones hauled up across the street, stepping down and throwing his reins. His gaze fixed Red Mike's as he said to me, "You get in the store and stay there." I didn't, but I got back on the walk out of the way, and he didn't even look at me.

"Carradine!" That was Jones's silence-shattering voice. A big voice for a little man. Maybe as big as the real Jones.

After a little, the batwing doors parted and Tod Carradine stood tall in the shadow of the weatherbeaten false-front. Stepping off the walk, bareheaded, the sun caught on his face, showing it red with heat and whisky. He'd been drinking, but he wasn't drunk.

When he saw who it was hailed him, he looked ready to laugh. Almost. He peered sharp at Jones, and something seemed to shut it off in his throat before it started.

"Carradine," Jones said. "Carradine, you brag something fierce. Back it."

Carradine began to smile, understanding, his teeth showing very white. He cut a mighty handsome figure in the sun. "All right, bravo," he said. "All right, bravo."

But I watched Jones. And I watched it happen.

Carradine was fast. Mighty fast. But Jones was the man. The last of a dying breed. Not one of your patent-leather movie cowboys with their gun-fanning foolery and their two fast-blazing six-guns. The man Jones knew you couldn't hit a barn fanning. He got his gun out right fast, but then took his time as you had to when it was a heavy single-action Colt you were handling. Carradine got two fast shots off before Jones's one bullet buckled him in the middle and smashed him into the walk on his back . . .

He didn't touch Jones; the other fellow did. The one in the alley between the store and the feed-barn, at our back—stationed there in case this happened. I heard this dirty son's gun from the alley and I saw Jones's scrawny body flung forward off balance. Before the shot sound died, I saw Jones haul around, his gun blasting, and this bushwhacker, hard-hit, fling out away from the alley with his gun going off in the hot blue face of the sky. He went down and moved no more.

Jones was sinking to his knees, the light going from his eyes and a funny little smile on his face. It was the first and the last time I saw him smile with all a smile should mean.

When I reached him and caught him as he

302

slipped down, he looked up, recognizing me, and said, "Tell your unc—you tell him to keep that peg dusted, Howie. My hat won't be on it . . ." The smile was gone as he lifted his head to stare at me with a fierce intensity. "Howie, mind what I say. If you forget everything else about me, never forget what I learned—the hard way. You can't run from what you made of yourself. You can't run that far . . ."

The voice trailed, and the eyes looked on, not at me . . . or at anything.

I eased down the meager body of the man we called Jones, and wanted to cover his face from the prying, question-rattling crowd. I remember I had to do that, and there was only my ragged pocket bandana. When I'd finished and looked up, there was someone standing over me I didn't at first recognize for the wet blurring in my eyes. But then I blinked and saw it was Gavin.

He was holding his cigar in his arrogant way, frowning around at his two dead hirelings and at Jones, and not believing it. I went up and after him with my fists doubled. Then a big man with a close-clipped Vandyke threw a beefy arm across my chest.

"Hold it, son. I have a word for Mr. Gavin."

Gavin fixed his cold stare on the newcomer. "Who the hell are you?"

"Baines, special agent for the U.S. Land Office. Washington has been getting notices about your terrorizing government homesteaders. And I've seen enough to validate it. You and I'll discuss that shortly." The big man turned back to me and nodded down to Jones. "He a friend of yours, son?"

I managed to find words. "Jones was the best."

"Jones?" Baines eyed me closely. "I reckon you didn't know him very well. Suggest you write to the sheriff at Cheyenne. He'll give you particulars. So can a lot of others."

That's about all. Within weeks, a new flood of homesteaders filled the valley. I saw Gavin a few times after, a broken old man. I don't know what Baines told him, but the hand of the government can be right heavy.

About Jones?

Yes, I could've written to Cheyenne and found out. But I didn't. I never wanted to find out.

All I can tell you is what he was to me—friend of the Devereuxs, the bravest and best man I ever knew. The man we called Jones.

*A prolific writer in a variety of fields, Bill Pronzini has published four Western novels under his own name (*The Gallows Land, Starvation Camp, The Last Days of Horseshy Halloran, *and* Quincannon), *three others under pseudonyms, and a score of Western short stories. In addition to the Best of the West series, he has edited or coedited several other anthologies of frontier and Old West fiction. "The Gunny," a tale of life and sudden death in a small New Mexico town, is his most successful variation on the gunfighter theme.*

The Gunny

Bill Pronzini

The old man sat smoking his pipe in the shade in front of Fletcher's Mercantile, one of the rows of neat frame buildings that made up the town of Bitter Springs. It was midafternoon, the sun brassy hot in the hard summer sky, and he was the only citizen in sight when the lanky stranger rode into town from the west.

Horse and rider were dust-spattered, and the lean Appaloosa blew heavily and walked with weary slowness, as if ridden long and hard. But the stranger sat the saddle tall and erect, shoulders pulled back, eyes moving left and right over the empty main street. He was young and leaned-down, with sharp features and a dusty black mustache that bracketed lips as thin as a razor slash. Hanging low on his right hip was a Colt double-action in a Mexican loop holster thong-tied to his thigh.

The old man watched him approach without moving. Smoke from his clay pipe haloed his white-maned head, seeming hardly to drift in the overheated air. He had a frail, dried-out appearance, like leather left too long to cure in the sun; but his eyes were alert, sharply watchful.

As the stranger neared Fletcher's Mercantile, he seemed to take notice of the old man sitting there in the shade. He turned the Appaloosa in that direction, drew rein, and swung easily out of the saddle.

"Hidy, grandpop," he said as he looped the reins around a tie rack. He stepped up onto the boardwalk.

"Hidy yourself."

"Hot, ain't it?"

"Some."

"I been riding three days in this heat and I got me a hell of a thirst. You know what I mean?"

"Don't look senile, do I?"

The stranger laughed. "No, you sure don't."

"Saloon up the street, if a beer's what you're after."

"It is, but not just yet. Got me a little business to attend to first."

"That a fact?" the old man asked conversationally.

"Where can I find Sheriff Ben Chadwick?"

"Most days you could find him at the jailhouse, down at the end of Main here. But he don't happen to be there today."

"No? Where is he?"

"Rode out to the Adams' place, west of town. Somebody's been runnin' off their stock."

"When's he due back?"

"Don't rightly know. What kind of business you got with the sheriff, son?"

"Killin' business."

"So? Who's been killed?"

307

The young stranger laughed again, without humor. "Nobody yet. Ben Chadwick ain't here, like you said."

The old man took the pipe from his mouth and stared up at the youth. Downstreet somewhere, a dog barked once and was still. The only other sound, until the old man spoke after several seconds, was the faint muffled beat of the hurdy-gurdy in the Oasis Saloon.

"You aimin' to kill Ben Chadwick, that what you're sayin'?"

"That's what I'm sayin', grandpop."

"Why?"

"He shot up a couple of men on the trail to Three Forks two weeks ago. I was in Arizona Territory when I heard about it. Else, I'd of been here long before this."

"What's them two fellas to you?"

"One of 'em, Ike Gerard, was my cousin."

"Well, now," the old man said dryly, "looky what we got here. Johnny Goheen, ain't you?"

"That's right, grandpop. Johnny Goheen."

"Your cousin and his sidekick robbed the bank in Three Forks. Killed a deputy. But I reckon that don't cut no ice with the likes of you."

"No, it don't."

"A damn gunny," the old man said, and spat on the worn boards alongside his chair. "Quick on the shoot, are you?"

"Quick as any there ever was."

"Huh. How many men you shot dead, Goheen?"

"Four. All in self-defense."

"Oh sure—self-defense." The old man spat again. "You kill Ben Chadwick, it'll be murder."

"Will it?"

"They'll hang you, Goheen."

"No warrant out on me. Ben Chadwick draws first, sheriff or no sheriff, it's self-defense."

"And you aim to make him draw first."

"That's right."

"Suppose he don't?"

"He will. Yessir, he will."

"Maybe he's faster than you."

"He ain't," Goheen said.

"He's got friends in this town, Ben Chadwick has. They won't let you get away with it."

"You one of 'em? You figure you can stop me?"

The old man said nothing.

Goheen laughed his mirthless laugh. "Tell

you what, grandpop. You sit right here in the shade and rest your old bones. No use gettin' all worked up on such a hot day."

Again the old man was silent.

"Nice talkin' to you," Goheen said. He tipped his hat, turned, went upstreet to the Oasis, and pushed in through the batwings without a backward glance.

The old man sat for a minute or so, staring downstreet to the east—the direction Ben Chadwick had ridden out earlier in the day. The road and the flats in that direction seemed empty, motionless except for the heat haze, unmarked by the billows of dust that foretold the arrival of a rider or wagon. Then he knocked the dottle from his pipe, stowed the briar inside his shirt, and got to his feet. He shuffled down to the mercantile's entrance.

Howard Fletcher, an elderly, balding man in shirtsleeves and suspendered trousers, looked up from behind the counter at the far end of the room and smiled. "Well, Jeb, you get tired of setting out there and decide to come in for a game of cribbage?"

The old man didn't return the smile. "I come in to ask a favor, Howard. I need the use of a six-gun."

The curve of Fletcher's mouth turned

310

down the other way. "Now what would you be wanting with a gun, Jeb?"

"I got my reasons."

"Mind my asking what they are?"

"Howard, you and me been friends for a long time and I ain't never asked you for much. I'm asking you for a six-gun now. I'll get it elsewhere if you got objections."

"No objections," Fletcher said. "I just don't understand what's got your hackles up."

"You will soon enough. Colt Peacemaker, if you got one in stock."

"I have."

Fletcher went to a locked window case, opened it with a key attached to his watch chain, and took a new Colt Peacemaker and a box of cartridges from inside. He brought them to where the old man stood, laid them on the counter. His eyes were troubled, but he held his peace.

The old man opened the box of cartridges, removed six, and fitted them into the Peacemaker. Then he spun the cylinder, hefted the weapon in his hand. "Pay you for the cartridges later, Howard, if I use any."

"Just as you say, Jeb," Fletcher said.

The old man nodded, turned, and went outside again. The street and the road and desert flats to the east were still empty under the hard sunglare. He hesitated for a moment, then walked slowly upstreet toward the saloon with the Peacemaker pointed muzzle-downward along his right thigh.

But when he was two buildings away from the saloon, he veered off at an angle, stepped onto the boardwalk, and took up a leaning position against the wall of Henderson's Feed Company. He spat onto the planking at his feet, watching the entrance to the saloon with narrowed eyes. Goheen might do all his waiting inside there, but then again he might not. It would be better if he made up his mind to come outside again. If the old man had to go in after him, some citizen might get hurt.

Five minutes he stood there. Ten. Frank Harper drove by, his wagon loaded with fresh-cut lumber. He waved, but the old man didn't wave back.

Another five minutes vanished. And then the saloon's batwings popped open and Goheen appeared, rubbing the back of one thin arm across his mouth and squinting against the bright sunlight. He moved down off the boardwalk, past the hitchrails into the dusty street.

"Hey, boy!" the old man called sharply. "Come over here, boy!"

Goheen's head jerked up and around; he stopped in midstride with his hand poised over the handle of his revolver. His face registered surprise when he realized who had spoken to him.

"Grandpop, you better not take that tone of voice with me again. What you want?"

The old man pushed away from Henderson's wall, bringing the Peacemaker up in a level point. When Goheen saw it his expression turned to one of slack-jawed amazement.

"What I want," the old man said, "is for you to unbuckle your gunbelt, slowlike, and drop it."

"You gone crazy?"

"Not hardly. I'm makin' a citizen's arrest and puttin' you in jail."

"The hell you are. On what charge?"

"Threatin' an officer of the law. Disturbin' the peace."

"You can't make charges like that stick!"

"Circuit judge is a hard man. He don't like a gunny any more'n I do. You'll do time, boy."

"You ain't arrestin' me," Goheen said.

"Be damned if you are. Now put that iron away, grandpop, or—"

"Or what? You'll draw on me?"

"That's right. And I'll kill you dead, too."

"Welcome to try, if that's how you want it." The old man lowered the Peacemaker, slowly, until he was holding it as he had been before, muzzle pointed downward. "Well, boy?"

Seconds passed—long, dragging, tense. Goheen's gaze didn't waver; neither did the old man's. Then, swiftly, Goheen's hand darted down, came up again filled with his weapon—but when he pulled the trigger it was only in belated reflex. The Peacemaker roared first and a bullet kicked up dust from the front of his shirt, drove him half around; his slug went straight down into the dust. His legs buckled and he dropped to his knees. The impact jarred the double-action from his grip; he made no move to pick it up. His face bore the same expression of slack-jawed amazement it had minutes earlier, tempered now by shock and pain.

The old man jumped off the boardwalk and kicked Goheen's gun to one side. Men were spilling out of buildings along the street, and from behind him the old man could hear Howard Fletcher calling anxiously, but he kept his eyes fixed on the fallen youth at his feet.

Goheen tried to stand, couldn't, and toppled sideways clutching at his bloody chest. Groaning, he twisted his head to look up at the old man. "Damn you, grandpop, you hurt me bad. Why? I didn't figure you for no . . . no hero."

"I ain't one," the old man said. "I'm just a retired gunsmith that knows how to shoot."

"Then why? Why?"

"Sheriff's got a bad arm, Goheen. Hurt it when his horse shied at a rattler three days ago. I couldn't stand by and let you kill him in cold blood. I'd lay my own life down, and gladly, before I'd let that happen."

"What're you talkin' about?"

"My name's Chadwick, too," the old man said. "Sheriff Ben Chadwick's my son."

Few writers can boast of a career that has lasted more than half a century; William R. Cox is one of those few, having sold his first piece of fiction in 1934. Cox was a regular contributor to Western, sports, and detective pulps until the end of the pulp era and has since authored numerous novels. His Western credits include the superb Commanche Moon *(1959), and such recent Fawcett successes as* Cemetery Jones *and* The Maverick Kid. *"Billy the Button" is vintage Cox, and its hero, Billy Choke, is one of his most memorable creations.*

Billy the Button

William R. Cox

Billy Choke was eighteen that day but few people in Silver knew it. He was so small everyone thought of him as a button and his ears bugged out and his eyes squinted and he was so all-around homely that people laughed at him a lot.

Red Morgan, who owned the Knave of

Spades Saloon, had taken Billy in when he was twelve and his parents had lost out to Victorio's raiders, and Red was fine, but Billy had to work around the saloon pretty hard, waiting on every sport who hit Silver and running errands like mad. But, of course, that was good fun, too, because Billy was a curious lad and his short legs carried him into every piece of gossip in the bustling town and his wide ears did not fail to hear what was said and done.

Tom Lancaster, foreman for Foster Deal's ranch up Bear Mountain way, had called him "Billy the Button" after the business had come out about Billy practicing with the old beat-up Colt Mick Bland had given him.

As Billy the Kid was reputed to have killed his first man in Silver—with a knife, from behind, in a bar—the joke contained a local flavor and was much savored, and men like gray-haired Mr. Carey, of the bank, would solemnly enquire of Billy if he had eaten his man for breakfast that day, and when Foster Deal himself had taken a few smiles at the bar he would launch into a long prophesy of how Billy would some day provide Silver with another legend of deeds done and man slaughtered.

Billy did not mind. He lived in a pleasant

world, with kindly limp-legged Red Morgan and lovely Molly Crane, the milliner, and dark Mick Bland as his town friends, with Foster Deal and Tom Lancaster ready to loan him a horse or rifle for hunting, with the miners throwing him coins and making merry with him. Silver was bustling in those days and Billy was a very busy little boy.

He trotted his short legs along the main stem and stopped before Molly Crane's shop. Mick was in there, asking her for a date. It was early Saturday morning and Tom Lancaster was out on the ranch at his duties.

Shamelessly, Billy eavesdropped.

Bland said, "We could ride up the mountain trail. There's a spot I'd like for you to see, Molly."

Bland had been at Dodge, at Abilene. Bland was town marshal, and Silver never had much gun trouble, because Bland was too quick and too well known and even badmen usually gave the town a wide berth.

Bland was not a gunslinger in the bad term, though. He was just sincere about guns, about their care, their handling. He had taught Billy to think of his old Colt as an orange he was squeezing, to hold it steady on the target without flourish, to inhale and exert gentle but firm pressure on the hair trigger. He was one grand hombre and Billy stretched his ear a mile to hear Molly's answer.

Molly said hesitantly, "I have a lot of sewing to do this weekend. I promised—"

Bland said, "I'll be busy myself after noon. It's Saturday and the boys'll be frisky. Mornin's my only free time."

He did not beg, but he had to tell her, and his deep dark eyes were hungry. He was not a man to lay up a dollar, he was not a steady man, perhaps. Or at least he never had been. He owned guns and a horse he kept behind Red's saloon and the dark, sober clothes he wore and he drew a hundred dollars per month from the city for his job and that was about all.

Bland did not drink a lot, like some, but he bought a lot of drinks. He was very handsome, with his rather long hair, his swarthy, smooth skin, his bright piercing eyes, but he owned no cattle, no mining interest.

Molly was fair, in contrast, and round and soft and lovely to touch and look at. She had been courted by everyone in town, even old Mr. Larue, Billy knew, but it had narrowed down to Tom Lancaster and Mick Bland.

Lancaster, now, was a fine, curly-haired cowboy. He ran his own cattle with Foster

Deal's herd and one day would own his own place. He was steady-going, he was a fighting, hard-riding fool. He was all man, no getting around that, Billy conceded. He would be in later, but would only have one drink with his boss, at the Knave of Spades, then he would hang around Molly until time to get back to the ranch. He was a solid fellow.

Billy listened and Molly said, "We-ell, Mick, I guess I really ought to go. I guess we should have a talk. Things have been running along—"

"I'd admire to talk a bit, too," Bland said in his slow strong voice. "There's things to be settled between you and me."

Billy had to go. Red would be looking for him and anyway Molly was going for her riding habit and Mick was looking serious and a bit worried, too. Billy trotted along. He felt solemn and doubt gnawed at him. He knew Mick's worry. He had pieced it all out for himself. How Tom Lancaster was maybe a better-seeming man for a woman to marry.

Furthermore, Billy knew something Mick did not. He knew that Silver had calmed down so much while Mick had been marshal that Mr. Carey and the council were considering reducing Mick's salary or letting him go and hiring a cheaper man.

That, Billy thought contemptuously, was penny-pinching damn nonsense, but that was the way with Carey and Larue and the other businessmen. And it would certainly put a crimp in marriage plans for poor Mick.

The stage came in off the Butterfield Trail and Billy paused one instant to listen to Andy, the driver. Andy said in his whisky voice, "Seen four men hit off the road comin' down off the mountain. I'd a swore one was Hack Wallack. Knowed Wallack afore he turned train robber. He allus traveled with Squint, Ford, and Deal—and there was four of them I seen. If there's a payroll around, you better git a guard on it!"

Andy was an alarmist of the first water, but the news about Wallack was exciting. Billy ran all the way to the Knave of Spades to tell Red about it.

Red Morgan had lost a leg in a scrape and was gimpy, but still tough. He pounded about on his peg and said, "Ain't no payroll for the mines this week. Anyhow, Wallack only hits the trains. He's a tough one, all right. Saw him down there in El Paso five years ago, cool as ice!"

Billy said, "Mick Bland'll want the mare

for Miss Molly. They're going up Bear Mountain."

Morgan shook his head mournfully. "Won't do him no good. Tom's got the inside track there, all right. Mebbe you better run up and tell Foster Deal I got a shipment of that bourbon whisky he likes an' if he wants a barrel he better come git it."

Billy said, "That's sure a good idee, Red!"

He went out back to the stable where Red Morgan kept a couple of horses for the use of his friends, because Morgan was an old wrangler and couldn't keep entirely away from horse nohow. He saddled the mare, wiping her to a shining red, then curried Mick's big black and polished a bit of the silver on Mick's bridle, to make it look good for Molly. Then he took the roan pony and lit a shuck for Bear Mountain.

It was fine riding into the hills that piled on one another everywhere he looked. He beat his way up along the ridge and came onto the level plain, which miraculously unfolded green with grama in the midst of stone. The ranch lay low, with white paint and red roof, a pleasing sight. Billy whooped at the grinning wrangler and slid off his pony outside the kitchen door. Cooky grunted at him, but Tom Lancaster strode long-legged from the corral, calling, "You got a message for me, Button?"

"Nope," said Billy. "For Foster." He added innocently, "Miss Molly's ridin' with Mick."

Tom Lancaster said, "Nobody asked you."

Billy shrugged and went in search of Foster Deal. He found that bluff gentleman disgustedly shaking an empty five gallon keg and repeated his message from Morgan. Foster Deal said, "Sho 'nuff? It just couldn't be a more pro-peetious time! You eat, Button?"

Billy said, "No. And I'm eighteen today."

"Law-dee," grinned the gray-thatched rancher. "You kill yore man this mawnin'?"

"Two of 'em," said Billy, but it was no use trying to keep up the badinage. It just didn't set well, now that he was eighteen. The ranch was mighty pleasant, if they only wouldn't treat him like a boy.

He ate heartily and mounted again and rode about the near pasture, critically surveying the cattle, derisively shooing off an old milch cow and her calf. It was time to think about his future, he knew. Ranching was certainly fine. He made a self-conscious inspection of things within short ride, then knew Red Morgan would be expecting him.

It was nearly noon, and he set the pony at the trail.

He thought a lot about ranching, riding down. Every button aspired to a horse and a gun and room to swing a wide loop. He was no exception and he had a lot of cattle lore and tracking knowledge and one thing and another he had gleaned up on the table land with Foster Deal and his men. Maybe he had ought to start thinking about moving on.

There were people in town who didn't like him staying at Red Morgan's Knave of Spades. Miz Carey had made a fuss once, and when she saw him practicing with his Colt, which Mick Bland had given him, she tried to take it away from him. But Red Morgan had a way with him and Bland and Mr. Carey himself had sided Morgan, and Billy had remained with his mentor. But he wondered now if ranching wasn't the life.

Turning off the main road for the short cut, he went past the small waterfall, which in this season was no more than a trickle. He could see beyond it into the glade where pinyons nodded low to the ground and there he saw Molly and Dick. He reined in, staring, holding his breath, wondering.

They were reclining on the soft earth. The

girl's hat was off and her hair shone like dull gold. She said, "Mick, you are good. You are true. The things you are, the good things, are not the things you do. That I know. But—"

He said, "I thought to open a gun shop. All I know best is guns. I thought I could save and start a business in them."

"You?" she said sadly. "Mick Bland, in a shop? Mick Bland, who has killed his men in Abilene, in Dodge? No, Mick. If you lay aside your trapping, your star, you are no longer Mick Bland."

"Other men have done it," he said. "For you, Molly, I would put aside life itself. You know that."

"What good are you without life?" she asked. She was as sad as Mick, Billy thought. "I wish I could feel it out within me, the way you want. I truly do. But you are a man who requires violence, who lives with guns. A woman wants peace, a home, a man to come home to her."

They were silent then, and Billy knew both were thinking of Tom Lancaster. Tom was the very one she was describing. He would soon be able to provide a cabin, a piece of land. His beefs were waxing fat, running with Foster Deal's herds. Foster was behind Lancaster, a steady man, a man to tie to.

Mick Bland stood, leaning a little over the girl. He said, "Perhaps you are right. A woman has to think of such things. But that which is between us, Molly, is a deeper emotion than measuring sticks can plumb. I want you and I am almost sure you want me. I have offered to meet your requirements to the best of my ability. I can do no more. Some day, Molly, it will come to a show-down."

She dropped her head, so that not even Billy could see her expression. It was funny, Billy thought, the way Mick talked, with a drawl, but different than most. More like Preacher Eddison. Mick was a strange one, all right.

Billy rode away, the unshod pony making no noise on the dirt of the back trail. Now that he was started, he did not return to the main road. He slid along easily, making good time, topping the rise at the edge of the dry stream that pointed straight for Silver and in the springtime sent flash floods into the town streets.

He caught sight of the horse's head as he munched the pinyons, or else he would have missed the whole thing. No horse belonged

326

to be in this place at this time, he knew. The glade beyond the cottonwoods was not mining country and Foster Deal's cattle lay beyond the ridge.

When the man jerked hard, hauling the horse back out of sight, Billy ducked over his pony's head and rode in a circle, like an Apache buck.

But he swung in at the end of the cottonwoods and pulled up the rise. He dropped between two rocks, dismounted. He slipped forward onto the little table of land and stared down.

There were four of them. The leader was sandy-haired and tall and rode a Montana saddle; otherwise he looked like anyone else. The others were just riders, assorted. Yet, with their heads together, conferring, there was no doubt about them.

The tall one was Hack Wallack. There had been posters for the sheriffs, and a reward offered. He did not look like the picture very much, but Billy could tell.

Old Andy hadn't been yarning, then. The outlaws, coming down from the North, were shabby, their clothing dusty, their boots cracked. They had the hungry look of broke men.

Billy wriggled backward, got to the pony.

He headed silently for the main road. He debated, riding, the pony lathering a little. He wiped the sweat from his own brow. It was getting hot and he was pretty excited.

He decided to get to town. He hadn't the heart to disturb Mick and the girl. Wallack was plotting something, all right. Lingering in the hills outside Silver, he was planning to get a stake to go south, maybe to hit the U.P. He was a train robber, but he had to eat and make expenses for his men.

Wallack had the reputation of being the hardest man in his profession. He was a shooter. He had killed several trainmen who had not obeyed his commands, without turning a hair. He had shot two law officers, beating them to the draw. He was becoming a tradition in his own time, a real badman. He was a worthy foe to a marshal like Mick Bland.

Billy wrestled with a problem, going swiftly down the road to town. If Mick did come in and Wallack was trying to pull something, there would be a shootout. Four against one, it would be. The others, Squint and Deal and Ford, were no less deadly than their leader. Mick would get hurt.

But that was not all. Molly had spoken against violence. She felt strongly about guns and shooting. If Mick got into it and killed even so unsavory a character as Wallack, what would Molly do? Would she marry Tom Lancaster at once? Billy knew little about women, but he suspected they would be hasty and ill-advised.

A stone had rolled down from an over-hanging boulder. The pony tried to dodge it with that sixth sense ponies have, but the stone was unavoidable and the pony struck it with his off-front leg. He did a prancing step, then went down to his knees.

Billy managed to land soft, in a heap. The dust was in his nostrils and Silver was four miles ahead. He scrambled up and examined the pony. The leg was not broken, but it was swelling.

Cursing with the fluency of eighteen, Billy began walking. On three legs the pony fol-lowed patiently. They made it very slowly, what with Billy's boots and the pony's lame-ness.

He knew he must not keep looking back, yet he had to do it. When the cloud of dust came, he estimated it at four men. He drew the pony over to the side and made himself even smaller.

Wallack came swirling to a stop, saw the tiny figure, the limping pony. He did not look twice, but waved his hand. The man came up, sitting, staring down. Wallack said harshly, "Button, which saloon in Silver is across from the bank?"

Billy made his voice high and quavery. "The Knave of Spades."

"Red Morgan's place," grunted the squint-eyed man.

"I'll handle Morgan," snorted one of the others. "Come on."

Wallack said, "Old man Carey close the bank at noon?"

"For lunch," nodded Billy. Inspired he said, "Gimme a lift to town behind yuh. My pony knows the way home."

Wallack said in his harsh voice, "Don't yuh know enough to stick with a lame hoss?"

Billy cowered. "He knows the way home."

"Pah!" spat Wallack. "Yuh'll never make a rider." He waved again, a lordly motion. He was a flamboyant man—his guns were tied low, in decorative holsters. The four rode on.

Billy plodded along. There was nothing else to do. The pony was coming as fast as Billy could walk, anyway. No use to stampede just because Wallack was planning to take the bank.

It was past noon, anyway. Only Mr. Carey also closed at three, for the weekend, staying in behind locked doors to count up the money or something, him and old Larue. This was Saturday, but the boys never came in until late, not even the miners.

Wallack had plenty of time. He could plan and hit when it was right.

Billy kept walking. The road wound about and went down past the arroyo.

An hour passed and Billy was dry in the throat and a bit dizzy in the head. He thought about Red Morgan and the man called Squint and the other, narrow-eyed man who had offered to take care of Red. With only one leg and his shotgun on a hook under the bar, how could Red do anything?

There was no leader in town, not with Mick Bland away and Foster Deal on his ranch and Tom Lancaster busy. These were the fighting men. The others would follow, but without these Silver would be disorderly, confused by such deadly workers as Wallack's gang. Billy had listened to so many stories that he could almost figure out how it would work.

He was looking back again, along the road. If Mick brought Molly home early, if they fought, he could warn Mick. It would be a bad business for Mick to get into, but he would be better off warned. Going against men like Wallack was what finished many a lawman of the day. Vaguely, Billy was beginning to know that men who lived by the gun generally perished by the same instrument. He could even see what Molly had in her mind when she refused Mick.

Nevertheless, Mick was his friend. Mick had given him the gun and had taught him to use it and about Mick there was a glamorous aura that blinded a button to the facts of violence as pure destruction. Billy was no longer a button, of course, but deep within him was a clinging to Mick Bland and what he stood for—the Old West, which knew no law save the six-gun in the hands of a man who could use it.

The last mile was the hardest. He measured every step, coming across the wooden bridge and turning, going down behind the Mex buildings, going across littered yards to the stable behind the Knave of Spades. He even watered the pony and turned him into the corral to rest his leg. Then he crept into his room at the rear of the saloon and washed himself and changed his clothing. He looked in the cracked glass and wondered if Wallack would recognize him. It would not be good if Wallack did.

He opened the door to the barroom cautiously. The shutters were slatted and it was dim. They were in there.

Wallack was at the blind, looking out. Red Morgan stood behind the bar, his hands carefully in sight. Red was cornered and he knew it and did not like it. Billy slipped in and the man at the bar said, "Who the hell is that?"

"My boy, Ford," said Red Morgan. "He's just a button."

Wallack never turned around. He said, "Take him, Squint."

The man with the funny eyes came over and slapped at Billy. Against the wall, Billy trembled despite himself. Squint searched him, peering in the dimness, and Billy knew Squint was near-sighted. Another slap sent him away from the bar, toward the pool table.

Squint snarled, "Jest sit tight, button. Mebbe yuh won't get kilt."

Mr. Larue pushed open the batwing doors and puttered into the Knave. He was very old and very rich and he quavered. "Whisky from the good bottle, Red. Got a lot of work this afternoon."

Red Morgan poured the drink. Not many people were in town yet. Larue drank and did not notice anything about the men, the old fool. A cowman or even a hardrock miner might have noticed, but not Larue. Billy stayed against the wall beyond the pool table and his mind rushed about like a cornered mouse.

Ford, at the bar, said conversationally, "Remember the time down in El Paso yuh ran that blazer on me? I never forget it, Red."

"Yuh run like a rabbit," said Red Morgan contemptuously.

"That's why I'm here," said Ford, grinning. "That's why you ain't gonna git a chance to do me agin."

"Shut up!" said Wallack.

Old Larue never tumbled. He just went out and tottered across the street and went into the bank. It was almost three o'clock. In a moment the bank would close. Then Wallack would go over and hit it. They would shoot Red Morgan, because they knew Red was brave and had a gun somewheres.

Billy caught his breath. He had seen a man or two shot before Mick had come to town. He had heard numberless bloody tales. He was a Western boy, brought up on six-gun stories. But this was different. This was Red Morgan being shot.

If only Mick would come, he thought now. He was getting panicky and he recognized it. He wanted Mick to come and make a play. He wanted Foster Deal and Tom Lancaster. They had to come to save Red. He cared nothing about the bank and the money, nor had he from the beginning. He just didn't want his friends killed in cold blood by this badman and his gang.

He looked at Red Morgan, whose homely face was serene as he stood on his one leg, watching Ford. Morgan did not look at Billy. Morgan would make a play of some kind, of course, but he was four feet from the shotgun, and getting it off the hook and up over the bar would take precious seconds and by that time he would be dead.

The clock on the wall ticked doomsday seconds away. Wallack said, "Get ready. No, wait! Dammit!"

Billy's heart leaped. He could have cried with joy, then, his mind began working again, clear as a bell. He saw the tall hats of Foster Deal and Tom Lancaster above the swinging doors. Foster had ridden in quickly after his precious bourbon!

They came through, but not before Wallack had made a motion and his men spread out. Billy moved softly laterally, his eye on all the scene. There was a chair, higher than the others, where he had always watched the pool and other life in the saloon. He wanted to get to that chair.

He froze. Foster Deal and Tom Lancaster were inside, and Deal said, "Whyn't yuh let some light in this joint, Red?"

Then the four men closed in, and Foster Deal saw it. He made a motion, but Billy almost wept for sure. Deal was not wearing his gun! Lancaster was weaponless!

Mick Bland had made them careless, cleaning up the town the way he had. They rode down thinking of whisky and a soft-shouldered girl and they left their guns behind. Maybe there was a rifle on the saddle, but Silver had become a town where a man could go without his hand weapons.

Wallack said, "Line up by the bar. Steady does it."

Wallack hadn't even drawn. He just shot the words at them out of the corner of his mouth. None of the outlaws had pulled a gun, yet Death entered the Knave of Spades and walked about, searching for his victim.

It was Foster Deal's immobility, in Tom

336

Lancaster's face, Billy could almost smell it. The outlaws had come at the most propitious moment. Their timing was nearly perfect. They had three unarmed men to contend with, and these were the town's leading fighters, save one.

Wallack said, "Bland's moonin' with the gal. He'll be in purty soon, though. The bank is closin'."

Squint said, "When you say, Hack."

They were trying to conceal the fact that they meant to kill Red and Foster and Tom, but Billy knew they must. Unless they left one man here to guard them, it was necessary. And the man called Ford wanted Red to die because of something that had happened in El Paso.

Even if Mick came in, someone would die. They might not get Mick for keeps, because Mick was a man in a gunfight who scarcely ever got hit, but someone would die. Foster or Tom or Red—they were Billy's friends. They were, he saw clearly in these moments of his growing up, his life. Molly and Mick . . . the ranchman and his foreman . . . his adopted parent . . . all mixed up, but all of his existence. All that counted.

Wallack had his eyes glued to the slatted

337

blinds. He growled, "There's an old woman, jawin' to Carey."

Wallack knew an awful lot about the town and the set-up. Someone had come in and spotted everything. Wallack was not a bank robber, but this was a bank he meant to take. He was cautious, making sure of every detail of an unfamiliar business. Desperately Billy tried to think of something Wallack had overlooked. It was no good. The sandy man had the quality of leadership, of being right. Billy could see that even through his new panic.

Red Morgan was drumming silently with his fingers, and that was a sign that made Billy's heart stop, then leap ahead. That was what Red Morgan always did before he stopped taking nonsense from a drunk and reached for a weapon. The time was getting close now.

It was in the taut, high shoulders of Wallack, in the queer eyes of Squint, the jerky hands of Ford, the slick cat quality of the silent man named Dowd. Wallack meant to surprise the men in the bar with sudden action, taking no chances they might make a bare-handed fight. When Miz Carey stopped jawing at Mr. Carey, the ball would open.

Molly and Mick came cantering down the

street as though nothing in the world was happening. Molly's face was sad, Mick's was set and withdrawn. Wallack saw them, everyone saw them. The millinery shop was halfway down the block. They went out of Billy's sight and the end of the world appeared, directly before his eyes like a high, sheer bluff. Mick was out of it, now. Wallack had seen him and that was that. They would get Mick Bland as he came back leading the horses, preoccupied with his spurned love.

The triumph in Wallack was something else again. He had, Billy knew now, feared only Mick. He said, "Well, that ties it. There goes the old gal. Ready, fellers?" He swaggered with his shoulders. Billy had not thought he was a swaggering man, but he saw now that with four aces in his hand he was a mean customer.

Squint said, "Ahhh!" and belted out viciously with the back of his hand. They never missed a detail, these trained robbers. He hit Billy in the jaw and knocked him sideways to the floor. Then Squint had drawn his gun and was peering in the dimness like a vulture, seeking prey.

Billy rolled over an extra time. He came to the feet of the high chair. He saw Ford leaning across the bar, calling Red Morgan foul names, referring to El Paso, working himself up to it. He saw Foster Deal turn and throw himself full length on the floor, seeking something for a weapon as he went. He saw Dowd covering the door as Wallack turned.

Tom Lancaster said loudly, "You can't murder us!"

Billy grabbed a leg and pulled himself up. There was, he discovered, a moment when even cold-blooded killers pause before striking. They had to be quick, as the shots would warn Mick, and then they would have to move and shoot and get Mick right away.

They had confidence in doing it, but they needed a last instant to gather themselves. Wallack was ready to give the signal, but something in his soul may not have been ready.

There was a cache beneath the chair. Some miggles and a fish line and an outgrown top and a snakeskin or two. Billy's hand went over them, shaking a little. He had repaired the chair himself and built this little box under the seat. He came to the butt of the Colt and closed down on it. He had to slip it from its holster, which was lined with the fur of a rabbit to keep it dry and ready.

He got it out. It was, for a moment, heavy,

but time could not be measured and he had to swing around.

He held it up and his voice did not shake. He stood against the chair, supporting himself, his cheek cut a little where Squint had struck him. He said, "All right, reach for it!"

Squint swung first. Tom Lancaster, the fool, was standing in the middle of it. Foster kicked hard and Lancaster stumbled and went down as Wallack shouted something and fired the first shot. That saved Tom Lancaster, for the time being.

Billy was thinking straight enough. He squeezed, like he was squeezing an orange. The Colt belched, kicking a little. Squint canted sideways, looking very foolish. He fell down.

Wallack, still shouting, tried to see in the dimness, but there was smoke, too, and it made trouble for him. Ford fired one shot at Red Morgan. Dowd crouched, steadiest of them all, watching for Mick.

Billy threw down, without flourish, without sparing an extra gesture, and his sight line on Ford. It was hard to shoot a man in the back, but he squeezed again. Ford flung up his arms and tumbled backward, screaming. Red Morgan ducked below the bar.

Then Wallack found him. He made a tiny figure, but he stood braced, where they could get at him. Dowd whirled around at a new noise.

Wallack said, "You dirty little whelp!"

The gun belched and Billy could see the fire come out of it. He was picked up, slammed against the chair. It broke again, and the holster fell on his hand. He tried to shake himself loose, to get the gun up. He had to fire at Wallack, at Dowd.

Mick came in the back, then. He just walked in, without word or expression. He held his gun waist high, like he had taught Billy, for close quarters work. He fanned the hair trigger—you never fan at a target, but against gunmen in a bar it can be very effective. He threw lead like another man would toss coins at a line. Billy's head was raised by a rung of the chair which had caught him and he saw it all.

Wallack, cursing, came at Bland, leaping, brave. Dowd squatted and shot over folded elbow, a cool thing to do. But Bland just stood there, his face without a wrinkle, serious, doing his job. His gun lanced flame and Dowd fell forward, arms spread out on the floor, unmoving.

Wallack was almost at arm's length. Bland

disdainfully shot again. Wallack doubled over the belt around the middle. His forehead came down and struck violently against the floor. Billy thought crazily, "He'll have a lump on his head. He shouldn't move when he's shootin'. Why, he wasn't a real shooter at all! He was just ready and bad. He missed Mick plenty."

Then it was over. The bad men lay still. It was easy to see that none of them lived. They had the still look of men through with life. Billy closed his eyes. There was a tearing pain in his chest and he was afraid he was going to be sick.

Bland was listening to Foster Deal, who was coming toward Billy. Foster roared, "The Button called 'em slick as a whistle. By Gawd, Mick, you taught him right! He stood there and he called 'em and then he shot Squint and then that other one that got Red."

Morgan's voice boomed, "Ford only pinked me. Get Doc Stewart. Hurry and get the Doc, Tom. Do somethin', for Godsake!"

Tom Lancaster went out. He did not walk steadily, but he went fast.

Foster Deal was picking Billy up and putting him on the pool table. Billy gasped. "No! You'll ruin the cloth."

343

Bland stood, his face terrible. He said, "Billy, they would have had me. Billy, they shot you. If I could kill them all again, one by one, slowly, Billy."

"No," said Billy. "Shhh! Molly'll hear you. Molly—"

She was there, shoving the men aside. She had never been inside the Knave before, but she made the place look better. She cut away his shirt with the shears and had white cloth from her shop to staunch the blood. She said, "Billy, what happened? What made you do it, Billy?"

He said, with effort, "Aw, Red mighta got hurt. And Tom and Foster, too. And they would a sure got Mick . . ."

She said, "Who was it? What happened here?"

Foster Deal told her, loudly, while Billy rested. He said, at the end, "And I wanta say here and now, when Tom leaves me for to go on his own, I got my new foreman picked. He can come out and start tomorrow."

Doc Stewart fussed in and began probing around. Bland hadn't said anything after Molly came in, but he stood there, his eyes still terrible, watching. Once his face went white and pinched in, and that time Billy fainted. But when he awoke that steady regard was still upon him. He managed to grin.

Doc said, "Too high to kill him."

Bland's tautness did not lapse. He said softly, "You did it for your friends, Billy. It's a thing we can't ever forget around here."

Mr. Carey and old Larue and lots of others were coming in, now that it was over. Men were toting out the corpses. Morgan's shoulder was being bandaged and he was watching Billy, too. Bland said, "I'm thinking about leaving for the East, Billy. If you wanted to go to school, I'd admire it if you went along."

Molly was holding the basin and she trembled so it spilled a little on the green baize. Billy said, "What you shakin' about, Molly? You and Mick are goin' to leave?"

He said it pretty loud and he saw Mick waver. He said, "Molly, you couldn't call me no gunslinger, could you?"

She shook her head silently. Mick said, "Now wait, son."

"I'm eighteen," said Billy stubbornly. "I don't want to go East to no school. I can learn from you like always. An' there's Red. I ain't goin' to no ranch. Foster's all right. Tom's all right. They're my friends. But Red raised me. Mick taught me what I know. I wanta stay here, with my folks."

He was exhausted for a moment and thought he was going to faint again. He bit his lip and managed to skip it. Molly said softly, "Go on, Billy."

"Foster and Tom didn't have guns. You know why? Because Mick made this town safe," said Billy.

Mr. Carey and old Larue were listening, he made sure. He wanted them to hear this good. He said louder, "Them men rode in—there's plenty more men like 'em in the West. It could happen again. They woulda had the bank and killed Red an'—an' everything. Only Mick give me a gun. And then he had sense enough to come in the back door and finish 'em. I only did what Mick taught me, and I hadda kill two men. But you can't call me a gunman, Molly."

He was getting mixed up and Mr. Carey wouldn't understand, but Molly would, he knew. He had seen Tom flinch when the odds were against him and he was sure about Tom, now, a good man, but not like Mick. He had to get his message to Molly.

She put down the bloodied water. She said, "I don't think you'll be going East."

She held her head high, looking straight at Bland. Then she walked out and the men parted, touched their hats politely in admiration of her, and she went out through the swinging doors. Foster Deal was behind the bar, pouring drinks at his expense for everyone. Men were beginning to come up and say things to Billy. Nobody called him "Billy the Button."

Bland lifted him tenderly. He was as strong as a bigger man. He carried him into the back room and put him on his own bed. He worked off Billy's boots. Billy was pretty drowsy. He said, "I was thinkin' about the ranch this mornin'. Thought I might try it. Takes experience to learn about things an' people. I wouldn't leave Red. Nor you."

Bland said, "You're my partner, aren't you?"

Red Morgan came in and propped himself in the doorway. His voice was very deep. He said, "He's my boy, don't forget!"

But he didn't mean that Billy was only a button. He meant he was proud. Billy grinned at the two of them and said, "You're awful damn serious, you two!"

Then he went to sleep. They didn't even cuss him out for swearing.

Donald Hamilton is justifiably famous for his rousing spy-adventure novels featuring Matt Helm. His Western fiction, which is every bit as accomplished and entertaining, is unjustifiably less well known—for instance, such excellent novels as Mad River, The Big Country, *and* Texas Fever, *and such outstanding short stories as* "The Guns of William Longley," *reprinted in the first Best of the West anthology,* The Lawmen, *and the suspenseful tale that follows. Among his other Western credits is editorship of the 1967 Western Writers of America anthology,* Iron Men and Silver Stars, *published by Fawcett Books.*

The Last Gunman

Donald Hamilton

The big man got on the train at Abilene. He came down the aisle with a pair of saddlebags over his shoulder and stopped by Paul Clyde's seat.

"Mind if I sit down, sir?" he asked politely.

"Not at all," Clyde said, a little surprised at the courtesy of the fellow, since he looked rather like a man who'd sit where he darn well pleased.

The stranger stowed his saddlebags under the seat and settled himself comfortably. He leaned back, drew his big hat over his eyes, and promptly fell asleep.

Clyde turned to watch the plains outside the window, wondering if there was any chance, in this year 1882, of seeing a buffalo, or perhaps an Indian tribe on the move. The big man awoke late in the day, sat up, yawned, rubbed a hand over his mouth, and leaned forward to look out the window. As he did so, a lurch of the train threw him against Clyde.

"My apologies, sir," he said. "This roadbed gets worse all the time. I figure they must have laid the rails direct on the prairie grass. I heard you mention Prairie Junction to the conductor."

"Yes, that's my destination."

"My stop, too. I live there." The big man held out his hand. "Name's Bannerman. Hank Bannerman."

"I'm Paul Clyde, from Boston." Clyde managed to keep from wincing as his fingers were crushed by the other's powerful grip.

Retrieving his hand, he said, "Perhaps you can tell me something about the town. All I know is that it must be big enough to have a bank, since I'm to work there."

Bannerman gave him a measuring look, obviously adding up his pale skin, well-cut Eastern clothes, and slight stature and arriving at some sum, which he did not reveal, saying only, "A banker, eh?"

"Hardly that. Just the man at the little window."

The big man grinned. "It's about time George Jarvis got somebody into that place who can count."

"Oh, you know Mr. Jarvis?"

Bannerman's smile cooled somewhat. "Yeh, I know Mr. Jarvis," he said in a dry tone. "Well, you'll find Prairie Junction a peaceful and pleasant place nowadays, Mr. Clyde. It was a tough town once, but the country's grown up and the cattle trail's moved still farther west, taking most of the rough element with it. Of course, there's a few of the old crowd still hanging around trying to make trouble—like this Bannerman gent some folks figure should have been run out of town long since."

He chuckled and leaned back in his seat. He seemed to be about Clyde's own age of twenty-eight. He had a face that was saved from heaviness only by the long and humorous mouth; and his hair was thick and yellow.

"This was a fine country ten years ago, when I first came up the trail—a fine, wild, hell-raising country, Mr. Clyde. But it's grown up and civilized now. Reckon a man should get grown up and civilized, too, in that many years. Even three years ago, coming this way at this season, there'd be herds of Texas cattle as far as the eye could see, awaiting shipment East. Well, the barbed wire killed the trail. . . . There's the old loading pens now; we're coming into town."

He reached down for the saddlebags, opened one, and before Clyde's startled eyes, drew out a heavy cartridge belt supporting a holstered revolver. Standing up, he buckled the belt about him. Then he turned back to Clyde.

"It's been a pleasure to make your acquaintance, sir. I hope you'll like our city." He grinned abruptly, reaching into his pocket, and produced a silver badge, which he pinned on his shirt. The badge read: MARSHAL. "You may consider that an official greeting, Mr. Clyde, in case there is no band to welcome you." He moved away down the aisle.

Prairie Junction seemed to be lined up opposite the railroad tracks. There was a wide, dusty, unpaved main street, a school, a church, a long row of false-front frame buildings, and the solid brick building that was the Farmers' and Merchants' Bank, situated on a corner. Up the side street, Clyde managed to read the names on a couple of once gaudy, now faded signs: the Cattleman's Rest and the Bulls-eye Saloon.

He picked up his coat and valise and stepped down to the ground. There was a trunk to be seen to, and he looked around for the proper official, but paused as he recognized the tall, broad-shouldered shape of Marshal Bannerman, standing with a girl only a few yards away. The girl was speaking, and her voice held a hint of amused reproach.

"Well, was it a good trip, Hank? Did you get drunk and disorderly in some other lawman's town?"

Bannerman chuckled. "Why, a man can't give rein to his baser impulses in the place where he wears the badge, Sally. It would lead to disrespect among the citizens. Yes, it was a good enough trip. But the ending was the best of it, seeing you standing here. Although I can't flatter myself you're here for my sake."

The girl laughed. "I might have been, if you'd let me know when you were coming back. No, Dad had some business with the stationmaster; and I'm supposed to be keeping an eye out for a man he's expecting, to work in the bank. I haven't any idea of what kind of a person I'm supposed to be watching for, except that he's from Boston."

"I can help you there," Bannerman said. "I made his acquaintance on the train." He turned, letting his glance sweep the platform. It came to rest on Clyde, who was already moving forward. The marshal waited for him to reach them, and said formally, "Miss Jarvis, allow me to present Mr. Paul Clyde, your dad's new—"

He broke off. The girl was not even looking at Clyde. Her smile of greeting had died abruptly; now her hand went out to grasp the marshal's arm. "Hank! Isn't that Rios, the man who tried to—Over there by that wagon!"

The marshal's voice was calm. "I saw him. Yeh, that's Johnny Rios. I'm waiting to see who comes to welcome him home. And here's Jud Haskell, right on schedule. Excuse me."

The girl retained her grip on his sleeve. "Hank, be careful! Rios is wearing a gun!"

"Which is illegal in this town," the marshal said. "It is my duty to remind the gentleman." When she did not release him immediately, he said gently, "Sally, never interfere with a man's business."

Sally Jarvis flushed slightly. Bannerman raised his hat to her, nodded to Clyde, and moved away. Beyond the marshal, Clyde saw two men shaking hands by a baggage cart. One, balancing a canvas-covered bedroll on his shoulder, was narrow, young, and swarthy. There was a holstered pistol at his hip. The man who had come to greet him was considerably older and had a fleshy white face. Both men turned at Bannerman's approach. The younger one, Johnny Rios, let the bedroll slide from his shoulder in a casual way and set it on the ground.

The older man, Haskell, spoke to Bannerman. The distance was too great for Clyde to catch the words. He was aware that the girl beside him, watching this scene, had moved closer to him. He heard her breath catch sharply.

"Hank! Hank, watch out!" It was only a

whisper, but it had the quality of a scream. She had seen it before Clyde did: the younger man's hand striking snakelike toward the butt of his holstered weapon. What happened next was so nearly instantaneous that Clyde could not be sure his eyes had caught all the details of the action. All he knew was that Bannerman was in motion; his left hand knocking Rios' pistol aside as it cleared the holster, his right whipping out his own weapon and laying the barrel brutally across the younger man's head.

A moment later, everything was still again. Johnny Rios was on the ground, and Bannerman was aiming his pistol at the older man, whose hand seemed to be frozen just inside the lapel of his coat. Slowly, Jud Haskell drew his hand into sight, empty. Bannerman spoke. Haskell hesitated, shrugged, reached inside his coat again, brought out a small revolver, and held it out, butt first. Bannerman took it and dropped it into his pocket; then, almost casually, he turned and kicked Rios in the face.

The wicked sound of the boot going home echoed across the depot. Rios, whose hand had been creeping out toward his fallen pistol, was lifted into the air and dropped on his back, unconscious. Bannerman scooped up the pistol, bent over the unconscious man, unbuckled the heavy gun belt, and pulled it free.

He straightened up and spoke to Haskell, "Tell your boy, when he wakes up, that he can pick up his property at the marshal's office whenever he decides to leave town. The same goes for you. Don't put it off too long. Good day, Mr. Haskell."

He walked away across the wide and sunlit street, looping the confiscated gun belt over his arm. The people drawn by the rumor of conflict made way for him. The girl beside Clyde had not moved at all and did not move until Bannerman was out of sight; then Clyde heard her pent-up breath go out in a sigh.

"Well, Mr. Clyde," she said, "you have something to write home about."

He was shocked to see on her face only relief that the incident was over. She displayed none of the horror and disgust and faintness proper for a gently reared young lady who had just witnessed a scene of brutal violence. In other respects, also, he found her a disconcerting person. He had come West with the notion that the female population would consist entirely of weather-beaten frontier matrons and buxom prairie belles.

Sally Jarvis fitted into neither category. She was of no more than medium height, blue-eyed, and slim-waisted, differing in appearance from the young women he had known back East only in a certain look of vigor and directness, and in being considerably prettier than most of them.

He looked away from her to where Johnny Rios, half conscious, his face streaming blood, was being led away between Haskell and another man. With some revulsion, Clyde said, "I thought that sort of thing belonged to the past."

Sally Jarvis glanced at him sharply. "Out here, the past isn't quite dead yet, Mr. Clyde."

"Your Mr. Bannerman seems to be doing his best to revive it."

There was clear dislike in her voice when she replied, "I might find some things to criticize if I visited your home town of Boston, Mr. Clyde. But I don't think I'd speak out until I'd been there long enough to know what I was talking about. Here comes my father."

A portly, gray-mustached man was marching down the platform toward them.

"Sally, I've told you—" he burst out.

"Dad, this is Mr. Clyde," she said quickly.

Mr. Jarvis ignored the introduction. "I have strictly forbidden you to have anything to do with that roughneck, and yet I'm informed that you just greeted him like a long-lost friend, with the whole town watching! I hope this latest display of his brutality will bring you to your senses! Bannerman should be shot for having the effrontery to address you; his place is on Texas Street with the people it's his business to control, his own kind of people! As a matter of fact, I don't understand why the city council keeps him on, at his inflated wages, now that we no longer have the yearly influx of cattle drovers to contend with. I shall bring it up again at the next meeting. In the meantime, I must insist that you—"

"Dad," the girl said gently, "this is Mr. Clyde."

"Oh." Mr. Jarvis put out his hand abruptly. "Glad to have you here, Clyde. You run along, miss. I'll speak to you later!" He watched the girl walk lightly away. Then he said in a tired voice, "I don't know. Clyde, do you have a daughter? No, I suppose not. You're not even married, as I recall your letters. Well, let's see to your baggage; and

358

then I'll show you around the bank, if you're not too tired from your journey . . ."

The following days were busy ones for Paul Clyde, since it developed that Mr. Jarvis had for years run his bank as a typically one-man business, keeping half the records in his head. Now, at the age of sixty, urged on by his family and doctor, he was taking steps toward ridding himself of at least part of the burdens of management. Clyde, with his rigid Eastern training, found himself continually shocked by the casual and trusting way this institution had been operated—at a considerable profit, he had to admit. One evening toward the end of the first week, he walked over to the Jarvis house to pick up a ledger Mr. Jarvis had forgotten at home, and incidentally to let Mrs. Jarvis know that her husband would be working late.

It was a pleasant evening, which, Clyde told himself, was why he had volunteered for the errand instead of sending a boy. He knew the way, having been to the big white house for supper a few nights before—Sally Jarvis had been noticeably cool to him, despite her parents' cordiality. He had not consciously been thinking of her as he walked; but when her mother, a small, handsome, white-haired woman, opened the door, he found that he was disappointed.

The discovery startled him; and as he was shown into the living room to wait while Mrs. Jarvis went upstairs for the ledger, he told himself firmly that he could have no possible interest in the headstrong daughter of a smalltown banker—a girl with so little taste and modesty that she would let her name become linked with that of a man who, although wearing a badge, was certainly no better than the crude and violent people with whom he had to deal.

Then there were footsteps on the veranda, and, as if in response to his thoughts, a voice he recognized as Marshal Bannerman's came clearly through the open window: "He's tried before. There's nothing to fear, Sally."

"Nothing to fear!" The girl's voice was sharp. "You know why he brought Rios back. And Rios will hate you twice as much now, after what you did to him at the depot."

"I can handle Johnny Rios. And Jud Haskell, too. It's what I've been waiting for."

There was a short silence. Sally's voice had a strange, flat sound when she spoke again. "Oh," she said, "is that what you've been waiting for, Hank?"

"I do not like to leave unfinished things

behind me. Haskell fought me all the way down the line when I was cleaning up Texas Street some years back. I closed up his Bullseye Saloon until he got in some dealers and girls who'd give the trail hands half a chance. He had men try for me on several occasions; Johnny Rios was the last one, and almost made it. It was in the cards there'd be a final showdown. The Street is dead now except for small sins, and Haskell's pulling out. He's waited a long time to do it. I wondered why. Now I know. He was waiting for Rios. He wanted one more try at me. This time, I think, he'll be out there with a gun himself. Well, I've waited a long time for him to hate me enough for that. It will finish my job here in Prairie Junction."

It occurred to Clyde that he was eavesdropping. He rose and walked across the room to the bookshelf, taking no pains to move quietly; but the two people on the porch were too concerned with their own affairs to hear him.

Sally's voice came through the window, clearly audible: "So all these last months—this last year—you've been waiting around to kill a man?"

The marshal's voice held a smile. "Well, there were some other things to hold me."

The girl spoke swiftly. "And if you succeed—if you survive, what then?"

"There's a town called Lagos Springs, to the west. The Texans coming up the trail take it apart each summer. The citizens have to spend all winter putting it back together again. A committee came to see me the other day—"

"Are you taking the job?"

"I thought I would."

"And after that?"

"What do you mean?"

"After you have—tamed Lagos Springs, where do you go? And was it your thought that I would be with you?"

"It was my hope that you would be, Sally."

There was a silence. It lasted so long Clyde thought they must have moved away; then Sally's voice said, "No. No, Hank. I'm sorry." She paused, as if to let Bannerman speak; when he remained silent, she went on swiftly: "If this were twenty years ago, or even ten years ago, my answer would be different. It was that kind of a country then. It needed your kind of man. But the cattle trail is dying, Hank; and the country's changing, and if you don't change with it, what's left for you—for us, if I should accompany you?

Oh, there are a few years left. There will be a few more trail towns, perhaps, trying feebly to live up to Abilene and Dodge City and Prairie Junction. But after that, where do you go? To the gold towns, the silver towns, one or another mining camp that needs a tough man with a gun?

"Oh, Hank, you've sowed your wild oats, and they've been wild enough, heaven knows, but I don't mind that. But when I get married, it will be to a man who can give me a home and children, not a room above a roaring street of sin in which to wait—wait for my husband to be brought home dead. That may make me less of a woman than you thought, my dear; but this pursuit of violence, for its own sake, also makes you less of a man. You're thirty years old, Hank. If you can't see it yet, I'm afraid there's not much hope for you. I will not be going with you!"

Her footsteps ran along the porch, and the front door opened and closed. Then Mrs. Jarvis was coming down the stairs; and Clyde, crossing the living room, heard her say: "Why, Sally, dear, I didn't know you were home. Is something wrong?"

"No. No, everything's fine, Mother," the

girl said, and hurried upstairs. She did not glance in Clyde's direction—he did not think she was aware of his presence—but he saw her face as she passed and read the heartache of the words she had spoken on the porch. He took the ledger from Mrs. Jarvis, thanked her, and started to turn away.

"Mr. Clyde. Paul. Did Mr. Bannerman bring her home?" Sally's mother asked.

Clyde hesitated, but saw no reason to lie. "Yes," he said.

"I see," she said slowly. "Well, as I told Mr. Jarvis, forbidding them to meet was no answer, no answer at all. But—" She drew a long, unhappy breath. "Thank you. Good night, Paul. Don't let Mr. Jarvis work too late."

The following day, Clyde was leaving the bank on his way to lunch when Sally Jarvis came out of her father's small office and started for the front door. Bareheaded, she looked like a schoolgirl. She saw him, paused, and smiled coolly.

"Which way are you going, Mr. Clyde?"

"Up toward the Chinaman's," he said. "Cheap and nourishing."

"Then you can walk with me as far as the corner," she said.

He bowed, and held the door for her. The sunshine struck them solidly as they emerged from the building. Clyde squinted, half blinded by the glare, and the girl laughed at him.

"You've been at your books and ledgers too long; you've got the look of a mole, my friend." She hesitated, and glanced at him in a sudden, speculative way. "I have a suggestion. Being new in town, perhaps you don't know that there's a dance at the schoolhouse Saturday night."

She left it there. He looked at her as they walked. The warm prairie wind was blowing her skirts ahead of her and playing with a few liberated tendrils of her fair hair. Her face was slightly flushed, perhaps from the sunlight. She threw him a quick glance, and he caught the challenge in her eyes.

"Why, it sounds interesting, but I would need a partner, would I not? Unfortunately, I'm acquainted with only one young lady in this town, Miss Jarvis, and she seems to have a fairly low opinion of me."

Sally Jarvis laughed. "But you're a man of the world, Mr. Clyde; you must know that a lonely young lady will put up with just about anybody for the pleasure of an evening of dancing."

Clyde laughed abruptly. "Well," he said, "in that case—will you do me the honor, Miss Jarvis?"

"Naturally," she said. "Why do you think I brought the matter up? Eight o'clock. We can walk if you don't have a rig."

"For such an occasion," he said, "I will certainly rent one."

Saturday evening was quite warm and windless, and the sun had just set red when Clyde drove away from the Jarvis house with Sally Jarvis at his side. The girl turned to wave to her parents, who were sitting on the veranda.

"They approve of you, Mr. Clyde," she said. "Of course, right now they'd approve of just about any man who didn't wear a gun."

"I seem to have come along at a fortuitous time," Clyde said dryly. "I will not question my luck."

She favored him with a sharp glance. "You've a funny, sarcastic way of talking, haven't you? I don't think I like it very much." She hesitated. "Tell me, why did you come out to this country, anyway?"

He looked at her, but the light was already too poor for him to see her clearly. He found himself, instead, visualizing her as she had looked descending the stairs toward him a few minutes earlier, in a blue silk dress that outlined the shape of her upper body, with gentle fidelity, the skirt drawn smoothly back to a generous fullness in the rear, after the fashion of the period. She had no longer looked in any way like a schoolgirl; she had been a poised and breathtakingly beautiful woman, and there was no longer any doubt in his mind about his feelings toward her. However, he had been taught the propriety of keeping his feelings to himself, and when he spoke, his voice was level and impersonal.

"You sound as if you disapproved of my coming here, Miss Jarvis."

She said, "No, but you just don't look like the kind of person—I mean, I don't think you left home to hide a broken heart or a criminal record."

He smiled. "Are those the only reasons for coming West?"

"Some come to find adventure or make a fortune. But you certainly don't look adventurous, and as far as money is concerned, Dad says you were being paid a better salary back there than he's paying you now, with much better chances of advancement in a much bigger bank. He's very pleased to have you here, I must say; but this worries him a little."

"It shouldn't," Clyde said. "Back home, I was one of a row of men sitting at a row of desks. In twenty years, perhaps, I would have worked my way to the head of the row of desks; in another twenty, I might have become a member of the firm. By then, I would have been almost ready for retirement. I would have been a substantial, respected, and very dull member of the community—"

"It's funny," she said, interrupting him. "I must be wrong about you, because my impression is that that's exactly what you'd like."

He grinned. "In other words, you think I'm naturally a dull and pompous fellow, Miss Jarvis?" She did not speak, and he went on: "Granted that I have certain tendencies that way; in my favor, let me say that I do try to overcome them. Which is one reason why I decided to break out of the pattern of my life and come out here. The other reason is that the next few decades of this Western land are, I think, going to be very interesting from a financial standpoint. There is half a continent to be opened up; the process has hardly begun. A man on the ground, with a little capital and sound training . . . I don't expect ever to make the fortune you mentioned, Miss Jarvis. I am not a gambling man; and it takes a gambler, usually, to make money in great quantities—or lose it. I do expect, however, to make some small contribution to the country's development, receiving in return enough profit to guarantee a fairly comfortable, as well as interesting, life for myself and such family as I may have."

For a long time the only sound was the chopping noise of the horse's hoofs. At last she turned to look at him directly. "I don't quite understand why you're telling me this," she said.

He said gently, "I think you do." Before she could speak, he went on: "I have a confession to make. I was in your house the other evening, waiting for your mother to bring me something from upstairs, when Mr. Bannerman brought you home. I could not help overhearing the conversation. He was telling you his plans for the future. You did not approve of them. I thought I'd take this opportunity to tell you mine."

It was the first time he had seen her visibly disconcerted. She frowned, and said stiffly, "Aren't you taking a good deal for granted,

Mr. Clyde? Just because I talked you into bringing me to a dance—"

He laughed and shook his head. "You had a disagreement with Mr. Bannerman, and decided that it would be well for you to be seen in public with some other man—any other man—so that the marshal would realize that your decision was irrevocable. It was my good fortune; and it gave me a chance to speak to you like this; but I'm giving it no more weight than it deserves, I assure you."

She had been studying him in a half-puzzled way; now she said, "You look like an unadventurous man; still you leave a good job to come out here, and speak like this to a girl on no more than a week's acquaintance. There must be more to you than I thought, Mr. Clyde."

He said, "I usually know what I want." After a little, he added, "I usually get it."

"Indeed?" she said sharply. "At least you have confidence in yourself, that's something. Well, there's the schoolhouse. Do you know, this will be the first time I've danced in well over a year?"

He looked at her in surprise; then he realized that, of course, Bannerman could hardly have escorted her to public functions over her parents' disapproval. They pulled into the schoolyard. There were people around of all ages, dressed in their best; and Sally introduced him to one group and another as they moved toward the open school-house door. She seemed unaware of the glances they drew and the whispers that were passed behind them; but once inside the door she turned to face him.

"I hope you don't mind," she said. "It really wasn't very fair of me to put you in this position."

"They mean no harm," he said. "It's something to gossip about." He looked at her in the yellow lamplight. "Would it be presumptuous of me to tell you that you look very lovely?"

She laughed. "No woman considers that a presumption, Mr. Clyde—Paul. I think I'm going to like—"

She checked herself abruptly; and Clyde realized that the room had suddenly become very quiet. He turned to look at the door. Bannerman stood there. His big frame seemed to fill the doorway. He came forward slowly, and Clyde realized, apprehensively, that he was a little drunk. It made him no less deadly; it only made his deadliness blind and unpredictable.

371

"Sally," he said, speaking slowly and quite clearly, "I want to talk to you."

She said quietly, "I don't think there's anything more to be said, Hank."

"I want to talk to you," the big man repeated, standing above her. "Not here." He reached out and took her arm.

Sally threw a quick and warning glance toward Clyde, and stepped forward obediently. "All right, Hank. All right."

Bannerman turned and started toward the door. His grip on the girl's arm was strong and awkward, so that she had difficulty in walking erect beside him. Clyde saw her face whiten with pain; suddenly his own chest seemed to be full of something that was not air, something thick and unbreatheable; and he took one step after them.

"Just a minute!"

To his surprise, his voice came out strong and distinct. A rustle went through the room, which had forgotten his presence. Sally turned her head quickly.

"No, Paul; no! It's all right. Don't—"

"The lady came with me," he said, looking up at Bannerman. "She will leave with me."

He could see himself clearly, standing in front of the big man, a slight dapper figure with a piping voice, inviting destruction. It was ridiculous, and he expected to hear laughter, but none came.

Bannerman shook his head, as if to clear it of the fumes of alcohol. "Get out of my way," he said.

"You're drunk, Marshal," Clyde said. "Let Miss Jarvis go."

"Little man," Bannerman said, "don't interfere."

He swung an arm to brush Clyde aside. There was no choice, and Clyde ducked and hit him, putting all his strength into the blow, and directing it just above the belt buckle. The man was built of leather, it seemed; nevertheless, the blow knocked some wind out of him, set him back a pace, and caused him to let go of Sally's arm. It also seemed to sober him miraculously; suddenly his eyes cleared and his jaw tightened, and his whole posture became taut and dangerous. His right hand swung casually into the neighborhood of the holstered gun; and the two men faced each other like that for measurable seconds—the longest seconds in Paul Clyde's life—then Bannerman straightened up slowly.

"You are quite right, Mr. Clyde. I've had a little too much to drink. My apologies."

He looked at Sally. "To you, too, ma'am. I will not bother you again."

He turned on his heel and strode away. Two steps from the door he came to a sudden halt, listening. They all heard it then, the distant sound of gunfire in town. A horseman was approaching at a dead run. They heard him dismount in the yard and hurry toward the door; then he was in the doorway, a grubby little man with thinning red hair.

"Marshal Bannerman!" He saw the marshal standing there, and caught his breath with an effort. "Haskell and Johnny Rios are shooting hell out of Texas Street. A drunk got hit in the Cattleman, and one of the girls in Lou Dance's place was cut by flying glass; they'll kill somebody yet if you don't stop them quick!"

A slow smile formed on Bannerman's face; his voice was gentle. "Why, you go on back, Pinky. Tell your boss and his shadow to save their cartridges; I'll be right with them."

The red-haired man flushed. "Ah—" he said, turning quickly away. They heard him run across the yard to his horse and ride off. Inside the schoolhouse Bannerman stood, looking idly about him. Abruptly he grinned, dug into his vest pocket, and produced a small, shiny badge. He tossed this into the air and caught it.

"I'm told this town's too poor to afford a permanent deputy marshal any longer," he said. "Tonight I could use a man to watch my back. Any of you fine, taxpaying citizens want to feel what it's like to wear a badge when the chips are down, here's your chance."

The room was silent. Bannerman laughed, tucked the badge back into his pocket, and walked out. Presently they heard him ride out of the yard at an easy trot.

Clyde heard a man nearby speaking to another in an angry voice: "The arrogance of the fellow! They're three of a kind, I say, Haskell, Rios, and Bannerman. Whichever of them goes down, it will be good riddance for the town!"

"Well, it will be Bannerman who goes down tonight. Did you note that he'd been drinking? That's one thing that will make him reckless; and there is another thing also—" His glance touched Sally Jarvis briefly. "He will march straight down Texas Street, taking no precautions. Haskell's a sly and careful one who's never exposed himself before; and Rios never faced a man without big odds in his favor. There'll be a marksman in the alley behind the bank, perhaps, to take the marshal in the rear as he goes up the street. Well, I hold no brief for anyone who lives by the gun, but that man will leave an emptiness behind him, dying. A brave man always does."

Clyde glanced at Sally Jarvis, whose face had gone pale. He touched her arm and said, "Wait here."

"Paul, what—"

"Wait here," he said.

Then he was out of the door, in the darkness, hurrying toward the rented buggy. The livery stable nag felt the cut of the whip, and broke into a lumbering run as they cleared the yard. Far ahead, Clyde could see the shape of a solitary rider, a big man on a gray horse that looked silvery in the darkness.

To the right, the railroad tracks were pale and shining ribbons in the night. The depot was dark except for a pair of illuminated windows marking the stationmaster's office. Well before he reached the bank, Clyde dragged the panting horse to a stop. He covered the rest of the distance on foot. The lock of the front door yielded to the key he had been given by Mr. Jarvis; he pushed the door open and looked around. Front Street was empty except for his deserted buggy. He stepped into the bank and pulled the door gently closed behind him.

Inside the familiar building, the night lights gave him plenty of illumination. The silence was complete, and his footsteps sounded loud and arresting as he crossed to the teller's cage and found the pistol beneath the counter. There was also a box of ammunition. He dropped a handful of cartridges into his pocket and walked quickly to the side door of the bank. It took a little time to throw off the locks without making a noise; then the door swung open under his hand to let him look out upon Texas Street.

Usually at night one could hear the constant beat of pianos and the sound of drunken laughter. Tonight, the street was silent. Directly across from him, Clyde saw, was the marshal's gray horse, riderless, standing at a hitching rail. Clyde stepped out cautiously. Looking up Texas Street, he saw Bannerman's tall and square-shouldered form striding away from him at a deliberate pace, holding the center of the street. Beyond him, awaiting him, were two men, whose shapes were familiar to Clyde: He had seen them once before, at the depot on his first day here. As he watched, they moved slowly apart, one to each side of the street.

Now there was a rustle of movement much closer at hand. Clyde drew back into the arch of the doorway, lifting the heavy pistol. He knew enough about firearms to have considerable respect for their deadly potentialities, but very little for the knowledge it took to operate one. It was a manual skill like any other. To become really expert took practice, no doubt; but there was nothing mysterious about the mechanics of putting a bullet into a large target at close range.

He watched two men step out from the alley behind the bank. One had a rifle in his hands. The barrel reflected the shine of the lights along the street. The other carried a holstered revolver, which he drew as he came to a halt. This one spoke: "Better take him now. Make it good; he's nobody to fool with."

The man with the rifle put it to his shoulder and sighted carefully. As he did so, Clyde aligned the barrel of the bank's weapon against the rifleman's hunched, black silhouette. His mouth was a little dry, and his voice came out softer than he had intended. "Look this way, gentlemen."

Soft though it was, it was loud enough for them to hear, punctuated by the metallic sound of the hammer of the pistol coming to

378

full cock. They turned instantly, throwing themselves in opposite directions. Clyde had had some thought of disarming them and holding them at pistol point while Bannerman fought his battle at the other end of the street, but he saw at once that it was not going to work that way. He reminded himself that these men had come here for the purpose of shooting an officer of the law in the back, and he pulled the trigger as the rifleman was swinging his weapon around for a shot.

The muzzle flame was a startling thing to a man who had never before fired a short gun at night; it blinded him momentarily. The bright, answering flame of the rifle cut through his blindness, but the bullet came nowhere near him, and he heard the man fall heavily to the ground. Now, as if these two shots had been a signal, the street seemed to pulse and echo with gunfire. A bullet went by high overhead with a strange, sucking sound. He had the pistol cocked again when something struck him a savage blow in the side, driving him back into the doorway and causing him to discharge his weapon ineffectually. He saw the second man, on one knee in the street, taking careful aim for another shot; and he knew he had no time to recock his piece and fire. This was the man who had carried the message, he saw, whom Bannerman had called Pinky; there was wicked triumph on his face. Then a shot sounded up the street, and the face went slack and dead, and the man fell over in the dust.

Clyde drew a cautious breath. There was some pain, and his side was wet with blood, but he did not think the injury was critical. He pressed his arm against it and straightened up. Marshal Bannerman came striding toward the bank and stopped to look at the two men on the ground and the third standing in the doorway.

"What the hell are you doing here, Boston?" he asked.

Clyde said, "Why, I intend to marry Miss Jarvis if she'll have me, Marshal. She would have blamed herself if you'd been killed tonight. I could not let that happen."

People were coming from everywhere now. A buggy pulled around the corner, and Sally Jarvis jumped out before it had stopped and came running up to them. Bannerman looked at her gravely for a moment and turned back to Clyde.

"Well, my work here is done," he said. "Take good care of her, Boston, and thank you for my life."

He turned and walked to his horse. They watched him mount, lift his hat, and ride up Texas Street past the two sprawled forms that lay there in front of the brightly lighted saloons. Clyde turned to look at the girl beside him. Her eyes were wide and questioning as she answered his look.

"What will become of him, Paul?" she whispered. "Where will he end?"

He knew that she was not thinking of death in a dusty street like this. She was thinking of a time when there would be no more streets like this; she was seeing a great, bowed, shabby figure in a barroom somewhere, buying another drink to drown the ghostly memories of a past glory, forgotten by everyone but himself. It was this, Clyde knew, that she had not been able to face; it was the reason she was here, with him. He was the tame and prosaic future; the man they were watching ride away was the wild and gaudy past.

Beyond the street and its lights, the darkness swallowed him. They never heard of him again.